# MEASUREMENTS AND METROLOGY


**AUTHOR (S)**

**Dr. A. Gnanavelbabu**
*Professor*
*Department of Industrial Engineering*
*College of Engineering Guindy*
*Anna University, Chennai – 600025,*
*Tamilnadu, India*

**Dr. M. Santhanakumar**
*Assistant Professor*
*Department of Industrial Engineering*
*College of Engineering Guindy,*
*Anna University, Chennai – 600025,*
*Tamilnadu, India*

**Mr. R. Saranraj**
*Teaching Fellow*
*Department of Industrial Engineering*
*College of Engineering Guindy*
*Anna University, Chennai – 600025,*
*Tamilnadu, India*

**REVIEWER**

**Prof. G. Ayyappan**
*Professor, Satish Dhawan*
*Professor, Indian Institute of Space Science and Technology (IIST)*
*DOS, Govt of India, Thiruvananthapuram, 695547, Kerala, India*



**KHANNA BOOK PUBLISHING CO. (P) Ltd.**
4C/4344, Ansari Road, Darya Ganj,
New Delhi, India

**All India Council for Technical Education**
Nelson Mandela Marg, Vasant Kunj,
New Delhi, India

Dear Readers,

To prevent the piracy, this book is secured with HIGH SECURITY HOLOGRAM on the front title cover. In case you don't find the hologram on the front cover title, please write us to at contact@khannabooks.com or whatsapp us at +91-99109 09320 and avail special gift voucher for yourself.

Specimen of Hologram on front Cover title:

Moreover, there is a SPECIAL DISCOUNT COUPON for you with EVERY HOLOGRAM.

How to avail this SPECIAL DISCOUNT:

Step 1: Scratch the hologram

Step 2: Under the scratch area, your "coupon code" is available

Step 3: Logon to www.khannabooks.com

Step 4: Use your "coupon code" in the shopping cart and get your copy at a special discount

Step 5: Enjoy your reading!

**ISBN:** 978-93-5538-599-4
**Book Code:** DIP477EN

**Measurements And Metrology**

*by* Dr. A. Gnanavelbabu, Dr. M. Santhanakumar and Mr. R. Saranraj

**First Edition:** 2026

*Originally Published by:*
**All India Council for Technical Education, Ministry of Education, GOI**

*Exclusively Published & Distributed by:*
**Khanna Book Publishing Co. (P) Ltd.**
4C/4344, Ansari Road, Daryaganj,
New Delhi (INDIA)

Visit us at: **www.khannabooks.com**
Write us at: **contact@khannabooks.com**

| To view complete list of books, Please scan the QR Code: | KPH |
|---|---|

*Printed in Bharat.*

प्रो. टी. जी. सीताराम
अध्यक्ष
Prof. T. G. Sitharam
Chairman

सत्यमेव जयते

आज़ादी का अमृत महोत्सव

अखिल भारतीय तकनीकी शिक्षा परिषद्
(भारत सरकार का एक सांविधिक निकाय)
(शिक्षा मंत्रालय, भारत सरकार)
नेल्सन मंडेला मार्ग, वसंत कुंज, नई दिल्ली–110070
दूरभाष : 011–26131498
ई–मेल : chairman@aicte-india.org

ALL INDIA COUNCIL FOR TECHNICAL EDUCATION
(A STATUTORY BODY OF THE GOVT. OF INDIA)
(Ministry of Education, Govt. of India)
Nelson Mandela Marg, Vasant Kunj, New Delhi-110070
Phone : 011-26131498
E-mail : chairman@aicte-india.org

# FOREWORD

Engineers are the backbone of any modern society. They are the ones responsible for the marvels as well as the improved quality of life across the world. Engineers have driven humanity towards greater heights in a more evolved and unprecedented manner.

The All India Council for Technical Education (AICTE), have spared no efforts towards the strengthening of the technical education in the country. AICTE is always committed towards promoting quality Technical Education to make India a modern developed nation emphasizing on the overall welfare of mankind.

An array of initiatives has been taken by AICTE in last decade which have been accelerated now by the National Education Policy (NEP) 2020. The implementation of NEP under the visionary leadership of Hon'ble Prime Minister of India envisages the provision for education in regional languages to all, thereby ensuring that every graduate becomes competent enough and is in a position to contribute towards the national growth and development through innovation & entrepreneurship.

One of the spheres where AICTE had been relentlessly working since past couple of years is providing high quality original technical contents at Under Graduate & Diploma level prepared and translated by eminent educators in various Indian languages to its aspirants. For students pursuing 2$^{nd}$ year of their Engineering education, AICTE has identified 87 books, which shall be translated into 12 Indian languages - Hindi, Tamil, Gujarati, Odia, Bengali, Kannada, Urdu, Punjabi, Telugu, Marathi, Assamese & Malayalam. In addition to the English medium, books in different Indian Languages are going to support the students to understand the concepts in their respective mother tongue.

On behalf of AICTE, I express sincere gratitude to all distinguished authors, reviewers and translators from the renowned institutions of high repute for their admirable contribution in a record span of time.

AICTE is confident that these outcomes based original contents shall help aspirants to master the subject with comprehension and greater ease.

(Prof. T. G. Sitharam)

## ACKNOWLEDGEMENT

The authors are grateful to the authorities of AICTE, particularly Prof. T. G. Sitharam, Chairman; Prof. Abhay Jere, Vice-Chairman; Prof. Rajive Kumar, Member-Secretary; and Dr. Sunil Luthra, Director and Reena Sharma, Hindi Officer Training and Learning Bureau, for their planning to publish the books on "Measurements and Metrology" We sincerely acknowledge the valuable contributions of the reviewer of the book, Prof. G. Ayyappan Professor, Indian Institute of Space Science and Technology, Department of Space, Government of India, for making it student-friendly and his unwavering support have been pivotal in bringing this book to its final form.

We want to extend our heartiest gratitude to our family members for their motivation and support during the period of book writing.

This book is the outcome of numerous suggestions from AICTE members, experts, and fellow authors who have shared their opinions and thoughts to develop engineering education in our country further. Acknowledgments are due to all the contributors and workers in this field, whose published books, review articles, papers, photographs, footnotes, references, and other valuable information have enriched us during the writing process.

*Dr. A. Gnanavelbabu*
*Dr. M. Santhanakumar*
*Mr. R. Saranraj*

# PREFACE

In an age where precision and accuracy govern the realms of engineering and manufacturing, the art and science of measurement stand as fundamental pillars of technological advancement. "Measurements and Metrology" is born from this necessity to understand, apply, and innovate within the world of measurement, offering a comprehensive introduction and an in-depth exploration of this critical field.

Our journey through this book is structured to provide a balanced blend of theoretical knowledge and practical application. We begin with the foundational principles in Unit 1: Introduction to Measurements, where readers will gain insight into the definitions, methods, standards, and instruments that form the backbone of metrology. This unit lays the groundwork by covering crucial concepts such as precision, accuracy, and error classification, equipping readers with the necessary tools to understand and conduct accurate measurements.

Moving forward, Unit 2: Transducers and Strain Gauges delves into the specifics of transducers, strain measurements, and various methods for measuring force, torque, and pressure. This unit highlights the significance of these elements in real-world applications, demonstrating their importance in fields ranging from structural engineering to everyday consumer products.

In Unit 3: Applied Mechanical Measurements, we expand our focus to include measurements of speed, displacement, flow, temperature, humidity, density, and liquid levels. This unit's practical approach ensures that readers not only understand the theory behind these measurements but also their application in diverse industries, including biomedical engineering.

The exploration continues with Unit 4: Limits, Fits & Tolerances, a critical section for anyone involved in manufacturing and quality control. Here, we address the principles of limits, fits, and tolerances, providing a detailed understanding of their application in ensuring product compatibility and quality. The discussion on angular measurement and screw thread measurements further underscores the precision required in mechanical design and inspection.

Unit 5: Gear Measurement and Testing offers a specialized focus on gear measurement's intricacies, addressing analytical and functional inspection methods. This unit is essential for professionals in the automotive and machinery sectors, where gear performance is paramount. The chapter on machine tool testing also provides insights into maintaining and ensuring the accuracy of machining operations.

Finally, the Measurements & Metrology Lab section is designed to bridge the gap between theory and practice. Here, we provide practical exercises and experiments that allow readers to apply their knowledge and hone their skills in a controlled environment. These hands-on activities are crucial for reinforcing the concepts discussed throughout the book.

"Measurements and Metrology" is intended for a diverse audience, from students pursuing engineering education to professionals seeking to deepen their expertise. We aim to present this complex and evolving field in a manner that is both accessible and comprehensive, fostering a deeper appreciation for the precision and intricacy involved in accurate measurement.

We are deeply grateful to the many educators, industry professionals, and researchers whose insights and feedback have shaped this book. We hope this work will serve as a valuable resource, inspiring a new generation of engineers and technicians to excel in the precise science of measurement.

With precision and dedication,

*Dr. A. Gnanavelbabu*
*Dr. M. Santhanakumar*
*Mr. R. Saranraj*

# OUTCOME BASED EDUCATION

For the implementation of an outcome-based education, the first requirement is to develop an outcome-based curriculum and incorporate an outcome-based assessment in the education system. By going through outcome-based assessments, evaluators will be able to evaluate whether the students have achieved the outlined standard, specific, and measurable outcomes. With the proper incorporation of outcome-based education, there will be a definite commitment to achieve a minimum standard for all learners without giving up at any level. At the end of the programme running with the aid of outcome-based education, a student will be able to arrive at the following outcomes:

Programme Outcomes (POs) are statements that describe what students are expected to know and be able to do upon graduating from the program. These relate to the skills, knowledge, analytical ability attitude, and behaviour that students acquire through the program. The POs essentially indicate what the students can do from subject-wise knowledge acquired by them during the program. As such, POs define the professional profile of an engineering diploma graduate.

The National Board of Accreditation (NBA) has defined the following seven POs for an Engineering diploma graduate:

**PO1. Basic and Discipline specific knowledge:** Apply knowledge of basic mathematics, science and engineering fundamentals and engineering specialization to solve engineering problems.

**PO2. Problem analysis:** Identify and analyses well-defined engineering problems using codified standard methods.

**PO3. Design/ development of solutions:** Design solutions for well-defined technical problems and assist with the design of systems components or processes to meet specified needs.

**PO4. Engineering Tools, Experimentation and Testing:** Apply modern engineering tools and appropriate techniques to conduct standard tests and measurements.

**PO5. Engineering practices for society, sustainability and environment:** Apply appropriate technology in the context of society, sustainability, environment and ethical practices.

**PO6. Project Management:** Use engineering management principles individually, as a team member or a leader to manage projects and effectively communicate about well-defined engineering activities.

**PO7. Life-long learning:** Ability to analyse individual needs and engage in updating in the context of technological changes.

# COURSE OUTCOMES

Upon successful completion of this course, students will be able to:

**CO1:** Understand and explain the fundamental principles of measurement and metrology, including the significance, methods, and standards

**CO2:** Identify and describe various types of measuring instruments and their applications in industry.

**CO3:** Analyze and interpret measurement data, including error classification and calibration processes.

**CO4:** Utilize transducers and strain gauges for force, torque, and pressure measurements effectively.

**CO5:** Apply principles of limits, fits, and tolerances in mechanical design and inspection.

**CO6:** Conduct precise angular, thread, and gear measurements using appropriate instruments and techniques.

### Mapping of Course Outcomes with Program Outcomes

| Course Outcomes (COs) | PO-1 | PO-2 | PO-3 | PO-4 | PO-5 | PO-6 | PO-7 |
|---|---|---|---|---|---|---|---|
| CO-1 | 3 | 2 | 2 | 1 | 1 | 1 | 3 |
| CO-2 | 3 | 3 | 3 | 3 | 2 | 1 | 3 |
| CO-3 | 3 | 3 | 3 | 3 | 2 | 2 | 3 |
| CO-4 | 3 | 3 | 3 | 3 | 2 | 1 | 3 |
| CO-5 | 3 | 2 | 2 | 2 | 3 | 1 | 3 |
| CO-6 | 3 | 2 | 1 | 3 | 2 | 1 | 3 |

# GUIDELINES FOR TEACHERS

To implement Outcome Based Education (OBE) knowledge level and skill set of the students should be enhanced. Teachers should take major responsibility for the proper implementation of OBE. Some of the responsibilities (not limited to) for the teachers in the OBE system may be as follows:

- Within reasonable constraints, they should manoeuvre the time to the best advantage of all students.
- They should assess the students only upon certain defined criteria without considering any other potential ineligibility to discriminate against them.
- They should try to grow the learning abilities of the students to a certain level before they leave the institute.
- They should try to ensure that all the students are equipped with quality knowledge as well as competence after they finish their education.
- They should always encourage the students to develop their ultimate performance capabilities.
- They should facilitate and encourage group work and teamwork to consolidate newer approaches.
- They should follow Bloom's taxonomy in every part of the assessment.

**Bloom's Taxonomy**

| Level | Teacher should Check | Student should be able to | Possible Mode of Assessment |
|---|---|---|---|
| Create | Students ability to create | Design or Create | Mini project |
| Evaluate | Students ability to justify | Argue or Defend | Assignment |
| Analyse | Students ability to distinguish | Differentiate or Distinguish | Project/Lab Methodology |
| Apply | Students ability to use information | Operate or Demonstrate | Technical Presentation/ Demonstration |
| Understand | Students ability to explain the ideas | Explain or Classify | Presentation/Seminar |
| Remember | Students ability to recall (or remember) | Define or Recall | Quiz |

## GUIDELINES FOR STUDENTS

Students should take equal responsibility for implementing the OBE. Some of the responsibilities (not limited to) for the students in the OBE system are as follows:

- Students should be well aware of each UO before the start of a unit in each and every course.
- Students should be well aware of each CO before the start of the course.
- Students should be well aware of each PO before the start of the programme.
- Students should think critically and reasonably with proper reflection and action.
- Learning of the students should be connected and integrated with practical and real-life consequences.
- Students should be well aware of their competency at every level of OBE.

# LIST OF FIGURES

## UNIT 1 INTRODUCTION TO MEASUREMENT



## UNIT -2 TRANSDUCERS AND STRAIN GAUGES

## UNIT 3 APPLIED MECHANICAL MEASUREMENTS

## UNIT 4 LIMITS, FITS & TOLERANCES

**UNIT 5 GEAR MEASUREMENT AND TESTING**

# LIST OF TABLES

# CONTENTS

## UNIT 2 TRANSDUCERS AND STRAIN GAUGES

## UNIT 3 APPLIED MECHANICAL MEASUREMENTS

## UNIT 4 LIMITS, FITS & TOLERANCES

## UNIT 5 GEAR MEASUREMENT AND TESTING

# 1 Introduction to Measurements

## UNIT SPECIFICS

*This unit presents information related to the following topics:*

- *Definition of measurement; Significance of measurement; Methods of measurements: Direct & Indirect; Generalized measuring system*
- *Standards of measurements: Primary & Secondary; Factors influencing selection of measuring instruments*
- *Terms applicable to measuring instruments: Precision and Accuracy, Sensitivity and Repeatability, Range, Threshold, Hysteresis, calibration*
- *Errors in Measurements: Classification of errors, Systematic and Random error*
- *Measuring instruments: Introduction*
- *Thread measurements: Thread gauge micrometre*
- *Angle measurements: Bevel protractor, Sine Bar*
- *Gauges: plain plug gauge, ring Gauge, snap gauge, limit gauge*
- *Comparators: Characteristics of comparators, Types of comparators*
- *Surface finish: Definition, Terminology of surface finish, Talysurf surface roughness tester*
- *Co-ordinate Measuring Machine (CMM)*

*This unit is designed to familiarize readers with the foundational aspects of measurements in engineering and metrology. It starts with defining what measurement is, why it's significant, and the methods used to achieve accurate measurements. The unit discusses both primary and secondary standards of measurements and explores various factors that influence the selection of measuring instruments.*

*Additionally, this unit covers essential terms related to measuring instruments, such as precision, accuracy, sensitivity, and repeatability, and explains different types of errors in* *measurements. An introduction to various measuring instruments and their applications is* provided, along with specific techniques for thread and angle measurements using tools like thread gauge micrometers, bevel protractors, and sine bars.*

*The unit further delves into the use of different types of gauges and comparators, and it explains how surface finish is measured using instruments like the Talysurf surface roughness tester. The concept and operation of Co-ordinate Measuring Machines (CMM) are also covered.*

*Apart from this, at the end of the unit, the overall broad concepts are provided in the form of a unit summary. Besides, a large number of multiple-choice questions as well as descriptive-type questions with Bloom's taxonomy action verbs are included. A list of references and suggested readings are given in the unit so that one can go through them provided such for practice. It is important to note that for getting more information on various topics of interest, some QR codes have been provided in different sections which can be scanned for relevant supportive knowledge. Video resources along with QR codes are mentioned for getting more information on various topics of interest which can be surfed or scanned through mobile phones for viewing.*

**RATIONALE**

*Measurement is critical in engineering and various industries, as it ensures accuracy and quality in manufacturing and design processes. Understanding measurement principles, standards, and instruments is essential for engineers to produce reliable and precise results. This unit provides a comprehensive introduction to the fundamental concepts of measurements and metrology, equipping students and professionals with the necessary skills to perform accurate measurements and understand the significance of metrological standards.*

**PRE-REQUISITES**

*Before reading this unit, the students are advised to revisit the following:*

- *Basic Mathematics: Understanding of fundamental mathematical concepts and principles*
- *Physics: Basic principles related to measurements and instrumentations*
- *Basic Engineering Concepts*

## UNIT OUTCOMES

*After studying this unit, students will be able to:*

- *U1-O1: Understand the definition, significance, and methods of measurements.*
- *U1-O2: Distinguish between primary and secondary standards and identify factors influencing the selection of measuring instruments.*
- *U1-O3: Explain terms related to measuring instruments and different types of errors in measurements.*
- *U1-O4: Demonstrate knowledge of various measuring instruments and their applications.*
- *U1-O5: Apply techniques for thread and angle measurements, understand the use of gauges and comparators, and measure surface finish and coordinates using advanced instruments like CMM.*

## EXPECTED MAPPING WITH COURSE OUTCOMES

*(1- Weak Correlation; 2- Medium correlation; 3- Strong Correlation)*

| Unit Outcomes (U1) | CO-1 | CO-2 | CO-3 | CO-4 | CO-5 |
|---|---|---|---|---|---|
| U1-O1 | 3 | 2 | 3 | 2 | 1 |
| U1-O2 | 3 | 3 | 2 | 2 | 1 |
| U1-O3 | 2 | 2 | 3 | 1 | 1 |
| U1-O4 | 3 | 3 | 2 | 3 | 1 |
| U1-O5 | 2 | 3 | 3 | 2 | 1 |

## 1.1 MEASUREMENT

**Definition:** According to the International Vocabulary of Basic and General Terms in Metrology (ISO 1993), "Measurement is the set of operations having the object of determining a value of a quantity." The act of measurement, commonly referred to as "to measure," involves experimentally comparing the unknown value of a quantity with a suitable standard unit, established by convention.

Measurement encompasses the process of quantifying and assigning numerical values to observable phenomena, properties, or attributes. It involves the comparison of an unknown quantity to a standard unit of measurement, thereby expressing its magnitude in a consistent and reproducible manner. Whether it be the length of a pencil, the temperature of a room, or the velocity of a moving object, measurement provides the means to describe and characterize the physical world with precision and accuracy.

### 1.1.1 SIGNIFICANCE OF MEASUREMENT

Measurement is more important than just a tool for quantification; it is the basis of everyday decision-making, scientific research, and technological advancement. Measurements are fundamental to many disciplines, including physics, chemistry, biology, engineering, and economics. The significance of measuring in various kinds of domains is,

**Scientific Inquiry:** Measurements form the bedrock of scientific inquiry, enabling observation, experimentation, and analysis across disciplines like physics, chemistry, biology, and astronomy. Accurate measurements are essential for formulating hypotheses, testing theories, and validating empirical observations, driving progress in understanding the universe's fundamental laws and principles.

**Technological Innovation:** Measurement underpins technological innovation by supplying critical data for designing, developing, and optimizing new technologies and products. Across sectors such as microelectronics, telecommunications, aerospace, and healthcare, precise measurements ensure reliability, performance, and safety. Without accurate measurements, technological advancement would stagnate, hindering our ability to tackle complex challenges and enhance quality of life.

**Quality Assurance and Control:** In industrial manufacturing, measurements are pivotal for ensuring product quality, consistency, and reliability. Metrology provides tools and methodologies for quality assurance and control, enabling monitoring, defect detection, and compliance with standards. Accurate measurements facilitate the delivery of high-quality products, fostering consumer trust and reputation. **Precision Engineering and Design:** Measurements are indispensable in engineering and design for achieving precision and accuracy in mechanical, electrical, and structural systems. Metrology offers techniques to measure dimensional, geometric, and functional properties, aiding in product design and optimization. Precise measurements help meet performance requirements, minimize errors, and optimize resource utilization.

**Global Trade and Commerce:** Measurements play a vital role in global trade by providing a common language for quantifying goods and services. Metrology establishes international standards, ensuring consistency and fairness in trade transactions. Accurate measurements promote market efficiency, transparency, and consumer protection against fraud.

**Healthcare and Safety:** In healthcare and safety-critical industries, measurements are crucial for monitoring and maintaining human health, safety, and well-being. Metrology supports accurate medical diagnostics, pharmaceutical formulations, and environmental monitoring. Precise measurements enable effective diagnosis, treatment, and safety in medical practices and procedures.

### 1.1.2 METHODS OF MEASUREMENT

Different methods are used when precise measurements are required to identify physical variables. These methods define the unit and magnitude of the quantity under examination. The choice of method depends on acceptable error margins and desired accuracy levels, all aimed at minimizing measurement uncertainty. Here are the conventional methods:

1) Direct Method: Compares either primary or secondary standards directly with the quantity being measured, using tools like bevel protractors, micrometres, and vernier callipers.
2) Indirect Method: Measures related quantities to calculate the desired value using mathematical equations. Examples include using a sine bar to determine angles or evaluating strain induced by force in a bar.
3) Fundamental or Absolute Method: Measures fundamental quantities defining a specific quantity, either directly or indirectly.
4) Comparative Method: Compares the quantity with known values, noting deviations from a master gauge. Examples include dial indicators and comparators.

5) Transposition Method: Balances the measured quantity with known values to determine its value, often used in determining mass with a balance and known weights.
6) Null Measurement Method: Minimizes the gap between the measured quantity and the specified value until it reaches zero.
7) Coincidence Method: Detects minute variations between the evaluated quantity and a reference using differential measurements.
8) Deflection Method: Directly displays the quantity by moving a pointer along a scale that has been calibrated.
9) Substitution Method: Substitutes the quantity under measurement with a known value, ensuring identical effects on the indicating device.
10) Complementary Method: Combines a known value with the quantity to be measured to meet a predetermined comparison value.
11) Contact Method: Involves making contact with the surface being measured and the sensor of the instrument, keeping the contact pressure constant. Dial indicators and micrometers are two examples.
12) Contactless Method: Measures the surface without direct contact using tools like profile projectors and optical equipment.
13) Composite Method: Compares the real shape of a component against its tolerance thresholds, especially useful for interconnected components with combined tolerances. Implemented using composite GO gauges, ensuring interchangeability.

### 1.1.3 GENERALIZED MEASURING SYSTEM

Evaluating the manufactured component quality is the purpose of measurement in industrial inspection. Several quality requirements, including tolerance limits, shape, size, surface finish, and flatness, must be satisfied by the components before they are considered complete. To do this, the quantitative data is compared to a reference standard for a process or physical object.

Measurement involves three essential elements as shown in Figure 1.1, the object or phenomenon being measured (measurand), the instrument or method used for measurement (reference), and the unit of measurement against which comparisons (comparator) are made.

Quantifying and characterizing a broad variety of physical qualities, such as length, mass, time, temperature, pressure, etc., are based on these elements taken together.

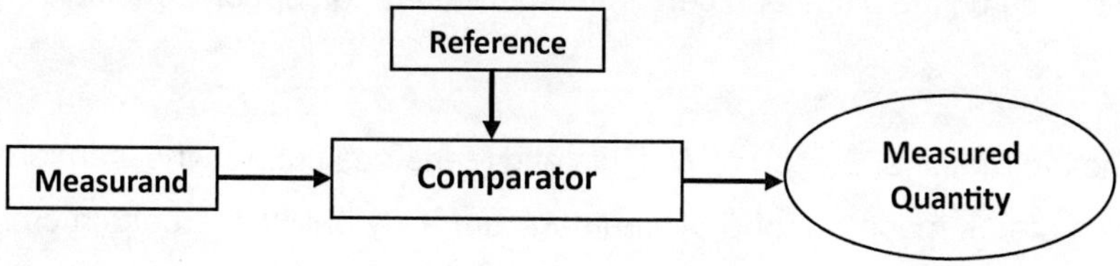


*Figure 1.1 Measuring System*

## 1.2 STANDARDS

**Definition:** A standard is defined as a benchmark or guideline established by an authority to determine the measure of quantity, weight, extent, value, or quality. For example, the meter serves as a standard unit of length measurement, established by an international governing body. The existence of robust standards is indispensable for the functioning of modern civilization, particularly in industries, commerce, and international trade.

Standards play an essential role in assuring the consistency, uniformity, and reproducibility of measurements on a global scale. They enable the interchangeability of parts and manufacturing processes, which underpin the entire industrial economy.

### 1.2.1 MATERIAL STANDARDS

Linear measurements of the material commonly rely on two standards:

- British/English system, represented by the ***yard***, and
- Metric system, utilizing ***meters***. The Metric system is widely used by most nations due to its convenience and practicality.
- The official definition of a yard or meter is the distance between two designated lines on a metal bar that is meticulously maintained under particular support and temperature parameters. Legislation passed by the Parliament governs the official usage of these lines, which serve as legally recognized norms.

**Yard**

The imperial standard yard (Figure 1.2) comprises a 38-inch bronze bar with a 1-inch square cross-section. It contains two 1/2-inch diameter, 1/2-inch-deep holes, each fitted with a 1/10-inch diameter gold plug. To avoid bending and unintentional damage, these plugs are placed on the bar's neutral axis. The gold plugs have a polished top surface that is engraved with longitudinal and transverse lines. The yard is the distance between the central transverse lines on the plugs at a certain temperature and support condition.

**Meter**

The International Bureau of Weights and Measures created the standard in 1875. The prototype meter is made out of a platinum-iridium alloy bar with a certain cross-section, as seen in Figure 1.3.

For accuracy, the meter's upper surface is polished and has two engraved lines. To reduce deflection, it is maintained at 0°C and supported by two rollers that are 58.9 centimeters apart. The distance between the center sections of a 102-centimeter-long bar made of platinum-iridium alloy with a web cross-section is know as a meter's length.

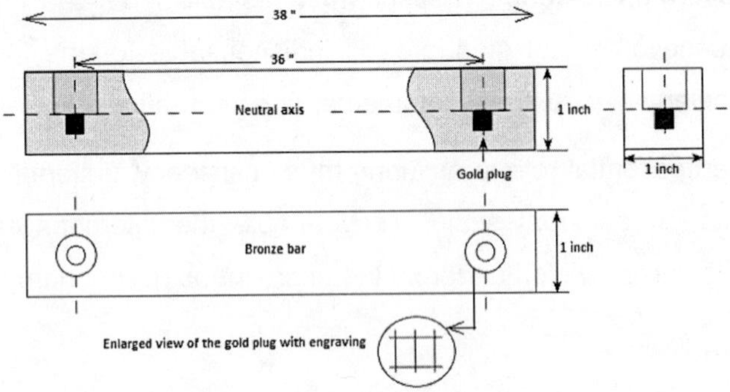


Figure 1.2 Standard Yard

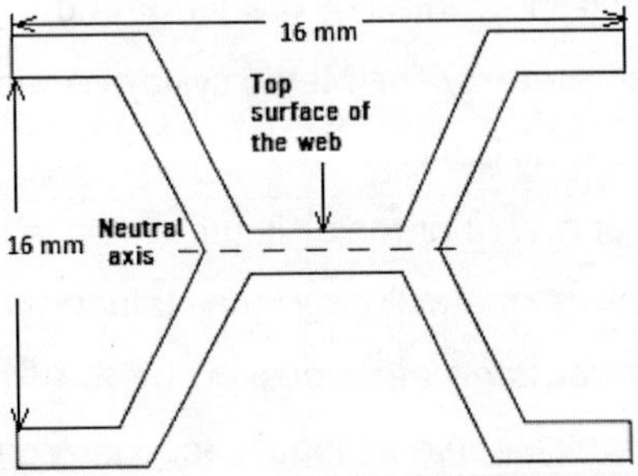


*Figure 1.3 International Prototype Meter*

The International Prototype Meter M is safeguarded by the BIPM in Sevres, France. The relationship between the yard and the meter was redefined as 1 yard = 0.9144 meters and 1 inch = 25.4 millimeters due to the stability of the prototype meter.

### 1.2.2 WAVELENGTH STANDARD

To address the limitations of metallic standards like the meter and yard, there arose a need for a more precise and consistent standard of length. Jacques Cabinet, a French philosopher, proposed utilizing the wavelength of monochromatic light as a natural and unchanging unit of measurement. In 1907, the International Angstrom (A) unit was established, defined by the wavelength of red cadmium in dry air at 15°C (with 6438.4696 A equalling one wavelength of red cadmium). The Seventh General Conference on Weights and Measures, held in 1927, approved a new definition of the standard unit of length, the meter, based on the wavelength of red cadmium as an alternative to the International Prototype Meter.

According to the new standard, a meter was defined as equivalent to 1650763.73 wavelengths of the red-orange radiation of krypton-86 gas, with an accuracy of about 1 part in 10. This refinement allowed for the meter and yard to be precisely defined in terms of the wavelength of krypton-86 radiation:

*1 meter = 1650763.73 wavelengths*

*1 yard = 0.9144 meters = 0.9144 x 1650763.73 wavelengths = 1509458.3 wavelengths*

While the Krypton-86 standard effectively met the growing technological need for precise standards, there was a belief that a definition rooted in the speed of light would offer both technical feasibility and practical benefits. This perspective led to a significant shift in the definition of the meter, which was agreed upon during the 17th General Conference on Weights and Measures on October 20, 1983. As per this new definition, **a meter is now defined** as the distance travelled by light in a vacuum within 1/299792458 of a second. This definition can be practically implemented through the utilization of an iodine-stabilized helium-neon laser.

### 1.2.3 SUB-STANDARDS

The international standard yard and prototype meter are not suitable for general use. Instead, there is a hierarchy of working standards for practical measurements. These standards are categorized into four grades based on the required level of accuracy:

1) **Primary Standards**: These standards offer precise definitions of units and are maintained under highly controlled conditions. Examples include the international yard and meter. Primary standards are rarely used, typically every 10 to 20 years, and only

for comparison with secondary standards. They have no direct application in engineering.

2) **Secondary Standards:** These are designed to closely replicate primary standards in terms of design, material, and length. Secondary standards are periodically compared with primary standards to record any deviations. They are stored in various locations for safekeeping and occasionally compared with tertiary standards as needed.

3) **Tertiary Standards:** Tertiary standards are the primary reference points in laboratories and workshops. They are exact replicas of secondary standards and are used for regular comparisons with working standards.

4) **Working Standards:** These standards are used more frequently in laboratories and workshops and are typically made from lower-grade materials than primary, secondary, and tertiary standards to reduce costs. Working standards are derived from fundamental standards and can be either line or end standards, with line standards often being manufactured in an H-cross-sectional form.

### 1.2.4 FACTORS INFLUENCING THE SELECTION OF MEASURING INSTRUMENTS

Factors influencing the accuracy of a measuring system encompass five key components:

1) **Standards:** This includes factors such as coefficient of thermal expansion, calibration interval, stability over time, elastic properties, and geometric compatibility.
2) **Workpiece:** Considerations here include cleanliness, surface finish, waviness, scratches, hidden geometry, elastic properties, appropriate datum, arrangement during support, and thermal equalization.
3) **Instrument:** The following factors influence the instrument's intrinsic properties: mechanical parts, repeatability, readability, contact geometry, scale error, friction effects, backlash, hysteresis, zero drift error, deformation during handling or use, calibration errors, and adequate amplification for accuracy.
4) **Person:** Training, skill level, feeling of precision, ability to choose tools and standards, knowledge of measuring costs, attitude toward achieving personal accuracy goals, and cost-effectiveness planning of measurement approaches all have an impact on the person doing the measurements.
5) **Environment: Environmental factors**, Factors including humidity, temperature, cleanliness, vibration, lighting, temperature equalization between the workpiece and

the standard, heat source-induced thermal expansion, and thermal expansion brought on by manual handling are also important.

6) To achieve higher accuracy, it is necessary to analyze and address sources of error within each of the elements.

## 1.3 TERMS APPLIED TO MEASURING INSTRUMENTS

### 1.3.1 ACCURACY OF MEASUREMENTS

The objective of measurement is to figure out a part's true dimensions. However, no measurement can be guaranteed to be 100% accurate. Errors occur constantly. The following variables affect the degree of error:

- Temperature fluctuations,
- Elastic deformation of the part or instrument,
- Operator skill, measuring method,
- Measuring instrument accuracy and
- Design, etc.

### 3.2 PRECISION AND ACCURACY

The terms precision and accuracy characterize the performance of a measurement device. An exceptional tool must exhibit both accuracy and precision.

Precision:

Precision measures consistency in measurements, reflecting agreement among multiple measurements under similar conditions. Repeatability, the ability of a measuring device to reproduce consistent results, is crucial. Precision ensures reliable consistency, with reproducibility being essential. Lack of precision yields varying results for repeated measurements, highlighting the importance of internationally recognized standards.

Accuracy:

Accuracy refers to the agreement between a measured dimension and its true magnitude. It represents how closely the measured value aligns with the true value. Achieving the exact true value is practically unattainable due to inherent uncertainties in the measuring process. Deviations from the true value leave uncertainty about whether the measured quantity truly represents its intended value. Figure 1.4 illustrates the relationship between accuracy and precision.

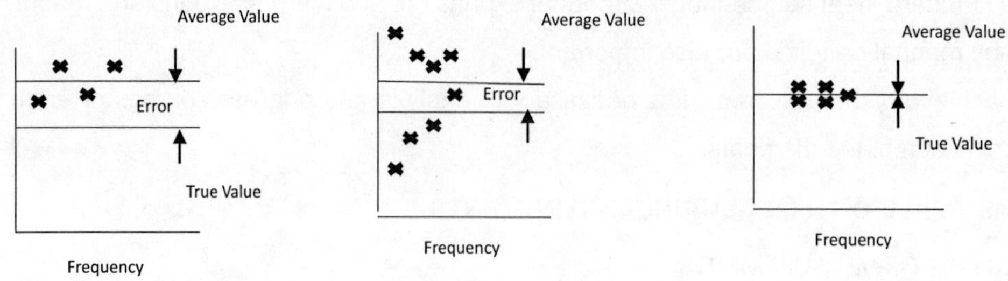


a. Precise but not accurate b. Accurate but not precise c. Accurate and precise

*Figure 1.4 Accuracy & Precision*

### 1.3.3 TERMS APPLICABLE TO MEASURING INSTRUMENTS

**Sensitivity:** Sensitivity refers to the capability of a measuring device to detect small differences in the quantity being measured. Unlike accuracy and precision, which are attributes of the measuring process, sensitivity is a characteristic of the measuring equipment itself. However, highly sensitive instruments may experience drift due to thermal and other factors, potentially affecting their repeatability compared to less sensitive instruments.

**Readability:** Readability pertains to the ease with which readings from a measuring instrument can be interpreted. It refers to the instrument's ability to present its indications clearly and understandably. Instruments with finely spaced graduation lines generally enhance readability, although excessively fine lines may hinder readability without the aid of magnification. Micrometres, for instance, may incorporate a vernier scale to improve readability, and additional magnification devices can further enhance readability.

**Repeatability:** Repeatability signifies the ability of a measuring instrument to produce consistent results when measurements are repeated under the same conditions. This includes consistency in measurements carried out by the same observer, with the same instrument, and without changes in location or measurement method. Repeatability is often quantified in terms of the dispersion of measurement results.

**Reproducibility:** Reproducibility refers to the consistency of variation patterns in measurements when individual measurements of the same quantity are conducted by different observers, methods, and instruments, or under different conditions, locations, and times. Similar to repeatability, reproducibility can also be quantified in terms of the dispersion of measurement results.

**Calibration:** Calibration is a critical process in ensuring the accuracy of a measuring instrument. It involves aligning the instrument's scale with known standard signals, typically performed by manufacturers before use. Calibration entails adjusting the instrument to produce zero output for zero input and to display accurate output for known input values, particularly near the full scale. Regular calibration checks are necessary to maintain accuracy, ideally performed under similar environmental conditions as actual measurements.

**Magnification:** Magnification involves amplifying the output signal of a measuring instrument to enhance readability. The degree of magnification should be balanced with the desired measurement accuracy, avoiding excessive magnification that may limit the instrument's measurement range. Generally, higher magnification leads to a narrower range of measurement.

**Range:** The range is a set of values over which a system or measuring instrument can function as intended and provide acceptable measurements. It establishes the upper and lower bounds on how accurately the device can identify and measure a physical quantity. A thermometer's range, for instance, might be -10°C to 100°C, meaning that it can measure temperatures precisely and accurately within this range. While a shorter range might make the instrument only useful for certain measurement jobs, a greater range enables the instrument to accommodate a wider spectrum of measurement values.

**Threshold:** The threshold is the minimum observable input value that triggers the instrument to respond or measure anything. It marks the beginning of the observed occurrence and is the point at which the instrument changes from a state of non-detection to detection. The threshold, for example, in a motion sensor is the minimum amount of movement necessary to trigger the sensor and record a measurement. Since they specify the lowest amount of input signal that the instrument can detect and measure with any degree of accuracy, thresholds are essential for assessing the sensitivity and accuracy of measurements.

**Hysteresis:** Depending on the direction of the input change, a measuring device's outputs may exhibit different values for the same input. This phenomenon is known as hysteresis. Put otherwise, hysteresis results in a lag or delay in the instrument's reaction to subsequent changes in the input variable. Measurements made under increasing and decreasing input circumstances may differ due to this non-linear behavior. For example, even when the input pressure values are the same, hysteresis in a pressure sensor may result in a minor variation in the sensor's output between rising and falling pressure.

## 1.4 MEASUREMENT ERRORS

A certain amount of error is always present when measuring a dimension, hence it is difficult to determine its true value. The measurement error denotes the difference between the actual value of the dimension being measured and its measured value. The actual value minus the measured value is the mathematical expression for the measurement error.

There are two primary ways to evaluate or express measurement errors: **absolute error and relative error**.

**Absolute error** refers to the algebraic difference between the measured value and the true value. Alternatively, if multiple measurements are taken, the apparent absolute error can be determined as the difference between one measurement result and the arithmetic mean of all measurements.

**Relative error**, on the other hand, is the ratio of the absolute error to the comparison value used for calculating that error. This comparison value can be the true value, the conventional true value, or the arithmetic mean for a series of measurements.

### 1.4.1 TYPES OF ERRORS

During the process of measurement, various types of errors may arise, which can be categorized as follows:

**Static Errors:** These errors stem from the physical characteristics of the components within the measuring system. There are three primary sources of static errors, and the precision of measurement can be determined by dividing the static error by the measurement range. Static errors include:

**Reading Errors:** These errors occur solely in the read-out device and are independent of other errors within the measuring system. Examples of reading errors include parallax errors and interpolation errors. Techniques such as using a mirror behind the readout pointer can mitigate parallax error, while interpolation error can be addressed by employing magnifiers or digital read-out systems.

**Characteristic Errors:** These errors refer to the deviation of the output of the measuring system from its theoretically predicted or nominal performance. Linearity errors, repeatability, hysteresis, resolution errors, and calibration errors fall under characteristic errors if the theoretical output follows a linear trend.

**Environmental Errors:** These errors stem from external factors such as temperature, pressure, humidity, magnetic or electric fields, radiation, vibrations, or shocks. Each component of the measuring system may contribute to environmental errors, which can be reduced by controlling the surrounding atmosphere to meet specific requirements.

**Instrument Loading Errors:** These errors arise from changes in the measurand itself when it is being measured, typically occurring after the measuring instrument is connected. Instrument loading error is quantified as the difference between the value of the measurand before and after the instrument is connected. For instance, delicate components may deform under the pressure exerted by the instrument, resulting in loading errors. Minimizing instrument loading error requires careful selection of sensing elements and measurement instruments.

**Dynamic Errors:** Time variations in the measurand cause dynamic errors, which are the outcome of the system's incapacity to precisely react to time-varying measurements. These errors are caused by factors such as inertia, damping, friction, or physical constraints within the sensing, readout, or display systems.

For statistical analysis and the examination of error accumulation, errors are typically categorized into two main types:

1. **Systematic or Controllable Errors**

Systematic errors exhibit regular repetition and maintain a consistent and uniform form. They arise from improper conditions or procedures that consistently affect measurements. Except for personal errors, which vary between individuals based on the observer's personality, systematic errors can be controlled in both magnitude and direction. Through proper analysis, systematic errors can be identified and minimized, earning them the moniker of "controllable errors."

**Random Errors**

Random errors lack consistency and occur sporadically and accidentally. They are inherent to the measuring system and are challenging to eliminate. The specific cause, magnitude, and source of random errors cannot be determined solely from knowledge of the measuring system or measurement conditions. Examples of random errors include

**(a).** Small variations in the positioning of setting standards and workpieces.

**(b).** Slight displacements of lever joints in measuring instruments.

**(c).** Operator errors in scale reading.

**(d).** Fluctuations in the friction of measuring instruments.

## 1.5 MEASURING INSTRUMENTS

Linear measurement encompasses the assessment of various dimensions, including lengths, diameters, heights, and thicknesses, both externally and internally. It serves as a fundamental aspect of metrology, facilitating accurate and precise quantification in diverse fields such as manufacturing, construction, engineering, and science.

Instruments designed for linear measurements can vary in their design and functionality based on the specific requirements of the application. For example:

1) **Micrometres:** These precision instruments are commonly used for measuring small distances with high accuracy, typically featuring a calibrated screw mechanism for fine adjustments and precise readings.
2) **Vernier Callipers:** Offering both inside and outside measurement capabilities, vernier callipers utilize a sliding jaw mechanism and a secondary scale (vernier scale) to achieve highly accurate measurements.
3) **Height Gauges:** Used for measuring the vertical distance between two surfaces, height gauges feature a vertical measuring spindle and a graduated scale for precise height measurements.
4) **Dial Indicators:** Employed for measuring linear displacements or deflections, dial indicators feature a needle or pointer that moves across a calibrated dial to indicate dimensional changes.
5) **Thickness Gauges:** These instruments are specifically designed for measuring the thickness of materials, such as sheet metal or paper, using various mechanisms such as spring-loaded probes or digital sensors.
6) **Non-Contact Measurement Devices:** Utilizing technologies such as laser or ultrasound, non-contact measurement devices enable precise measurements to be taken without physically touching the object being measured, ideal for fragile or delicate materials.

### 1.5.1 VERNIER INSTRUMENTS

The vernier principle enhances measurement accuracy by leveraging the minute difference in size between two scales or divisions. A vernier calliper comprises two steel rules sliding along each other. The main scale, on a solid L-shaped frame, divides into 20 parts, each small division representing 0.05 cm.

Here's a breakdown of their functions:

1) ***Inside jaws:*** Utilized for measuring the internal diameter of an object.
2) ***Outside jaws:*** These are employed to measure the external diameter or width of an object.
3) ***Vernier scale:*** Provides measurements in fractions, predominantly in inches.
4) *Vernier scale:* Facilitates measurements with precision up to two decimal places, usually in centimeters.

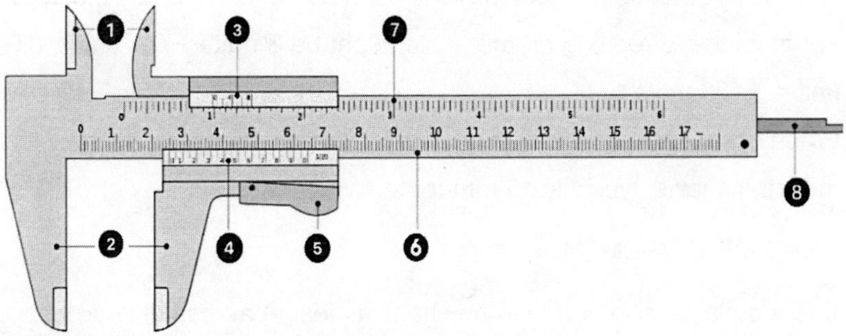


*Figure 1.5 Vernier Calliper*

5) ***Retainer*:** Serves the purpose of securing the movable part, enabling seamless transfer of measurements.
6) ***Main scale:*** Offers measurements in fractions, predominantly in inches.
7) ***Main scale:*** Provides measurements with precision up to one decimal place, typically in centimeters.
8) ***Depth probe:*** Designed for measuring the depths of objects or holes.

**Reading the Vernier Calliper**

1) The main scale is assumed to have small divisions of 0.02 units.
2) The vernier scale comprises 20 divisions, aligning precisely with 19 divisions of the main scale.
3) Each vernier division corresponds to 1/20 of 19 main-scale divisions, resulting in 0.019 units.
4) The difference between one main scale small division and one vernier division (the least count) equals 0.02 — 0.019, which is 0.001 unit.
5) When the main scale and vernier zero points coincide, the first vernier division reads 0.001 units less than one small-scale division.

6) Subsequent vernier divisions indicate 0.002 units less than two small-scale divisions, and so on.

7) If the zero vernier scale lies between two small divisions on the main scale, its exact value is determined by the coinciding vernier division.

8) To read a measurement from a vernier calliper, note the units and tenths indicated by the vernier's movement relative to the main scale zero.

9) Add the vernier division coinciding with a scale division to the previous reading, considering the number of thousandths of a unit indicated by the vernier divisions.

10) For instance, a reading on the scale might be 3 units + 0.1 unit + 0.075 unit + 0.008 unit = 3.183 units.

11) When using the vernier calliper for internal measurements, account for the width of the measuring jaws, typically 10 mm for the Metric System.

## 1.6 THREAD MEASUREMENT

Screw threads play a pivotal role in mechanical design across diverse applications, serving as vital components for controlled translational motion and facilitating dis-engageable connections through fasteners. The dimensional precision of screw threads is paramount, ensuring the reliable assembly of threaded mating components, the interchangeability of corresponding threaded parts, and the consistent correlation between rotational input and translational output. Furthermore, accurate thread dimensions contribute to the mechanical robustness of threaded connections, reinforcing structural integrity and enhancing overall performance.

### Thread Guage Micrometre

The vernier calliper boasts an accuracy of 0.02mm. However, for most precision engineering tasks, achieving component interchangeability necessitates a level of accuracy surpassing this value. To attain greater precision, more accurate and sensitive measuring equipment must be utilized. Among the most prevalent instruments for precise measurements is the micrometre, capable of achieving an accuracy of 0.01mm. Micrometres with even higher accuracy, such as 0.001mm, are also available as shown in Figure 1.6.

Micrometres can be categorized into various types, including outside Micrometres, inside Micrometres, screw thread Micrometres, and depth gauge Micrometres. Operating on the principle of a screw and nut, Micrometres utilize the rotation of a screw through a nut to advance by a specific distance corresponding to the pitch of the screw thread. By dividing the circumference of the screw into equal parts, the minimum length that can be measured can be determined. This accuracy can be further enhanced by reducing the pitch of the screw thread or increasing the number of divisions on the circumference of the screw.

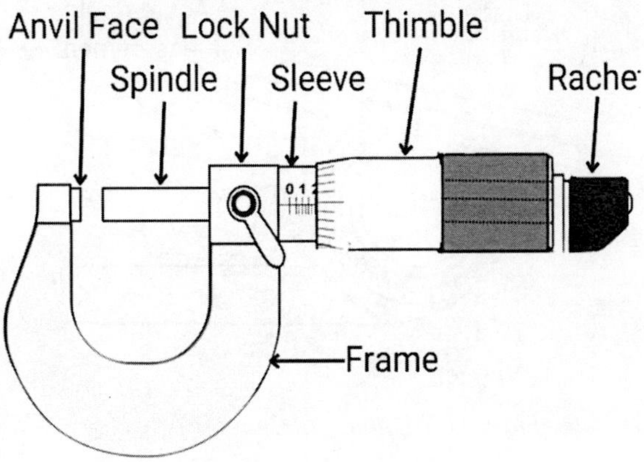


*Figure 1.6 Micrometer*

The pitch of the spindle screw divided by a number of spindle divisions gives the least count of a micrometre. The Micrometre's sensitivity and precision are indicated by this value, which is the smallest increment that can be measured with it. The outside diameter and length of small objects can be measured with an accuracy of 0.01mm using an outside micrometre, a precision tool. Outside Micrometres typically have a maximum opening of 25mm and are available in various measuring ranges, such as 0 to 25mm, 25 to 50mm, 125 to 150mm, and up to 575 to 600mm.

## 1.7 ANGULAR MEASUREMENTS

### Definition of Angle:

An angle is the space between two intersecting lines that meet at a common point. When a circle is divided into 360 equal parts, each part is known as a degree (°). Furthermore, each degree is subdivided into 60 smaller parts called minutes ('), and each minute is further divided into 60 parts known as seconds ("). Additionally, the unit of measurement known as the radian is defined as the angle formed by an arc of a circle with a length equal to the radius. For instance, if the length of arc AB is equal to the radius OA, then the angle θ is said to be 1 radian.

### Vernier Bevel Protractor (Universal Bevel Protractor):

The Vernier Bevel Protractor (figure 1.7), also known as the Universal Bevel Protractor, is a basic tool used for measuring the angle between two surfaces of a component. It consists of a base plate attached to a main body, along with an adjustable blade connected to a circular plate containing a vernier scale.

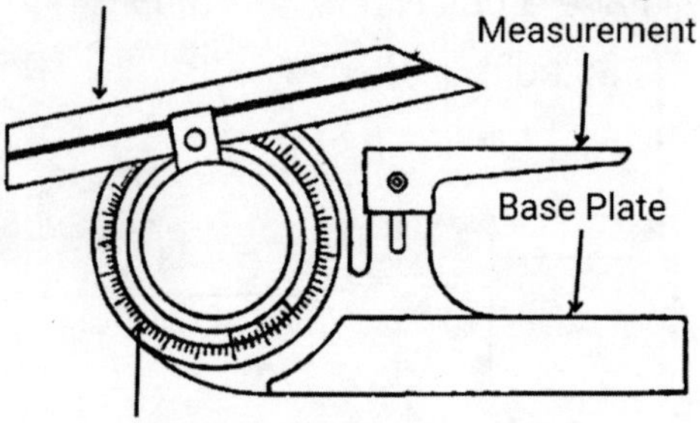


*Figure1.7 Universal Bevel Protractor*

The adjustable blade can freely slide along a groove and can be clamped at any desired length for convenience. Additionally, it can rotate around the centre of the main scale engraved on the instrument's body and can be securely locked in place using a clamping knob. The main scale is graduated in degrees, while the vernier scale features 12 divisions on each side of the centre zero. These divisions are marked from 0 to 60 minutes of arc, with each division representing 1/12th of 60 minutes, which is equivalent to 5 minutes. Furthermore, these 12 divisions occupy the same arc space as 23 degrees on the main scale, resulting in each division of the vernier scale measuring (1/12) 23 = 1(11/12) degree.

Measurement of acute and obtuse angles is facilitated by the use of a vernier scale. When the zero marking on the vernier scale aligns with a graduation on the main scale, the reading represents an exact measurement in degrees. However, if the zero marking aligns with a different graduation on the vernier scale, the number of vernier graduations multiplied by 5 minutes must be added to the main scale reading.

**Sine Bars**

Sine bars (figure 1.8), crafted from high-quality, corrosion-resistant steel, boast excellent hardness, ground surface finish, and stability. These bars feature two cylinders of equal diameter attached at the ends. They are available in various lengths, such as 100, 200, and 300 mm, and are primarily utilized for precise angle setting, often in conjunction with slip gauges and surface plates. The operational principle of sine bars relies on the principles of trigonometry.

In the diagram depicted above, the standard-length AB (L) serves as a reference, and by adjusting the stack of slip gauges (H), any desired angle (θ) can be obtained using the formula $\theta = \sin^{-1}(H/L)$

To measure unknown angles of a component, a dial indicator is moved along the work surface, and any deviation is noted. The slip gauges are then adjusted to ensure that the dial reads zero as it traverses from one end to the other.

## 1.8 GAUGES

### Limit Gauge

- A limit gauge is not a measuring gauge; it is primarily used as an inspecting gauge.
- These gauges are utilized in inspection processes based on attributes.
- They provide information regarding whether the products fall within the prescribed limits or not.
- Control charts, such as P and C charts, are generated based on the data obtained from limit gauges to monitor the consistency of products.
- Limit gauges are primarily employed for checking cylindrical holes of identical components in mass production.

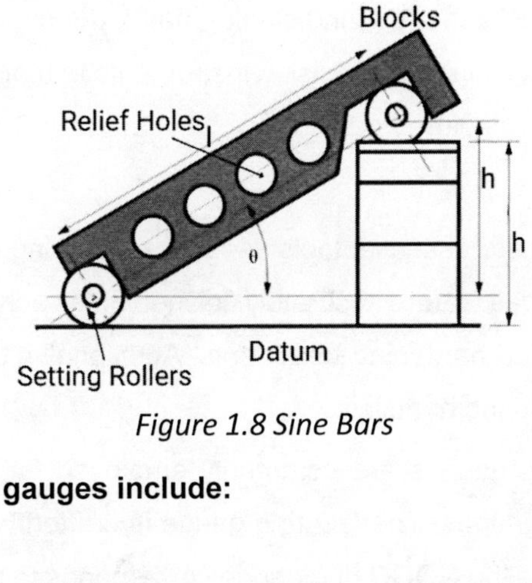


*Figure 1.8 Sine Bars*

**Common types of limit gauges include:**

1. *Plug gauges.*
2. *Ring gauges.*
3. *Snap gauges.*

### Plug Gauges

Plug gauges as shown in figure 1.9, are precision instruments used for measuring the dimensional accuracy of holes in mechanical components. They come in various types, each designed for specific applications and ease of use. There are three common types of plug gauges:

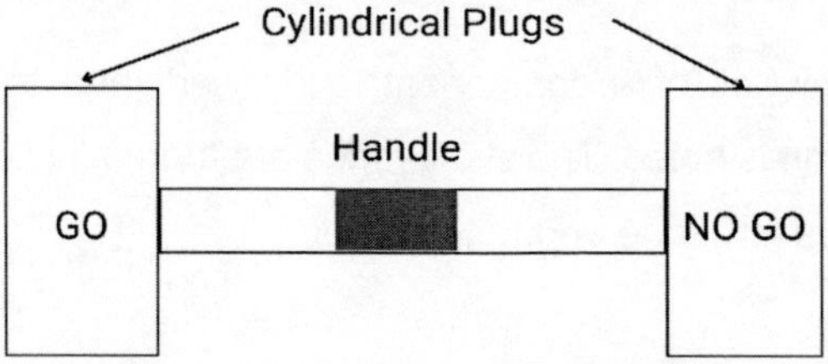


*Figure 1.9 Double-Ended Plug Gauge*

1. Single-Ended Plug Gauges
2. Double-Ended Plug Gauges
3. Progressive Type Plug Gauges

*Figure 1.10 Progressive Plug Gauge*

Plug gauges are indispensable tools for ensuring the dimensional accuracy of holes in mechanical components. Whether utilizing single-ended, double-ended, or progressive plug gauges, inspectors can rely on these precision instruments to maintain quality standards and uphold the integrity of manufactured parts.

**Ring Gauges**

Ring gauges (figure 1.11) are essential tools used for measuring the diameter of shafts with a central hole. These gauges feature accurately finished holes achieved through grinding and lapping processes following hardening treatments. Additionally, the periphery of the ring is knurled to enhance grip during handling.

Two distinct types of ring gauges are commonly employed for shaft inspection: GO ring gauges and NOGO ring gauges. The GO ring gauge is crafted with a hole set to the upper limit size of the shaft, while the NOGO ring gauge corresponds to the lower limit. During shaft inspection, the GO ring gauge should smoothly pass through the shaft, whereas the NOGO ring gauge should not.

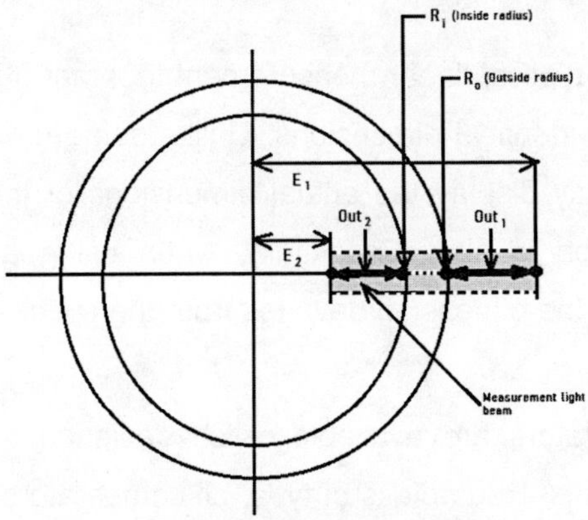


*Figure 1.11 Ring Gauge*

To facilitate easy identification of the NOGO ring gauges, a red mark or small groove is typically etched into the periphery. This visual indicator aids in distinguishing between the two types of gauges during the inspection process.

**Snap Gauges**

Snap gauges (figure 1.12), also known as gap gauges, serve as essential tools for inspecting external dimensions in manufacturing processes.

These gauges come in various types, each tailored to specific measurement needs. There are 5 type of snap gauges:

1. Double-Ended Snap Gauge
2. Progressive Snap Gauge
3. Adjustable Snap Gauge
4. Combined Limit Gauges
5. Position Gauge

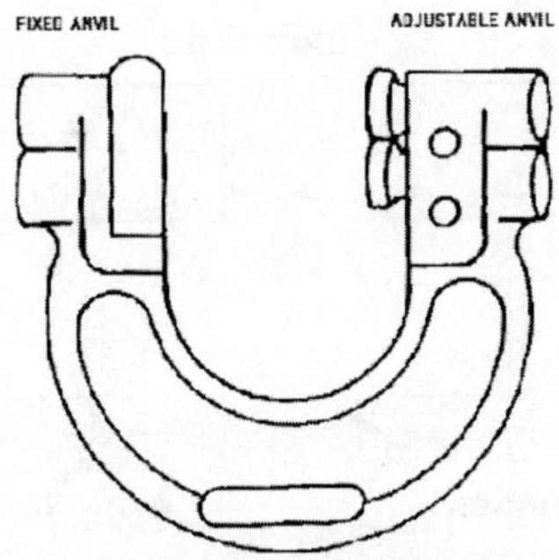


*Figure 1.12 Snap Gauge*

## 1.9 COMPARATORS

Comparators represent a type of linear measurement tool that offers rapid and convenient assessment of numerous identical dimensions. Unlike some other measurement devices, comparators do not directly display the actual dimensions of the workpiece; rather, they indicate only the deviation in size. Essentially, when using a comparator, it provides information on how much the dimension deviates from the specified dimension, rather than the exact measurement.

Various types of comparators are available, each designed to accommodate different conditions and requirements. Regardless of type, all comparators incorporate a magnifying device to enhance the visualization of the dimension's deviation from the standard size. The classification of comparators is based on the principles utilized for achieving magnification. The common types of comparators include 1. mechanical, 2. electrical, 3. optical, and 4. pneumatic variants.

### Mechanical Comparators

Mechanical comparators utilize mechanical mechanisms to amplify small deviations. These devices employ levers, gear trains, or a combination of both to magnify the slight movement of an indicator. They typically offer magnifications ranging from 300 to 5000 to 1, making them suitable for inspecting small parts machined to precise tolerances.

The dial indicators, sometimes referred to as a dial gauge (figure 1.13), is a common type of mechanical comparator. This instrument resembles a small clock, with a plunger protruding from the bottom. When the plunger experiences even a slight upward movement, it triggers a corresponding motion of the dial pointer, which is graduated into 100 divisions. A full revolution of the pointer corresponds to a 1mm travel of the plunger, meaning that each division represents a plunger travel of 0.01mm.

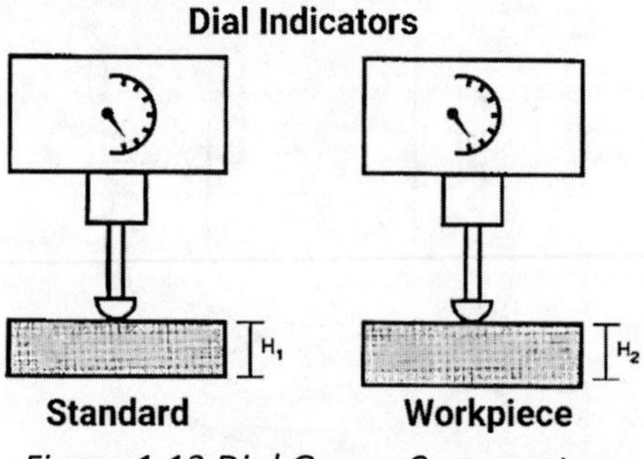

*Figure 1.13 Dial Gauge Comparators*

The experimental setup typically includes a worktable, a dial indicator, and a vertical post. The dial indicator is attached to the vertical post using an adjusting screw, allowing for vertical adjustment. The vertical post is then affixed to the worktable, which features a finely finished top surface. The dial gauge can be precisely adjusted vertically and secured in place using a locking screw.

**Advantages:**

1. Robust, compact, and user-friendly design.
2. Does not require external power sources such as electricity or air.
3. Simple mechanism resulting in cost-effectiveness.
4. Suitable for use in ordinary workshops and easily portable.

**Disadvantages:**

1. Accuracy relies heavily on the precision of the rack and pinion arrangement; any slackness in this mechanism reduces accuracy.
2. Increased friction due to multiple moving parts can compromise accuracy.
3. Limited range of measurement due to the pointer's movement being confined to a fixed scale.

**Electrical Comparator:**

An electrical (figure 1.14) is a precision measuring instrument used for comparing the dimensions of mechanical components with high accuracy. It comprises three main components:

1. **Transducer:** The transducer consists of an iron armature positioned between two coils, which are supported by a leaf spring at one end. The other end of the armature is in contact with a plunger. These coils function as two arms of an AC Wheatstone bridge circuit.
2. **Amplifier:** The amplifier is responsible for magnifying the input signal frequency received from the transducer. It amplifies the signal to a level suitable for further processing and display.
3. **Display Device or Meter:** The amplified input signal is displayed on a terminal instrument, typically a meter. This meter provides a visual indication of the measured displacement.

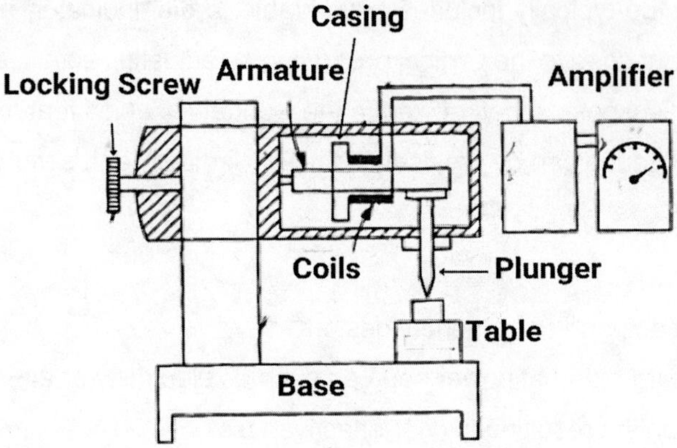


*Figure 1.14 Electrical Comparators*

To verify the accuracy of a specimen or workpiece, a standard specimen is initially placed under the plunger. The resistance of the Wheatstone bridge is adjusted until the meter reads zero. Subsequently, the standard specimen is removed, and the workpiece to be measured is introduced. Any height variation in the workpiece causes the plunger to move, which is then amplified and displayed on the meter. The least count of this electrical comparator is typically 0.001mm (one micron), allowing for precise measurements with high resolution.

**Electronic Comparator:**

The electronic comparator operates on the principle of transducer induction or the application of frequency modulation or radio oscillation.

**Advantages of Electrical and Electronic Comparator:**

1. It has fewer moving parts compared to mechanical comparators.
2. High magnification is achieved.
3. Multiple magnifications are provided in the same instrument for versatile usage.
4. The lightweight pointer enhances sensitivity to vibration.
5. The instrument is compact, saving space in the workspace.

**Disadvantages of Electrical and Electronic Comparator:**

1. An external agency is required to actuate the meter.
2. Variations in voltage or frequency may affect the accuracy of the output.
3. Accuracy decreases due to heating coils.
4. It is more expensive than mechanical comparators.

Electronic comparators offer advanced functionality and precision, making them valuable tools for accurate measurements in various industrial applications despite their drawbacks.

## 1.10 SURFACE FINISH MEASUREMENT

**Definition**: Surface finish refers to the texture, roughness, or smoothness of a manufactured surface, typically measured after the machining or finishing process. It encompasses both the irregularities and deviations from the ideal surface, as well as the overall appearance and tactile quality. Surface finish is crucial in various industries such as manufacturing, automotive, aerospace, and electronics, as it directly impacts the functionality, performance, and aesthetics of the final product. It is quantified using parameters such as Ra (average roughness), Rz (maximum height of profile), and Rt (total roughness), among others, measured using specialized instruments like profilometers.

**Factors Affecting Surface Roughness:**

1. **Work Piece Material:** The material from which the workpiece is fabricated plays a crucial role in determining surface roughness. Different materials exhibit varying degrees of roughness when subjected to manufacturing processes.
2. **Vibrations:** Vibrations during the machining process can introduce irregularities on the surface of the workpiece, affecting its finish.
3. **Machining Type:** The type of machining operation employed, such as turning, milling, or grinding, can influence the surface finish of the component.
4. **Tool and Fixtures:** The choice of tools and fixtures used in the manufacturing process can impact surface roughness, with different tool materials and geometries producing varying surface finishes.

**Classification of Geometric Irregularities:**

1. **First-Order Irregularities:** The machining tool moves on non-straight guide paths, which leads to these irregularities. They may have an impact on the surface's general shape.
2. **Second-order irregularities:** Vibrations during machining can lead to second-order irregularities, which manifest as periodic fluctuations on the surface.
3. **Third-Order Irregularities:** These irregularities are caused by the machining process itself and can include tool marks, grooves, and scratches on the surface.

4. **Fourth-Order Irregularities:** Improper handling of machines and equipment can result in fourth-order irregularities, which may appear as random deviations on the surface.

Surface finish measurement plays a critical role in ensuring the quality, functionality, and aesthetics of manufactured components. By understanding the factors influencing surface roughness and the various elements of surface texture, manufacturers can implement effective quality control measures to achieve desired surface finishes and meet customer specifications.

**Methods of Measuring Surface Finish**

Measuring the surface finish of a component is essential in various industrial applications to ensure quality and functionality. The methods employed for this purpose can be classified into two main categories: inspection by comparison and direct instrument measurements.

**1. Inspection by Comparison Methods:**

In these methods, the surface texture is evaluated through observation and comparison with known standards. Several techniques fall under this category:

- YYC Touch Inspection
- Visual Inspection
- Microscopic Inspection
- Scratch Inspection
- Micro-Interferometer
- Surface Photographs
- Reflected Light Intensity
- Wallace Surface Dynamometer

**2. Direct Instrument Measurements:**

These methods provide numerical values for surface finish and are quantitative. They are operated using electrical principles and are classified into two types:

- Carrier-Modulating Principle: Instruments operating on this principle modulate a carrier wave to determine surface finish.
- Voltage-Generating Principle: Instruments operating on this principle generate voltage to assess surface finish. In both types, the output is amplified for further analysis.

These direct instrument measurements enable precise quantification of surface finish, providing valuable data for quality control and process optimization in industrial settings.

Some of the commonly used direct measurement instruments along with their principles of operation, construction, and advantages/disadvantages:

**1. Stylus Probe Instruments**

**Principle:** These instruments (figure 1.15) utilize a stylus that traverses the surface of the workpiece to measure surface irregularities, thereby assessing surface finish.

Working: The instrument comprises a skid, stylus, amplifying device, and recording device. As the skid moves over the surface, following its irregularities, the stylus moves vertically, and its movements are amplified and recorded to produce a trace.

**Advantages:** Can record any desired roughness parameter.

**Disadvantages:** Fragile materials cannot be measured; high initial cost; requires skilled operators.

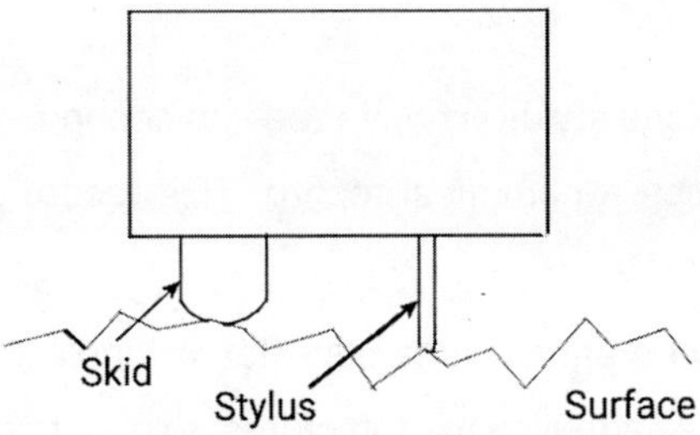


*Figure 1.15 Stylus Instrument*

**2. Tomlinson Surface Meter**

**Construction:** The instrument (figure 1.16) features a diamond stylus held against the surface of a lapped cylinder by spring pressure. The stylus moves in response to the probe's vertical movement, which is brought on by surface irregularities and leaves a trace on a smoked glass plate.

**Working:** A screw rotation moves the instrument across the surface, causing the lapped cylinder to roll and induce movement in the stylus, which produces a trace on the smoked glass plate.

**3. Profilometer**

**Description:** An indicator and recorder for roughness measurement in microns.

**Working:** The stylus, mounted in a pickup, is displaced up and down by surface irregularities, inducing movement in an induction coil. The resulting voltage is amplified and recorded.

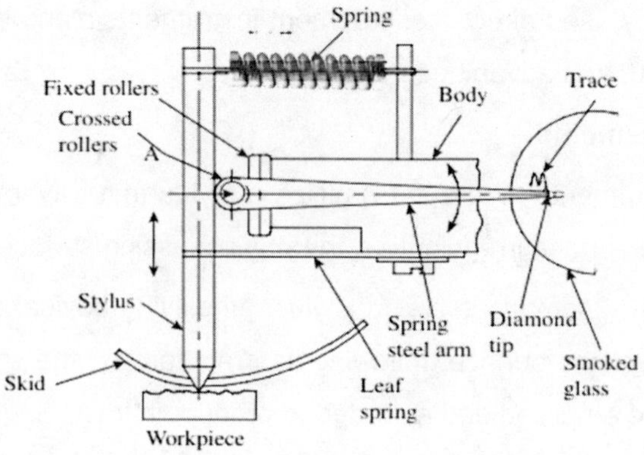


*Figure 1.16 Tomlinson Surface Meter*

**4. Taylor-Hobson Talysurf**

**Principle:** Utilizes a carrier-modulating principle to trace surface irregularities as shown in Figure 1.17.

**Working:** The movement of the stylus is converted into changes in electric current, which are then demodulated to produce a numerical record. This record provides a direct numerical assessment of surface features.

These direct measurement instruments offer valuable insights into the quality and characteristics of workpieces, enabling manufacturers to maintain high standards of precision and accuracy in their products. However, their effectiveness relies on skilled operators and careful calibration to ensure reliable measurements.

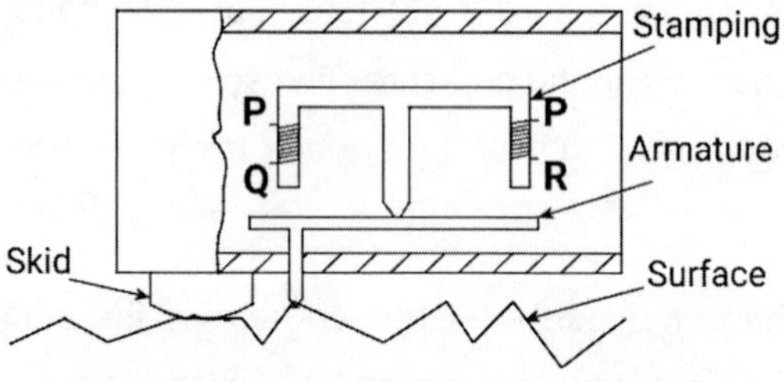


*Figure 1.17 Taylor Hobson Instrument*

## 1.11 COORDINATE MEASURING MACHINE

Measuring machines are employed to gauge the length over the external surfaces of lengthy objects such as length bars or similar members. These objects can vary in shape, being either rounded or flat and parallel. They offer distinct advantages over traditional tools like vernier callipers, micrometres, and screw gauges. The versatility of measuring machines allows them to be utilized across various types of work.

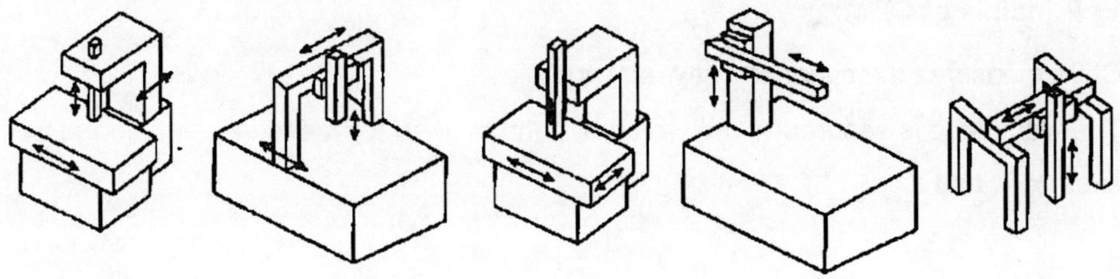

i) ii) iii) iv) v)

*Figure 1.18 Configuration of CMM*

*i) Moving lever cantilever arm type ii) Moving bridge type iii) Column type iv) Moving RAM horizontal type v) Gantry type*

**Coordinate Measuring Machine (CMM):**

- A specific type of measuring machine known as the coordinate measuring machine (CMM) (figure 1.19) is utilized for contact inspection of parts.
- In computer-integrated manufacturing setups, these machines are controlled through computer numerical control (CNC).
- General software is provided to facilitate the reverse engineering of complex-shaped objects.
- Components are digitized using CNC and CMM, then converted into computer models, streamlining the process.
- Automatic work part alignment on the table is a notable feature of these machines, enhancing efficiency.
- Time savings in inspections range from 5 to 10 percent when compared to manual methods.

**Types of Measuring Machines:**

a) Length Bar Measuring Machine
b) Newall Measuring Machine
c) Universal Measuring Machine
d) Coordinate Measuring Machine
e) Computer Controlled Coordinate Measuring Machine

**Types of Coordinate Measuring Machines (CMM):**

1. *Cantilever Type*
2. *Bridge Type*
3. *Horizontal Boring Mill Type*

**Working Principle of CMM:**

- CMM measures the distance between two holes.
- The workpiece is secured to the worktable and aligned for measurement along three axes: x, y, and z.

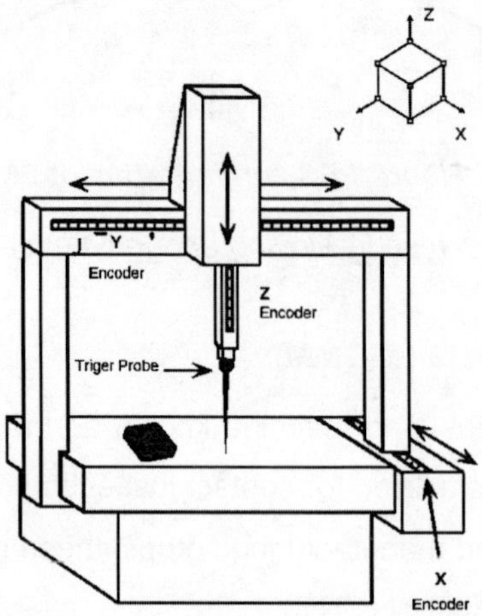


*Figure 1.19 Co-ordinate Measuring Machine*

- A taper probe tip is provided by the measuring head, seated in the first datum hole, and set to zero.
- Successive holes are measured, with the readout indicating the coordinates of the part print hole relative to the datum hole.
- Automatic recording and data processing units are integrated for complex geometric and statistical analysis.
- Special CMMs offer both linear and rotary axes for measuring features like cones, cylinders, and hemispheres.

**Advantages:**

1. Increased Inspection Rate
2. Enhanced Accuracy
3. Error Minimization
4. Reduced Skill Requirements
5. Cost Savings
6. Time Efficiency

**Disadvantages:**

1. Alignment Issues

2. Probe Runout
3. Perpendicular Errors in Z-Axis
4. Non-Square Movements
5. Digital System Errors

## 1.12 APPLICATIONS

Measurement, fundamental to metrology, is crucial for precision and consistency across industries:

1. Manufacturing: Ensures quality and process optimization.
2. Engineering and Construction: Guarantees proper fit and tolerance analysis.
3. Automotive: Verifies part quality and streamlines assembly.
4. Aerospace and Defence: Maintains precision and safety standards.
5. Medical and Pharmaceuticals: Ensures regulatory compliance and instrument reliability.
6. Research and Development: Supports experimentation and innovation.

## 1.13 UNIT SUMMARY

Introduction to Measurements serves as the cornerstone for grasping fundamental concepts and techniques essential across various fields. This unit covers a wide range of topics, including the definition and importance of measurement, measurement methods, standards, terms relevant to measuring instruments, measurement errors, and an overview of various measuring instruments such as thread gauges, angle measurement tools, gauges, comparators, surface finish assessment tools, and coordinate measuring machines (CMM).

This unit offers a comprehensive introduction to measurements, laying the groundwork for understanding advanced concepts and applications. Mastery of these principles is essential for accurate and reliable measurement practices across industries and disciplines.

## 1.14 EXERCISES

### Multiple Choice Questions

1. What is the primary objective of inspection in manufacturing?
    a. Ensuring mass production
    b. Maintaining customer relations
    c. Identifying shortcomings
    d. Streamlining operations

2. According to the International Vocabulary of Basic and General Terms in Metrology, what is measurement?
    a. Comparing unknown values with established standards
    b. Setting operational standards for manufacturing
    c. Experimenting with different measurement tools
    d. Scrutinizing components for compliance
3. What are the essential elements of a measuring system?
    a. Object, measurement, comparison
    b. Comparator, reference, measurand
    c. Measurand, instrument, comparator
    d. Standard unit, measurement, comparison
4. In which domain are precise measurements crucial for technological innovation?
    a. Finance and accounting
    b. Education and academia
    c. Healthcare and safety
    d. Engineering and design
5. How do accurate measurements contribute to global trade and commerce?
    a. By promoting market inefficiency
    b. By establishing internationally recognized standards
    c. By limiting fraud and deception
    d. By decreasing consumer protection
6. Which method of measurement involves comparing the quantity being measured directly to a known value of the same quantity?
    a. Indirect method
    b. Direct method
    c. Comparative method
    d. Transposition method
7. Which method of measurement utilizes mathematical equations to calculate the value of a quantity based on multiple related measurements?
    a. Null measurement method
    b. Coincidence method
    c. Indirect method
    d. Substitution method
8. What does the "Fundamental or absolute method" primarily involve?

a. Comparing the quantity to be measured with the known value of a similar quantity
b. Measuring a quantity directly, aligning with its definition
c. Utilizing differential measurement methods
d. Balancing the measured quantity with known values

9. Which method of measurement involves making contact between the instrument's sensor and the surface being measured?
   a. Contactless method
   b. Deflection method
   c. Complementary method
   d. Contact method
10. What does the acronym "SWIPE" stand for concerning factors influencing the accuracy of a measuring system?
    a. Standards, Workpiece, Instrument, Precision, Environment
    b. Standards, Workpiece, Inference, Precision, Efficiency
    c. Standards, Weight, Inference, Precision, Environment
    d. Standards, Workpiece, Instrument, Person, Environment
11. What term refers to the capability of a measuring device to detect small differences in the quantity being measured?
    a. Precision
    b. Sensitivity
    c. Reproducibility
    d. Calibration
12. Which of the following accurately defines precision in measurement?
    a. The agreement between measured values and true values
    b. The ability of a measuring device to consistently reproduce the same results
    c. The capability of a measuring instrument to detect small differences in quantity
    d. The difference between the mean value and the true value in a set of measurements
13. Accuracy is best described as:
    a. The degree of agreement among multiple measurements
    b. The consistency or repeatability of measurements

c. The level of agreement between a measured dimension and its true magnitude
d. The ability of a measuring device to detect small differences in the quantity being measured

14. What does hysteresis refer to in the context of measurements?
    a. The capability of a measuring device to detect small differences in the quantity being measured
    b. The ease with which readings from a measuring instrument can be interpreted
    c. The difference between the mean value and the true value in a set of measurements
    d. The phenomenon where the outputs of a measuring device vary for the same input depending on the direction of change
15. Of the following errors, which one's magnitude and direction can be controlled?
    a. Reading Errors
    b. Environmental Errors
    c. Dynamic Errors
    d. Systematic Errors

**MCQ Answers**

**1) c, 2) a, 3) c, 4) d, 5) b, 6) b, 7) c, 8) b, 9) d, 10) a, 11) b, 12) b, 13) c, 14) d, 15) d**

**Subjective Type Questions**

1. What is the definition of measurement and why is it significant in various industries?
2. Discuss the differences between direct and indirect methods of measurement, providing examples of each.
3. What are the key factors that influence the selection of measuring instruments in industrial applications?
4. Discuss the concepts of range, threshold, hysteresis, and calibration in the context of measuring instruments.
5. Classify errors in measurements, distinguishing between systematic and random errors. Provide examples of each.
6. Explain the use of thread gauge micrometres in precision measurement applications.
7. Discuss the principles and applications of bevel protractors and sine bars in angle measurements.

8. Outline the characteristics of comparators and discuss the different types commonly used in industry.
9. Define surface finish and elaborate on the terminology associated with it. Explain the significance of Talysurf surface roughness testers in assessing surface quality.
10. What is a Coordinate Measuring Machine (CMM) and how does it contribute to precision measurement processes?

## 1.15 PRACTICAL'S

**Practical Statement:**

**PS1.** Measure the diameter of the wire using a micrometre and compare the results with a digital micrometre

**PS2.** Measure the angle of the machined surface using a sine bar with slip gauges

**PS3.** Measure the thickness of ground MS plates using slip gauges

**Relevant Theory:**

Refer to the topic of 1.5. measuring instruments, 1.6. thread measurement, 1.7. angle measurement and 1.8. gauge measurement.

**Practical Outcome:**

**CO1:** Measure various components of linear measurement using vernier callipers and a micrometre

**CO2:** Measure various components of angle measurement using sine bar and bevel protractor

## 1.16 KNOW MORE

1. **Importance of Measurements:** Measurements are the foundation of scientific inquiry and technological progress, offering insights into natural phenomena, driving innovation, and ensuring quality in manufacturing.
2. **Measurement Uncertainty:** Every measurement carries some degree of uncertainty due to factors like instrument limitations, environmental conditions, and human error. Acknowledging and quantifying these uncertainties is crucial for validating measurements.
3. **Measuring Instruments:** A wide range of measuring instruments, from basic rulers to advanced spectrometers and oscilloscopes, cater to diverse measurement needs with

specific functionalities and accuracies. Understanding their principles aids in selecting the most suitable tool for each task.

4. **Recent Advancements:** Metrology is evolving rapidly with technological innovations such as artificial intelligence integration, nanoscale measurement techniques, and the use of quantum phenomena for ultra-precision measurements, demonstrating its continuous progress and impact across industries.

5. **Applications Across Industries:** Measurements and metrology play essential roles in aerospace, automotive, healthcare, telecommunications, and consumer electronics industries. Tailoring metrological solutions to industry-specific needs enhances efficiency and quality across various sectors.

From fundamental principles to cutting-edge advancements, the journey towards precision and accuracy is rich with exploration and discovery.

## 1.17 REFERENCES AND SUGGESTED READINGS

1. "**Fundamentals of Dimensional Metrology**" by Roger Harlow, Cengage Learning, 2011.
2. "**Introduction to Engineering Experimentation**" by Anthony J. Wheeler and Ahmad R. Ganji, Pearson, 2016.
3. "**Handbook of Dimensional Measurement**" by Mark A. Curtis, Wiley, 2013.
4. "**Metrology and Measurement Systems**" by Andrzej Stepinski, CRC Press, 2015.
5. "**Engineering Measurements and Metrology**" by Raghavendra, Krishnamurthy, and P. L. Srinivasa Murthy, Oxford University Press, 2019.

**Suggested Readings**

6. "**Statistical Methods for Quality Improvement**" by Thomas P. Ryan - Provides in-depth coverage of statistical techniques used in quality control and metrology.
7. "**Instrumentation and Measurement in Electrical Engineering**" by Roman Malaric - Focuses on instrumentation and measurement techniques specifically in the field of electrical engineering.
8. "**Measurement and Instrumentation Principles**" by Alan S. Morris - Offers a comprehensive overview of measurement principles and instrumentation across various engineering disciplines.

9. "**Metrology for Engineers**" by Donald J. Harding and David J. Owen - Provides practical guidance on metrological principles and techniques relevant to engineering applications.

**Additional Materials**

10. **YouTube Channels:**
    - "**Metrology & Quality Services**" - Offers tutorials and demonstrations on various metrology topics, including calibration techniques and measurement principles.
    - "**NPL Measurement**" - Provides educational videos from the National Physical Laboratory (NPL) covering a wide range of measurement-related subjects, from basic concepts to advanced instrumentation.
    - "**MIT Open Courseware**" - Features lectures and course materials from the Massachusetts Institute of Technology (MIT), including topics such as experimental methods and instrumentation.
11. **TED Talks:**
    - "**The Magic of Metrology**" by Dr. Janez Potocnik - Explores the importance of accurate measurements in addressing global challenges and fostering innovation.
    - "**The Art of Science and Metrology**" by John P. Hartnett - Discusses the intersection of art, science, and metrology, highlighting the beauty and precision inherent in measurement.

**Dynamic QR Code for Further Reading**

Measurement and Types    The Science of Measurement    National Physical Laboratory

# 2 Transducers and Strain Gauges

## UNIT SPECIFICS

*This unit presents information related to the following topics:*

- *Introduction to transducers: Characteristics, Classification of transducers, two coil self-inductance transducer, Piezoelectric transducer*
- *Strain Measurements: Strain gauge, Classification, mounting of strain gauges, Strain gauge rosettes-two and three elements*
- *Measurement of force, torque, and pressure: Introduction; Force measurement: Spring Balance, Proving ring, Load cell; Torque measurement: Prony brake, Eddy current, Hydraulic dynamometer; Pressure measurement: Mcloed gauge*

### *Applications*

*This unit is designed to familiarize readers with the fundamental aspects of transducers and strain gauges, which are essential components in various measurement systems. The unit begins with an introduction to transducers, discussing their characteristics and classification, and explaining specific types like the two coil self-inductance transducer and Piezoelectric transducer.*

*Furthermore, the unit covers strain measurements, including the use of strain gauges, their classification, and mounting techniques. It also introduces strain gauge rosettes and details the application of two and three-element rosettes for strain analysis.*

*In addition, the unit elaborates on the measurement of force, torque, and pressure, explaining the methods and instruments used, such as spring balances, proving rings, load cells for force measurement, Prony brake, Eddy current and hydraulic dynamometers for torque measurement, and Mcloed gauge for pressure measurement.*

*Apart from this, at the end of the unit, the overall broad concepts are provided as a unit summary. Besides, a large number of multiple-choice questions as well as descriptive-type questions with Bloom's taxonomy action verbs are included. A list of references and suggested readings is given in the unit so that one can go through them for practice. It is important to note that for getting more information on various topics of interest, some QR codes have been provided in different sections which can be scanned for relevant supportive knowledge. Video resources along with QR codes are mentioned for getting more information on various topics of interest which can be surfed or scanned through mobile phones for viewing.*

## RATIONALE

*Transducers and strain gauges are vital in various engineering applications for converting physical quantities into measurable signals. Understanding the principles and applications of these devices is crucial for engineers involved in designing and analyzing measurement systems. This unit provides a comprehensive overview of transducers and strain gauges, enabling students and professionals to accurately measure and interpret force, torque, and pressure in different contexts.*

## PRE-REQUISITES

*Before reading this unit, the students are advised to revisit the following:*

- *Basic Physics: Principles of force, torque, and pressure*
- *Basic Electrical Engineering: Understanding of electrical circuits and signal processing*
- *Basic Engineering Mechanics*

## UNIT OUTCOMES

*After studying this unit, students will be able to:*

- *U2-O1: Understand the characteristics and classification of transducers.*
- *U2-O2: Explain the principles and applications of strain gauges.*
- *U2-O3: Demonstrate the methods of force measurement using different instruments.*
- *U2-O4: Apply techniques for measuring torque using various dynamometers.*
- *U2-O5: Measure pressure accurately using instruments like the Mcloed gauge.*

## EXPECTED MAPPING WITH COURSE OUTCOMES

*(1- Weak Correlation; 2- Medium correlation; 3- Strong Correlation)*

| Unit Outcomes (U2) | CO-1 | CO-2 | CO-3 | CO-4 | CO-5 |
|---|---|---|---|---|---|
| U2-O1 | 3 | 2 | 3 | 2 | 1 |
| U2-O2 | 3 | 3 | 2 | 2 | 1 |
| U2-O3 | 2 | 2 | 3 | 1 | 1 |
| U2-O4 | 3 | 3 | 2 | 3 | 1 |
| U2-O5 | 2 | 3 | 3 | 2 | 1 |

## INTRODUCTION

Transducers and strain gauges are the essential building blocks of modern measurement systems. Their ability to translate physical phenomena into quantifiable electrical signals underpins precision across manufacturing, scientific research, and quality assurance. Transducers form the cornerstone of measurement by transforming various physical quantities into interpretable electrical signals. A transducer transforms energy between various forms. It converts physical non-electrical amounts (e.g., force, light, sound) into measurable electrical signals in measurement and control systems. They serve two key functions:

1. Sensing: Transducers detect changes in physical quantities, enabling their measurement.
2. Signal Generation: Transducers enable us to quantify and analyze various measurements by converting physical properties into proportional electrical signals.

## 2.1 TRANSDUCERS

Transducers play a pivotal role in metrology by facilitating the measurement of physical quantities like temperature, pressure, or force. They achieve this by converting these physical parameters into electrical signals, which can be conveniently measured, transmitted, and recorded. Since electronic instruments cannot often directly measure many physical quantities, the conversion process carried out by transducers becomes indispensable. Transducers enable the seamless integration of precise electronic circuits for measurement and analysis by translating physical properties into electrical signals. Moreover, these electrical signals can undergo amplification and conditioning, thereby mitigating the effects of noise and enhancing measurement accuracy. Furthermore, the electrical nature of these signals allows for easy transmission over long distances, facilitating real-time remote monitoring of physical quantities. This capability proves particularly beneficial in industrial environments and applications related to environmental monitoring.

### 2.1.1 ESSENTIAL CHARACTERISTICS OF TRANSDUCERS

Transducers are vital in transforming diverse physical quantities into quantifiable electrical signals in precise measurement science. Several key characteristics are paramount for transducers employed in metrological applications to ensure accurate and reliable measurements.

1) High Sensitivity: Transducers require exceptional sensitivity to detect minute changes in measurements, ensuring accurate representation by converting them into electrical signals.
2) Linearity: Maintaining a proportional relationship between input and output signals is crucial for transducers to ensure accuracy and reliability under all conditions.
3) High Accuracy: Metrological transducers must offer precise measurements to validate experimental results and product quality, avoiding errors and ensuring reliability.
4) Stability: Transducers should show minimal signal drift over time for consistent and reliable measurements without frequent adjustments.
5) High Resolution: Transducers with high resolution can detect and measure even the smallest changes in the measured quantity reliably.
6) Broad Frequency Response: Metrological transducers need a wide frequency response to measure dynamic physical quantities without distortion accurately.
7) Environmental Robustness: Transducers must endure environmental factors like temperature fluctuations and electromagnetic interference for dependable performance.
8) Calibration and Traceability: Regular calibration against standards with traceable measurements ensures confidence in transducer output and consistency across different applications.

### 2.1.2 CLASSIFICATION OF TRANSDUCERS

Transducers are categorized using various criteria, including their application area, energy conversion method, nature of output signal, electrical parameters, principle of operation, and typical applications. Broadly, transducers can be classified based on the principle of transduction as follows:

- Capacitive Transducers
- Inductance Transducers
- Resistive Transducers

#### 2.1.2.1 Capacitive Transducers

Capacitive transducers are a type of sensor that excels at converting various physical quantities, such as displacement and pressure, into electrical signals. Unlike a typical capacitor with a fixed plate separation, these have one movable plate. This allows external forces, like pressure or movement, to alter the spacing between the plates. The working principle relies on the fact that capacitance changes with the distance between the plates and the material filling the gap, known as the dielectric (which can be air, a specific material, gas, or liquid). As this distance or dielectric property changes due to the applied force, the capacitance of the transducer changes as well. This variation in capacitance is then directly measured as an electrical signal. One of the key strengths of capacitive transducers is their ability to measure both static (unchanging) and dynamic (continuously varying) quantities. Additionally, the movable plate can be directly connected to the object being measured, enabling it to operate in both contacting and non-contacting modes, making it highly versatile for various applications.

Upon detecting changes in capacitance, the transducers translate them into electrical signals for subsequent analysis or processing. Renowned for their elevated sensitivity, broad frequency response, and minimal power consumption, capacitive transducers find applications in diverse fields such as pressure sensing, proximity detection, and humidity measurement.

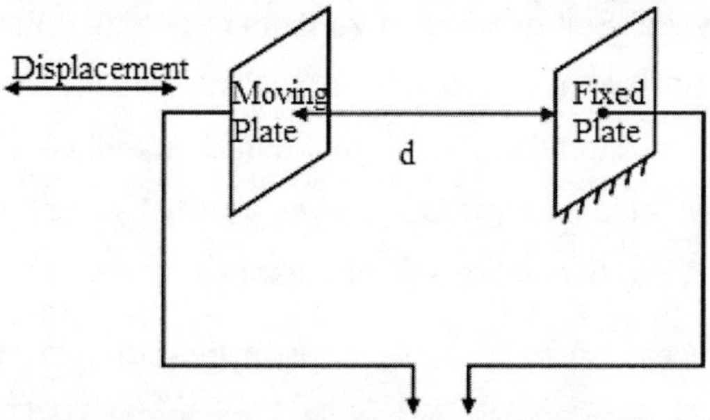


*Figure 2.1 Capacitive Transducers*

Common variants of capacitive transducers include:

- Capacitive displacement sensors: These sensors discern shifts in displacement by detecting capacitance fluctuations induced by the movement of either or both plates.
- Capacitive pressure sensors: These sensors gauge pressure alterations by sensing changes in capacitance stemming from the deformation of a diaphragm or membrane.
- Capacitive humidity sensors: These sensors assess humidity shifts by detecting variations in capacitance caused by moisture absorption or desorption within a dielectric medium.

The following are the applications of capacitive transducers.

1) Variable Capacitance Pressure Gauge works with the principle of operation that an externally applied force alters the distance between two parallel plates. It is used for measuring displacement and pressure.
2) Capacitor microphones detect sound pressure through variations in capacitance between a fixed plate and a movable diaphragm. They are commonly used for recording speech, music, and noise.
3) A dielectric gauge is utilized to measure liquid level and thickness. The changes in the dielectric result in variations in capacitance.

#### 2.1.2.2 Inductance Transducers

An inductance transducer is a device designed to transform a physical parameter, such as displacement, into an electrical signal by detecting variations in inductance. Inductance refers to a conductor's inherent resistance to alterations in the current passing through it. This property relies on the coil's geometry and the characteristics of the material, including its permeability, contained within the coil. Inductance transducers function as either self-generating or passive types. Self-generating variants capitalize on the principle of electrical generation, where the movement of a conductor within a magnetic field induces a voltage. This motion can stem from alterations in the measured quantity. An inductance transducer, also called an electromechanical transducer, serves as an electrical apparatus engineered to translate physical motion into fluctuations in inductance.

Inductive transducers come in two primary types: simple inductance and two-coil mutual inductance. The Linear Variable Differential Transformer (LVDT) is a notable example.

***1. Simple Inductance***

This type of inductive transducer uses a single coil as its primary element. When the measured mechanical component moves, the strength of the magnetic field generated by the circuit changes. As a result, the circuit's inductance and output are altered. This allows for easy adjustment of the circuit's output based on the input value, making it simple to calculate the value of the measured parameter.

When an inductive transducer operates on self-inductance, the inductance can be mathematically related to the reluctance.

$$L = \frac{n^2}{R}$$

Where,

n - number of turns of the coil

R- the reluctance of the magnetic circuit

The reluctance of the magnetic coil (R) is expressed as,

$$R = \frac{1}{\mu_o \mu_r A}$$

Where,

$\mu_o$ is the permeability of air, and $\mu_r$ is the relative permeability.

A is the cross-sectional area of the coil.

Therefore, the inductance of a coil is expressed in terms of the permeability of material (μ) and the geometric factor (K) since the inductance is a function of N, μ and K, i.e., L = f( N, μ, K). In the simple inductance-type transducer, there are three primary constructional arrangements for the inductive coil:

Type I: The inductance coil is wound over a rectangular magnetic material.

Type II: The inductance coil is wound on a cylindrical magnetic material.

Type III: Two coils are employed in the setup.

***Type I: The inductance coil is wound over a rectangular magnetic material.***

An inductive transducer of this design employs a ferromagnetic core shaped like a rectangle around which a single inductor coil with N turns is wound. This coil acts as the magnetomotive force (MMF) source, driving the generated flux through the established magnetic circuit.

An armature element is positioned opposite to the wound inductive coil. Any movement in this mechanical armature alters the permeability of the flux path, subsequently modifying the circuit's inductance. This change in inductance corresponds to an output, which can be directly calibrated to reflect the movement of the armature element

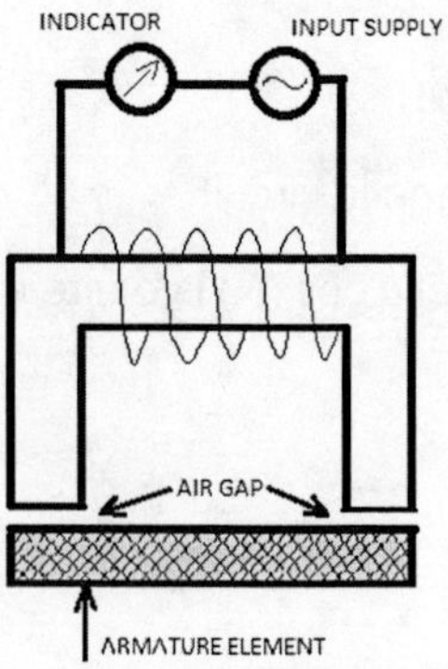


*Figure 2.2 Simple Inductance Transducer -Type I*

***Type II: The inductance coil is wound on a cylindrical magnetic material.***

In Fig 2.3, a round hollow magnetic material is the base over which the inductive coil is wound. Within this hollow tube, a movable magnetic core is situated. As the core moves, it induces a change in inductance, resulting in a corresponding output in the connected output indicator across the wound coil.

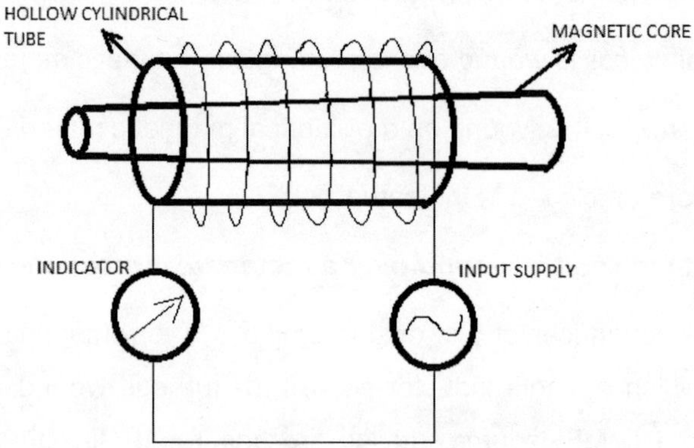


*Figure 2.3 Hollow Coil inductive Transducer -Type II*

***Type III:* Two-Coil Self-Inductance Transducer**

In this configuration, two coils are employed. When the magnetic core, positioned at the center of these two coils, moves, it alters the relative inductance of the coils. Consequently, the overall inductance of the circuit changes in proportion to the variation in the ratio of the two inductive coils.

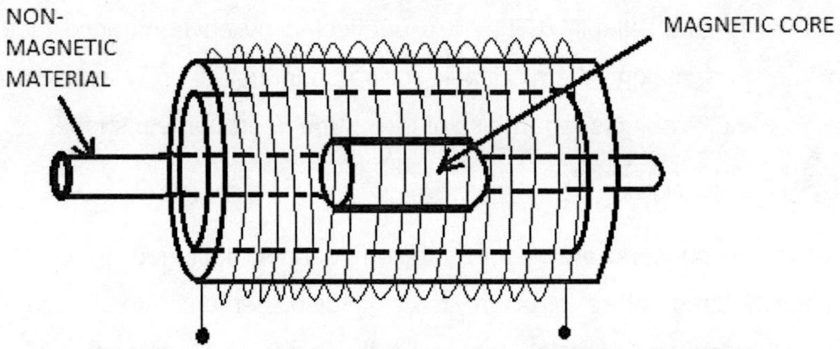


*Figure 2.4 Two Coil Inductance Transducer -Type III*

The two-coil self-inductance transducer comprises dual distinct coils organized in a specific configuration. The primary coil receives excitation from an external power source, while the secondary coil captures the output. Notably, both the mechanical input and output are directly proportional in this arrangement.

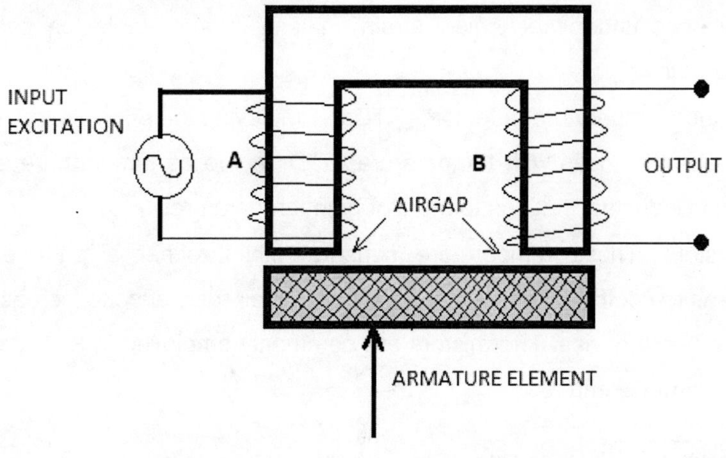


*Figure 2.5 Self-Inductance type transducer*

Two separate coils, A and B, are wound opposite to each other on a rectangular magnetic material in this setup. The excitation coil is denoted as A, while the output coil is represented as B. An armature is positioned opposite to both the input and output inductive coils. Any alteration in the armature's position changes the air gap between the rectangular inductive base material and the armature element. Consequently, the inductance of the output coil B changes in proportion to the mechanical displacement of the armature.

Advantages of two-coil self-inductance transducers include their non-contact operation, durability, and reliability. They are unaffected by environmental factors such as dust, dirt, or moisture, making them suitable for harsh industrial environments. Additionally, they can detect metallic objects regardless of their surface properties, shape, or colour.

#### 2.1.2.3 Resistive Transducers

Resistive transducers are electronic components designed to convert physical quantities, such as temperature, pressure, force, or displacement, into changes in electrical resistance. This variation in resistance facilitates easy measurement and subsequent conversion back into the corresponding physical quantity. These transducers find extensive use across various applications owing to their simplicity, cost-effectiveness, and precision. Among the common types are:

- Potentiometers: These are adjustable resistors allowing manual adjustment, frequently utilized as voltage dividers to regulate applied circuit voltage.
- Strain gauges: Consisting of small wire-based resistors, strain gauges exhibit changes in resistance under mechanical strain, making them suitable for measuring force, pressure, or weight.
- Resistance temperature detectors (RTDs): Employing the principle that the resistance of a metal wire rises with temperature, RTDs serve as temperature sensors, often applied in industrial settings to monitor high temperatures.
- Thermistors: These temperature sensors exhibit either a positive or negative temperature coefficient of resistance, causing their resistance to increase or decrease with temperature rise. Thermistors are commonly employed in low-cost temperature measurement scenarios.

### 2.1.3 PIEZOELECTRIC TRANSDUCER

The term "piezoelectric" comes from the Greek word "piezen," which means pressing or squeezing. The piezoelectric effect is a phenomenon where applying mechanical stress or force to a quartz crystal generates electrical charges on its surface. This effect was first discovered by Pierre and Jacques Curie. The amount of charge generated is directly proportional to the rate of change of the applied mechanical stress, resulting in a higher voltage with increased stress levels.

Piezoelectric transducers, also known as piezoelectric sensors, are instruments designed to convert various physical quantities into measurable electrical signals by harnessing the piezoelectric effect. A transducer is a device that converts energy from one form to another, and piezoelectric material is a specific type of transducer. When force or pressure is applied to this material, it induces a voltage that is directly proportional to the applied stress. This voltage can be easily measured using standard voltage-measuring equipment. The main advantage of piezoelectric transducers is the direct correlation between the measured voltage and the applied stress. This inherent relationship makes it easier to determine physical quantities such as mechanical stress or force based solely on voltage readings. As a result, piezoelectric transducers provide a convenient and efficient way to directly measure various physical phenomena, making them useful across a wide range of scientific and industrial applications.

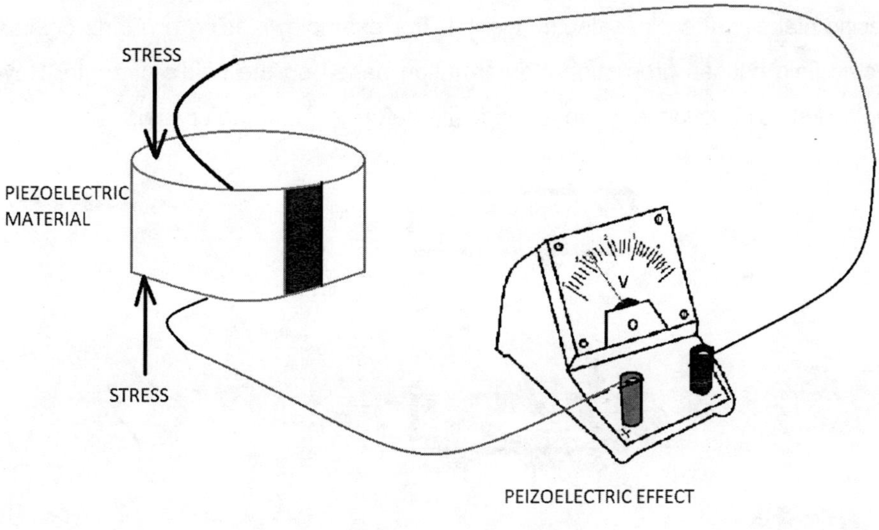


*Figure 2.6 Piezoelectric Effect*

Piezoelectric actuators and sensors operate in opposite ways. While sensors convert mechanical stress into an electrical signal, actuators use electric voltage to generate mechanical deformation in the material. By regulating the voltage applied, the actuator's movement can be precisely controlled, allowing for accurate positioning and actuation. Piezoelectric transducers are made up of a quartz crystal of silicon and oxygen arranged in a crystalline structure known as $SiO_2$. Although most crystals have a symmetrical unit cell, piezoelectric quartz crystals do not. However, despite the lack of symmetry, they maintain electrical neutrality. The arrangement of atoms inside the crystal may not be symmetrical, but the positive and negative charges are balanced, resulting in a net neutral charge. When mechanical stress is applied along a specific plane, quartz crystals generate an electrical polarity. This stress can be in the form of compression or tension, and its magnitude and direction determine the resulting deformation.

The piezoelectric effect is a fundamental phenomenon that occurs when certain materials generate an electric charge when exposed to mechanical stress. An unstressed quartz crystal remains uncharged, but subjecting it to compressive stress induces positive charges on one side and negative charges on the opposite side. This polarity shift causes a dimensional alteration in the crystal, elongating it and making it thinner. Applying tensile stress reverses this charge distribution, resulting in a contraction of the crystal, making it shorter and thicker. Piezoelectric transducers operate on this principle. The effect is reversible, meaning that applying an electric voltage induces a dimensional change along a specific plane in the piezoelectric crystal. For example, placing a quartz crystal within an electric field causes proportional deformation based on the field's strength. Reversing the electric field's direction leads to an opposite deformation in the crystal.

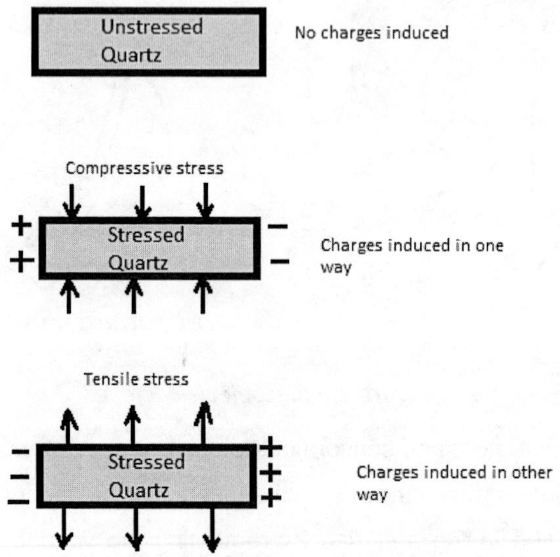


*Figure 2.7 Working of Piezoelectric Transducers*

Piezoelectric transducers serve as self-generating devices, obviating the need for an external electric voltage source. They produce an electric voltage directly proportional to the applied stress or force, making them highly sensitive and suitable for sensor applications. Due to their exceptional frequency response, piezoelectric transducers are widely used in accelerometers and find relevance across diverse fields. Applications of the piezoelectric effect extend to sound production and detection, electronic frequency generation, and ignition systems for cigarette lighters. Moreover, piezoelectric transducers are integral components in sonar technology and microphones, facilitating the measurement of force, pressure, and displacement with remarkable precision and reliability.

***Advantages of Piezoelectric Transducer and Disadvantages***

1. Piezoelectric transducers do not require an external power source to function. They generate their own electrical signal when subjected to mechanical stress.
2. Due to their small dimensions, piezoelectric transducers are often lightweight and easily integrated into various equipment and devices.
3. These transducers possess a broad range of operational frequencies, enabling them to detect and measure rapidly changing phenomena.

***Disadvantages of Piezoelectric Transducer***

1. Piezoelectric transducers are primarily suited for measuring dynamic or changing quantities like pressure fluctuations or vibrations. They are not suitable for measuring static (unchanging) values.
2. The output of a piezoelectric transducer can be affected by changes in temperature, requiring potential calibration adjustments or temperature-controlled environments.
3. The electrical signal generated by these transducers can be relatively weak, often necessitating additional circuitry to amplify the signal for effective measurement.
4. Shaping and achieving the desired strength in piezoelectric materials can be challenging compared to other materials.

***Applications of piezoelectric transducers using various piezoelectric materials***

Piezoelectric materials find versatile applications across multiple fields. Microphones convert sound waves into electrical signals through diaphragm stress, enabling amplification for audible sound production. Automotive safety benefits from piezoelectric sensors in seat belt pre-tensioners, where rapid force changes trigger tightening mechanisms during sudden deceleration. Medical diagnostics benefit from piezoelectric transducers in ultrasound machines, facilitating high-resolution imaging of internal organs. Electric lighters utilize piezoelectric elements to generate sparks for igniting fuel. Shockwave and blast wave studies utilize piezoelectric sensors due to their rapid pressure response, aiding in understanding high-speed phenomena. Inkjet printers employ piezoelectric crystals for precise ink droplet ejection, ensuring high-resolution printing. Automatic doors utilize piezoelectric sensors, responding to pressure changes when someone steps on them, triggering door opening mechanisms. Additionally, piezoelectric materials contribute to fuel injectors, noise-cancellation headphones, and vibration sensors in various applications.

## 2.2 STRAIN MEASUREMENT

Strain measurement involves quantifying the deformation or alteration in the shape of an object when exposed to external forces. It is a pivotal concept in engineering, material science, and specific areas of physics due to its ability to evaluate the structural integrity of loaded objects, ensuring they function within safe parameters and comprehend the mechanical characteristics of materials, including elasticity and strength. It also helps to identify potential issues and monitor structures and machinery to prevent major failures.

### 2.2.1 STRAIN GAUGES

A strain gauge is a pivotal instrument for quantifying strain or deformation across diverse material substrates and is crucial for monitoring mechanical stresses in engineering applications. Particularly vital in solid mechanics, strain gauges ascertain the extent of deformation incurred by objects under external forces. Typically fashioned from a thin wire or foil arranged in a grid or zigzag pattern, these gauges exhibit alterations in electrical resistance commensurate with applied mechanical strain. This resistance modification, directly proportional to the exerted strain, facilitates meticulous deformation measurement.

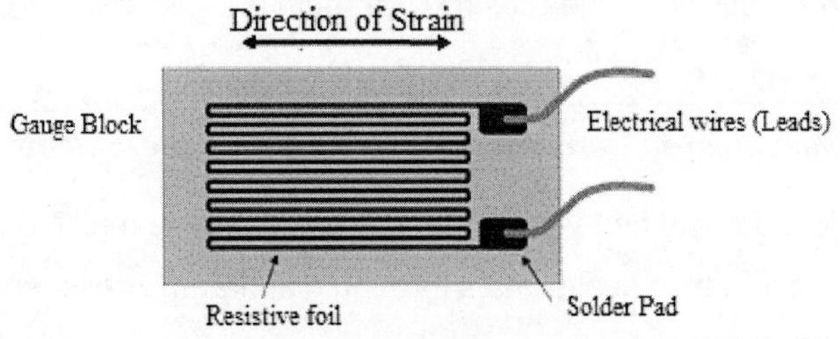


*Figure 2.8 Strain Gauge*

Extensive applications of strain gauges encompass diverse fields and they play a vital role in:

1. Monitoring and analyzing the behaviour of structures under various loading conditions.

2. Determining material properties like elasticity and strength.
3. Assessing the structural integrity of components and structures.
4. Optimizing designs by providing valuable insights into material behaviour under stress.

When an external force is applied to an object, it induces deformation, altering its shape and potentially causing variations in its length and cross-sectional area. These alterations affect the attached strain gauge, resulting in discernible shifts in its electrical resistance. To precisely quantify this change, a gauge indicator is affixed or soldered onto the surface of the object. As the object experiences deformation in response to the applied force, the strain gauge undergoes corresponding shape changes, thereby eliciting resistance alterations. This change in resistance directly indicates the object's response to the applied force, offering valuable insights into its mechanical properties and structural integrity. Through careful analysis of these resistance variations, engineers and researchers can glean critical information about the object's behaviour under stress, aiding in designing, testing, and optimising various mechanical systems and structures.

**Working Principle of Strain Gauges**

Strain gauges stand as essential tools in the realm of measurement, offering precise insights into the properties of objects by modulating electrical resistance in response to mechanical strain. These devices typically consist of a strain gauge affixed to a flexible substrate, often a slender wire or foil crafted from conductive materials like copper or constantan. When subjected to mechanical strain, this wire or foil undergoes deformation, inducing length and cross-sectional area alterations. These physical changes directly influence the electrical resistance of the gauge, facilitating measurements of the object's properties. In the realm of strain gauge systems, the assessment of resistance variation commonly employs a Wheatstone bridge circuit. This circuit, comprising four resistive arms, incorporates one arm housing the strain gauge while the remaining three arms contain fixed resistors. Upon the application of strain, the resistance of the gauge undergoes modification, instigating an imbalance within the Wheatstone bridge. This imbalance, in turn, yields a minute electrical output signal proportionate to the applied strain. The meticulous analysis of this signal enables the determination of strain magnitude, thereby facilitating the comprehensive evaluation of mechanical properties such as stress, load, and deformation in structural components. The ubiquitous utilization of strain gauges spans a multitude of industries, including civil engineering, aerospace, automotive, and materials testing. Within these sectors, strain gauges serve as indispensable instruments for unraveling the intricate behavior of structures and materials under various loads, thereby informing critical decision-making processes and fostering advancements in engineering and technology.

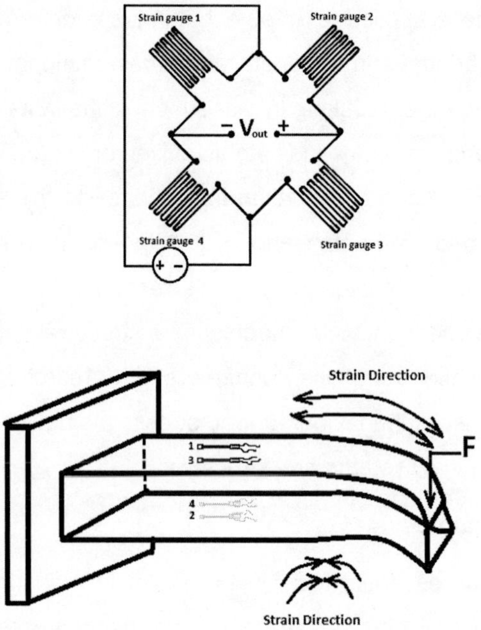


*Figure 2.9 Working principle of Strain gauge*

When a force is applied to a metallic wire, it undergoes strain, causing an increase in its length. The magnitude of strain experienced by the wire is directly related to the applied force. If the wire's initial length is denoted by $L_1$ and the final length after the application of force is denoted by $L_2$, the strain (ε) can be calculated using the formula:

$$\varepsilon = \frac{L_2 - L_1}{L_1}$$

When subjected to stretching, a wire experiences elongation along its length, concomitant with a reduction in diameter, thereby undergoing a transformation in shape that influences its electrical resistance. Precisely, the elongation of the conductor leads to a decrease in its electrical resistance. This alteration in resistance is amenable to quantification and correlation with the magnitude of the applied force. Strain gauges fulfill the essential role of quantifying force, displacement, and stress within structural components and materials. The relationship between the input, represented by the applied strain, and the output, symbolized by the resultant change in resistance, is encapsulated by the term "gauge factor" or "gauge gradient." This parameter denotes the ratio of the change in resistance (ΔR) to the applied strain (ε). In essence, the gauge factor provides a quantitative measure of the sensitivity of the strain gauge to mechanical deformation, thereby facilitating precise and accurate measurements of force, displacement, and stress in diverse engineering applications.

For instance, consider a wire strain gauge comprising a uniform conductor with resistivity (r), length (l), and cross-sectional area (A). The resistance (R) is contingent upon its geometry, given by:

$$R = \rho \frac{l}{A}$$

The rate at which the combined effects of changes in length, cross-sectional area, and resistivity determine resistance changes.

$$dR = \frac{\rho}{A} dl - \frac{\rho l}{A^2} dA + \frac{l}{A} d\rho$$

$$\Rightarrow \frac{dR}{R} = \frac{dl}{l} - \frac{dA}{A} + \frac{d\rho}{\rho}$$

When the strain gauge is properly attached and bonded to an object's surface, it is considered to deform in conjunction with the object. The strain experienced by the strain gauge wire in the longitudinal direction is equivalent to the strain experienced by the surface in the same direction.

$$\varepsilon_l = \frac{dl}{l}$$

When a wire undergoes deformation, its Poisson's ratio influences its cross-sectional area. For a cylindrical wire with an initial radius of r, any normal strain experienced in the radial direction is affected accordingly. The normal strain in the radial direction ($\varepsilon_\gamma$) can be calculated using the following formula:

$$\varepsilon_\gamma = \frac{dr}{r} = -\nu \cdot \varepsilon_l = -\nu \frac{dl}{l}$$

The rate of change of the cross-sectional area is two times of the radial strain when the strain is small.

$$\frac{dA}{A} = (1+\varepsilon_r)^2 - 1 = 2\varepsilon_r + \varepsilon_r^{\ 2} \approx 2\varepsilon_r$$
$$= -2v\frac{dl}{l}$$

The rate of change of resistance is

$$\frac{dR}{R} = \frac{dl}{l} - \frac{dA}{A} + \frac{d\rho}{\rho} = (1+2v)\frac{dl}{l} + \frac{d\rho}{\rho}$$
$$= (1+2v)\varepsilon_l + \frac{d\rho}{\rho}$$

The resistance sensitivity to the strain for a given material can be calibrated with an equation

$$S \triangleq \frac{dR/R}{\varepsilon_l}$$
$$= 1 + 2v + \frac{d\rho/\rho}{\varepsilon_l}$$

Strain gauge vendors typically provide the sensitivity factor S, which can be used to calculate the change in electric resistance and determine the average strain at the attachment point.

$$\varepsilon_l = \frac{dR/R}{S} \approx \frac{\Delta R}{SR}$$

**Applications**

1. Strain gauges play a vital role in structural monitoring, safeguarding structures like bridges and dams by measuring strains and stresses to detect potential weaknesses.
2. In experimental studies, strain gauges analyze material behavior under various loads, offering insights into material performance.
3. Aerospace relies on strain gauges to monitor aircraft structural integrity, detecting fatigue and stress concentrations to ensure safety.
4. Automotive testing utilizes strain gauges to assess component performance and durability, optimizing designs and enhancing safety.
5. Strain gauges monitor ground movements, aiding in assessing slope stability, predicting landslides, and monitoring structural performance.

6. Critical in infrastructure, strain gauges monitor the health of structures like bridges and tunnels, detecting degradation and ensuring safety.

**Advantages and Limitations**

The exceptional sensitivity of strain gauges allows them to detect even the slightest changes in shape, making them ideal for monitoring delicate structures and identifying potential issues before they escalate. This is particularly valuable in civil engineering for ensuring the safety and integrity of buildings and infrastructure. Strain gauges work effectively across various materials, from concrete and steel to composites. This versatility allows them to be used in a wide range of engineering projects. They can be attached directly to surfaces or embedded within structures, providing targeted strain data from specific locations of interest.

Strain gauges deliver continuous data, enabling engineers to monitor the behaviour of structures in real-time. This is especially crucial during load testing, construction phases, or seismic activity, allowing for immediate identification of any concerning strain levels or deformations. Compared to other techniques like extensometers, strain gauges offer a more economical way to measure strain. Their affordability and reusability make them ideal for conducting multiple measure-ments at different points within a structure.

**Limitations of strain gauges**

Installation of strain gauges can be challenging and requires expertise and meticulous attention to detail. Careful attachment, wiring, and calibration of strain gauges are necessary for accurate readings. This process can be time-consuming and add complexity to a project. Temperature fluctuations, humidity, and vibrations can affect strain gauge readings, introducing errors or interfering with measurement accuracy. Environmental controls or shielding techniques may need to be implemented to mitigate these influences.

Every strain gauge is designed to function within a specific range, ensuring the accuracy and reliability of the data it provides. When high strains are expected, such as during dynamic load testing or extreme events, accuracy may decrease beyond this limit. Strain gauges are delicate and susceptible to damage during construction or accidental impacts. Therefore, ensuring their protection is essential to obtaining reliable and consistent measurements.

## 2.2.2 CLASSIFICATIONS OF STRAIN GAUGES

Strain gauges are available in various types and configurations, each tailored to specific requirements and operating conditions. Understanding the classifications of strain gauges is essential for selecting the most suitable option for a particular application. These classifications are based on various factors, including construction, configuration, applications, attachment method, etc. Engineers can make informed decisions to ensure accurate and reliable measurements in diverse environments and conditions by categorizing strain gauges according to these characteristics.

***Types of Strain Gauges based on the principle of working***

1. **Mechanical:** The mechanical strain gauge comprises two plastic layers with a ruled scale on the bottom and a red arrow or pointer on the top. These layers adhere to opposite sides of the crack, allowing the pointer to move along the scale as the crack widens due to mechanical loading. In simpler versions, a piece of plastic or glass is affixed across the crack, and its response to strain is observed to determine the extent of deformation.
2. **Electrical:** These gauges typically encompass slender, rectangular-shaped foil strips adorned with intricate wiring patterns that ultimately converge onto a pair of electrical cables. When subjected to strain, the monitored material imparts subtle bending to the foil strip, prompting the labyrinthine wires to either undergo separation (resulting in slight thinning) or converge (leading to slight thickening). Consequently, as the cross-sectional dimensions of the metal wire fluctuate, its electrical resistance undergoes commensurate variations in response to the applied stress. Under conditions where the applied forces remain within a minimal range, the ensuing deformation remains elastic, eventually allowing the strain gauge to revert to its initial configuration. This characteristic highlights the gauge's resilience to mechanical loading, ensuring its longevity and reliability in diverse measurement applications.
3. **Piezoelectric**: Piezoelectric sensors are a type of strain gauge that generates electrical voltages when compressed or stretched, making them highly sensitive and reliable. This is because they exhibit piezoelectricity, which is the ability of a material to generate electricity when subjected to mechanical stress. By measuring the voltage output of these sensors, we can easily calculate the amount of strain that the material is experiencing. Due to their accuracy and reliability, piezoelectric strain gauges are widely used in various applications.

4. **Electrical Strain Gauge:** A strain gauge operates based on the physical principle of electrical conductance, which relies on the conductor's electrical conductivity and geometric properties. When an electrical conductor experience stretching within its elastic limits, it elongates and narrows without enduring permanent deformation or breakage. Conversely, under compression, it shortens and widens. The alteration in the resistance of the gauge wire stems from changes in its length and cross-sectional area.

   The Gauge Factor (GF) is a crucial parameter used in strain measurement, particularly in electrical strain gauges. It represents the ratio of the relative change in electrical resistance of the strain gauge to the mechanical strain experienced by the gauge. Mathematically, it is expressed as:

$$G.F.=(\Delta R/RG)/\varepsilon$$

   where, ΔR - Change in resistance.

   RG - Resistance of the undeformed gauge, and ε – Mechanical strain.

***Types of strain gauges based on the configuration***

1. Quarter- bridge
2. Half-bridge
3. Full -bridge

1. **Quarter bridge**: This setup features a single active strain gauge, making it the simplest configuration, albeit the least sensitive. Typically, the rheostat arm ($R_2$) is adjusted in the bridge circuit diagram to match the strain gauge resistance when no force is applied. Both ratio arms ($R_1$ and $R_3$) are set to equal values. Consequently, without any force acting on the strain gauge, the bridge is symmetrically balanced, resulting in zero voltage on the voltmeter, indicating zero force exerted on the strain gauge.

   The strain gauge changes its electrical resistance when subjected to either compression or tension. Specifically, when experiencing compression, the resistance decreases, whereas under tension, it increases. This resistance alteration perturbs the bridge circuit's equilibrium, inducing an imbalance that results in a voltage reading on the connected voltmeter. This configuration, in which a single element within the bridge circuit exhibits a change in resistance proportional to the measured variable (mechanical force), is commonly referred to as a quarter-bridge circuit. The strain gauge is pivotal in this circuit arrangement, serving as the primary sensing element that converts mechanical deformation into discernible electrical signals. This configuration can obtain precise measurements of applied forces, facilitating accurate analysis and evaluation of structural integrity and performance.

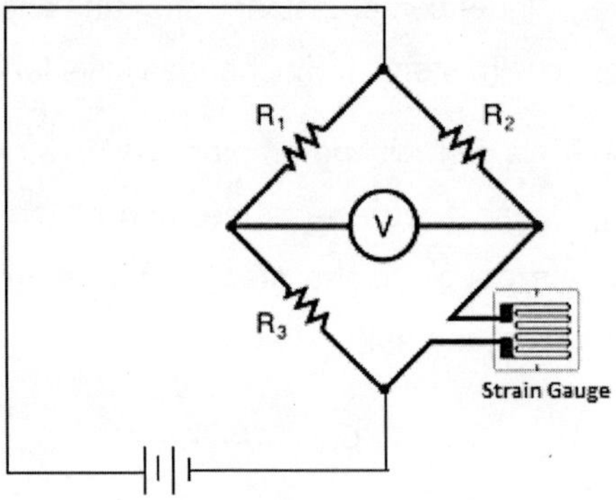


*Figure 2.10 Quarter-bridge Strain gauge*

2. **Half bridge**: In contrast to the quarter bridge setup, which incorporates a single active strain gauge, the half-bridge configuration employs two active strain gauges. This configuration offers heightened sensitivity compared to the quarter bridge but falls short of the sensitivity achieved with a full bridge setup. The selection of the appropriate configuration is paramount in designing a strain gauge circuit, ensuring the attainment of the desired levels of sensitivity and responsiveness. The half-bridge arrangement involves strategically placing two active strain gauges on a bending beam positioned at both the front and back sections. In this setup, half of the four resistors constituting the bridge circuit are strain gauges, allowing both to respond to the induced strain accurately. Consequently, the bridge circuit exhibits enhanced responsiveness to the applied force, resulting in a greater output voltage output for a given strain level. Compared to the quarter bridge configuration, the half-bridge circuit yields twice the output voltage for a given strain level, effectively doubling the circuit's sensitivity. This augmented sensitivity makes the half-bridge arrangement an enticing option for applications where high levels of sensitivity and responsiveness are imperative, ensuring precise and reliable measurements in critical engineering and scientific endeavours.
3. **Full bridge:** The Full Bridge Strain Gauge configuration entails the utilization of all four resistors within the Wheatstone bridge circuit as strain gauges. This configuration enhances sensitivity to applied forces and yields higher output voltages when

compared to half-bridge or quarter-bridge setups. It finds widespread application in sectors necessitating high sensitivity and precision, such as aerospace, automotive, and civil engineering industries. In this configuration, the two strain gauges on one arm of the bridge are connected in series, while those on the opposing arm are connected in parallel.

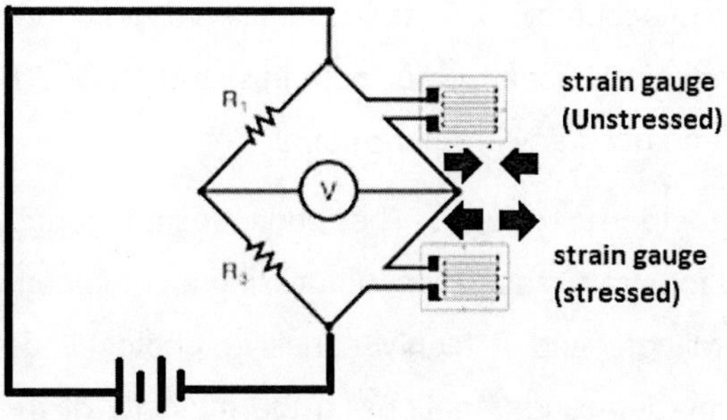


*Figure 2.11 Half-bridge Strain gauge*

This arrangement effectively balances the resistance and temperature sensitivity of the circuit, thereby enhancing measurement accuracy. Integration of a signal conditioning amplifier with the full bridge strain gauge circuit is common practice to amplify the output voltage to a level suitable for accurate measurement by a data acquisition system or other measurement instruments. Ensuring compatibility between the amplifier's input impedance and the output impedance of the bridge is imperative to mitigate signal loss or distortion.

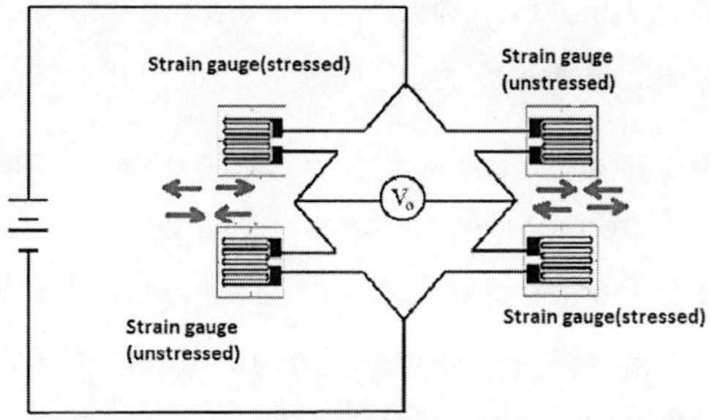


*Figure 2.12 Full-bridge Strain gauge*

**Types of strain gauges based on the construction**

1. **Optical sensors:** Despite their precision, optical sensors are not extensively utilized in industrial settings primarily due to their inherent fragility. These sensors analyse interference fringes generated by optical flats, offering exceptionally accurate strain

measurements. However, their delicate nature renders them less suitable for rugged industrial environments where durability is paramount. Optical sensors thrive in controlled laboratory settings where environmental conditions can be meticulously regulated to ensure optimal performance. In such environments, these sensors exhibit their full potential, delivering precise and reliable strain measurements with high levels of accuracy. Despite their limited application in industrial contexts, optical sensors remain indispensable tools in research and development settings where precision and accuracy are paramount.

2. **The photoelectric gauge:** The photoelectric gauge is a sophisticated device employed for strain measurement, utilizing a combination of a light beam, two finely crafted gratings, and a highly sensitive photocell detector. This intricate setup operates by detecting variations in the intensity of the light beam caused by the strain-induced displacement of the gratings. As the strain alters the spacing between the gratings, the intensity of the light passing through fluctuates accordingly. The photocell detector, capable of discerning these subtle changes in light intensity, converts them into an electrical current. This electrical signal is then proportional to the magnitude of the applied strain, providing a precise and reliable measure of deformation. Despite their exceptional precision and the ability to achieve gage lengths as short as 1/16-inch, photoelectric gauges are often characterized by their relatively high cost and fragility. These factors limit their widespread adoption, particularly in industrial environments where robustness and cost-effectiveness are essential considerations.

3. **Semiconductor strain:** Piezo-resistive strain gauges, also known as semiconductor gauges, are preferred for measuring small strains over foil gauges. They rely on the piezo-resistive properties of materials like silicon or germanium to detect changes in resistance under stress rather than directly measuring strain. Typically constructed from a wafer with a resistance element diffused into a silicon substrate, these gauges lack a backing and require careful bonding to the strained surface using a thin layer of epoxy. Precise bonding is crucial while semiconductor gauges are smaller and less expensive than metallic foil sensors. The same epoxy adhesives used for foil gauges are used for bonding semiconductor gauges. However, semiconductor strain gauges are more susceptible to temperature variations and tend to drift more than metallic foil sensors. Additionally, their resistance-strain relationship is nonlinear, although

this limitation can be addressed through software compensation techniques.

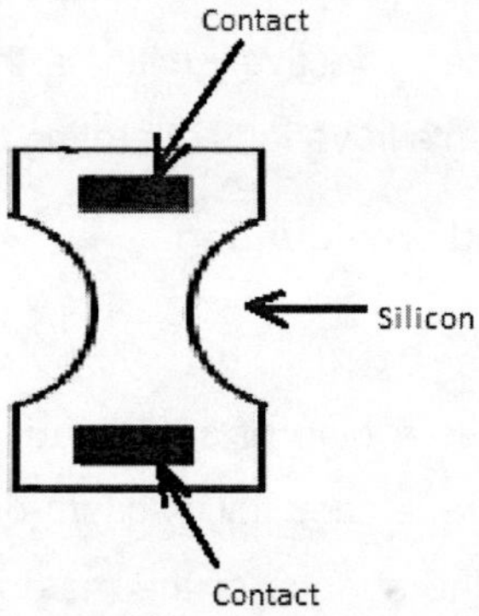


*Figure 2.13 Semiconductor Strain Gauge*

4. **Thin-film strain gauge**: This type of strain gauge offers the advantage of eliminating the need for adhesive bonding. They are created by depositing an electrical insulation layer, usually ceramic, onto the stressed metal surface, followed by the deposition of the strain gauge onto this insulation layer. Molecular bonding of materials is achieved through vacuum deposition or sputtering methods. The thin-film gauge is securely installed and maintains a stable resistance value with minimal drift over time. Additionally, the stressed force detector can be a metallic diaphragm or beam with a ceramic insulation layer deposited on it, providing an additional advantage.

5. **Diffused semiconductor strain gauges:** The advent of diffused semiconductor strain gauges represents a significant advancement in strain gauge technology, notably eliminating the requirement for bonding agents. This innovation effectively mitigates potential errors associated with creep and hysteresis. Employing photolithography masking techniques and boron solid-state diffusion, the diffused semiconductor strain gauge establishes molecular bonds with the resistance elements, circumventing the need for traditional bonding agents. Electrical leads are directly affixed to the pattern, simplifying the installation process. Despite these advantages, diffused semiconductor strain gauges are primarily suited for moderate-temperature applications and necessitate temperature compensation. However, they are widely utilized as sensing elements in pressure transducers owing to their compact size, affordability, accuracy, repeatability, and wide pressure range. Furthermore, they produce robust output signals, enhancing their appeal for diverse

applications. Nonetheless, the susceptibility of diffused semiconductor strain gauges to ambient temperature fluctuations necessitates careful consideration. Intelligent transmitter designs can effectively mitigate this vulnerability, ensuring reliable and accurate measurements in various operating conditions.

## Types of strain gauge based on mounting

### 1. Bonded strain gauge

A bonded strain gauge is a type of strain gauge where a sensing element, typically composed of metallic wire, etched foil, vacuum-deposited film, or semiconductor bar, is attached or bonded to the surface of the material undergoing strain. This bonding is usually achieved using a cementing agent. When the material experiences deformation due to an applied force or load, the strain is transferred to the bonded strain gauge, changing its electrical resistance. This alteration in resistance is directly proportional to the applied strain, enabling precise measurement and analysis of mechanical stress or strain in the material. Due to their high sensitivity and accuracy, bonded strain gauges are of extensive use in various industries for applications such as structural monitoring, load testing, and material characterization.

### 2. Unbonded Strain Gauge

An unbonded strain gauge configuration involves stretching a wire between two points within an insulating medium, commonly air. One end of the wire is securely fixed, while the other end is linked to a movable element. Deformation occurs Upon applying mechanical stress or strain to the structure or material under measurement, leading to a change in the distance between the two points. Consequently, the wire experiences a corresponding alteration in length, resulting in a change in its electrical resistance. This change in resistance is directly proportional to the applied strain, facilitating precise measurement of mechanical deformation. Unbonded strain gauges prove particularly beneficial in scenarios where direct bonding to the surface is impractical or where high flexibility and dynamic response are essential, as observed in the aerospace and automotive industries.

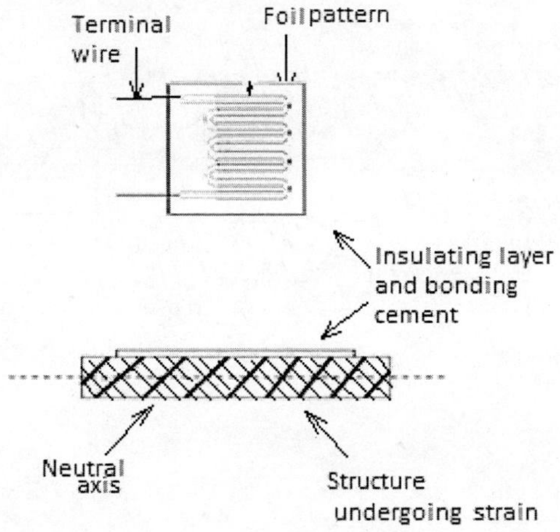


*Figure 2.14 Bonded Strain gauge*

***Based on the applications, the strain gauges are classified into four types***

1. **Electrical Resistance Strain Gauges**

   The most commonly used strain gauges typically consist of a finely crafted metallic grid firmly bonded to a backing material. These strain gauges function by detecting alterations in the wire's resistance in response to applied strain, a principle exploited in their measurement using Wheatstone bridge circuits. Renowned for their exceptional attributes including high sensitivity, accuracy, and stability, these strain gauges are extensively employed for monitoring minute strains in various structural components such as bridges, dams, and buildings. Their reliability and precision make them indispensable tools in ensuring the structural integrity and safety of critical infrastructure.

2. **Vibrating Wire Strain Gauges**

   Based on the principle of resonant frequency, these gauges utilize a taut wire whose tension varies with strain, consequently impacting its resonant frequency. The measurement of this frequency shift enables the determination of strain. Recognized for their robustness, long-term stability, and resilience against environmental factors, these gauges are particularly well-suited for geotechnical and structural monitoring applications.

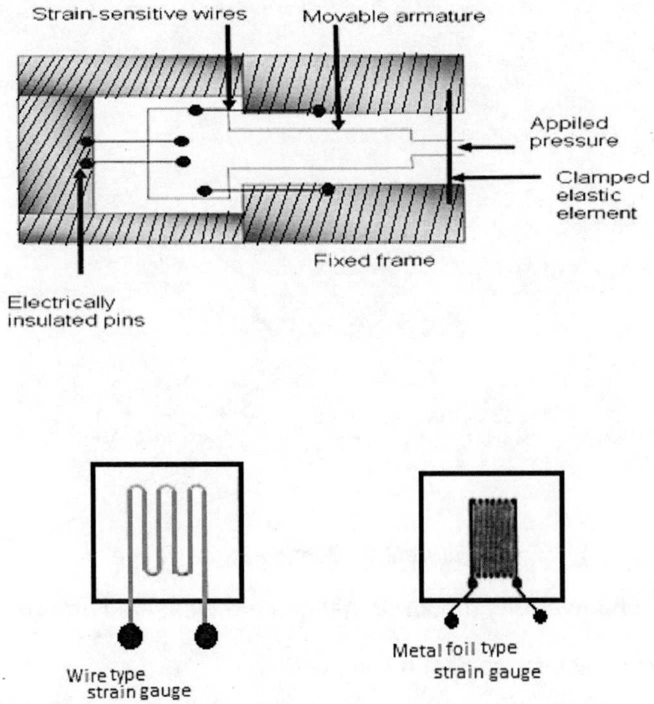


*Figure 2.15 Unbonded Strain gauge*

3. **Fiber Optic Strain Gauges**

   These innovative gauges harness optical fibers for strain measurement. Strain modifies the2.2. propagation of light through the fiber, influencing either its intensity or wavelength. Engineers can ascertain the strain by detecting and analyzing these alterations. Fiber optic gauges boast high accuracy, immunity to electromagnetic interference, and the capability to connect multiple sensors along a single fiber.

4. **Piezoelectric Strain Gauges**

   Utilizing the piezoelectric effect, these gauges incorporate a crystal or ceramic material capable of generating an electric charge when subjected to deformation. This charge is directly proportional to the applied strain and can be quantified using specialized equipment. Piezoelectric gauges excel in measuring dynamic strains, particularly in structures such as bridges, tunnels, and pavements, owing to their high sensitivity. Nonetheless, they exhibit sensitivity to temperature fluctuations and possess a limited linear range.

### 2.2.3 MOUNTING OF STRAIN GAUGES

When using a strain gauge to measure the strain on a test specimen, the measurements must be transferred accurately and without any loss. This requires a strong and proper connection between the gauge and the specimen. An incorrect or improper installation can affect the accuracy and validity of the test results. The necessary steps for installing a strain gauge, as well as the techniques used to protect the installation of the gauge.

**Case 1: Installing Strain Gauges on Metal Surfaces using Adhesives.**

***Preparation***

The first step in the installation process involves cleaning the surface of the test specimen where the gauge is to be bonded. To establish a clean, shiny metallic surface, it is critical to eliminate all traces of grease, rust, paint, and any other contaminants. To achieve this, it is recommended to use abrasive paper to uniformly and finely abrade an area larger than the bonding area. This will ensure the bonding surface is smooth and free from impurities. Next, clean the region with an industrial tissue or cloth soaked in chemical solvent until it is entirely free of contamination. Ensure that the solvent used is suitable for the material being cleaned. This will help to remove any remaining dirt, dust, or other residues that may interfere with the bonding process. After cleaning the surface, it is essential to let it dry completely before installing. This can be done by using a clean, dry cloth or by air-drying the surface for a few minutes.

***Adhesive Curing and Pressing***

Apply a precise quantity of adhesive onto the rear side of the strain gauge, considering its dimensions, and uniformly distribute it using a suitable nozzle. Subsequently, affix the gauge onto the test specimen, ensuring prompt attachment upon surface cleaning to prevent bonding onto contaminated surfaces. Then, overlay the gauge with a polythene sheet or translucent tape and apply continuous pressure using either your thumb or a gauge clamp to ensure secure adhesion.

*Figure 2.16 Strain Gauges on Metal Surfaces using Adhesives.*

Additionally, it is crucial to allow adequate curing time for the adhesive to be fully set before subjecting the assembly to any strain or testing procedures. This procedure ensures optimal bonding strength and reliability of the strain gauge installation, which is essential for accurate strain measurement and analysis in various engineering applications.

***Bonding Connecting Terminals***

Once the adhesive beneath the polyethene sheet has fully cured, carefully raise the gauge, which leads to a position inside the gauge base. Using tweezers, meticulously affix the terminal near the gauge leads and apply solder to encapsulate the metal foil of the terminal. Utilize tweezers to eliminate any surplus gauge leads. Subsequently, the end of the lead wire is soldered to the terminals, ensuring cautious application to prevent overheating the terminal and potential detachment of the metal foil.

Moreover, verifying the integrity of the solder joint and the electrical connection is imperative to guarantee accurate signal transmission during strain measurement. This meticulous soldering process is essential for maintaining the reliability and performance of the strain gauge system in various engineering applications.

**Case 2: Installing Strain Gauge on Concrete Surface.**

***Preparation***

To prepare the surface for installation, start by meticulously clearing away any debris, paint, or other contaminants from the designated area. Utilize a surface preparation agent to ensure thorough cleansing and drying of the surface. It's crucial to note that the adhesive may not effectively set if the surface remains damp. Proceed by using abrasive paper to carefully sand an area approximately 20mm to 30mm larger than the intended installation area. Once the sanding process is complete, meticulously wipe the area using a cloth or industrial tissue dampened with a small quantity of solvent, such as acetone. This step is essential to guarantee the surface is entirely impurities-free and primed for installation.

***Pre-coating***

Before bonding the strain gauge, surface preparation is crucial to establish a barrier against any potential moisture released from the concrete or mortar surface. This barrier aims to prevent moisture absorption by the underside of the strain gauge. Initially, cut the gauge binder provided with the strain gauge approximately 5mm inward from the fold. Next, apply packing tape around the perimeter of the binder, effectively masking an area roughly 10mm larger than the binder on each side. Subsequently, the adhesive must be applied thoroughly onto the mortar or concrete surface. Ensure that the adhesive is applied to form a layer measuring 0.5mm to 1mm thick on the installation surface. This meticulous surface preparation is essential to optimize the bonding strength and reliability of the strain gauge installation, ensuring accurate strain measurement and analysis in concrete or mortar structures.

***Bonding the Strain Gauge***

When installing a strain gauge on concrete or mortar, it's crucial to consider the gauge length relative to the strain. These materials are heterogeneous, meaning that using strain gauges with short gauge lengths may lead to measuring partial strains in pebbles or individual sections of the hardened cement paste. Therefore, it's recommended to use a gauge length that is at least five times longer than the largest grain size. To install the gauge, begin by placing the cut piece of the gauge binder over the applied adhesive gradually pressing it into place from one end to ensure no air bubbles are trapped underneath. Once the adhesive has cured, remove the piece of gauge binder and proceed to install the strain gauge. For optimal results, employ a robust, pore-filling adhesive that forms reliable bonds, even in the presence of residual moisture in the concrete. As described earlier, the same procedure should be followed for bonding the connecting terminals for installation on metal surfaces. This meticulous installation is essential to ensure accurate strain measurement and analysis in concrete or mortar structures, enabling reliable mechanical behavior and structural integrity assessment.

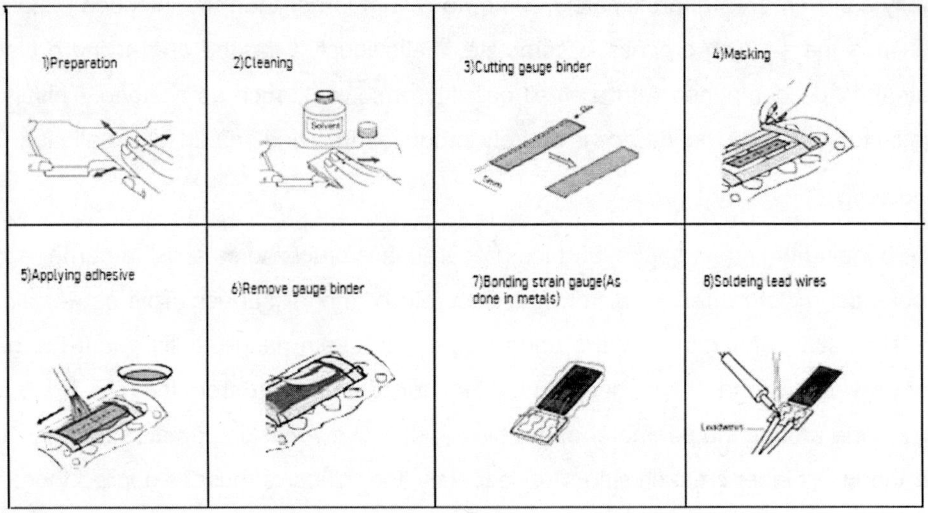


*Figure 2.17 Installing Strain Gauge on Concrete Surface*

**Case 3: Installation of Weldable Strain Gauges**

A weldable strain gauge offers the advantage of facile spot welding to a metallic surface, requiring minimal preparation conditions compared to adhesive bonding. This method significantly reduces the structural impact, eliminating the need for stringent surface preparation typically associated with adhesive bonding processes.

***Preparation***

Preparing the surface for installation involves the straightforward removal of any dirt and oil using a surface preparation agent to achieve a clean surface. Upon receiving the weldable strain gauge, it comes equipped with a metal ribbon intended for trial welding. This ribbon includes a securing sleeve and an MI cable. The trial welding process is initiated to adjust the welding power of the spot welder. During this process, if cracks or holes appear in the ribbon, it indicates that the welding power should be reduced. Conversely, if the ribbon remains unmarked, it suggests that the power should be increased accordingly. This iterative adjustment ensures optimal welding conditions for secure, reliable strain gauge attachment to the metallic surface.

***Welding Process***

Before initiating the welding process, it's essential to precisely align the strain gauge at the centre of the installation area. Utilize a spot welder and metal ribbon to apply pressure on both sides of the gauge. During the installation, it's critical to carefully plan the number and sequence of welding points to ensure they do not form a crisscross pattern. This precaution is vital to prevent the inclusion of any mechanical stresses in the steel substrate. Secure the MI cable with the metal ribbon to alleviate any strain on the secured sleeve. Additionally, gently curving the cable between the gauge and the connecting terminal can help avoid undue strain on the MI cable. It's worth noting that various types of strain gauge installations exist, depending on the connection technique and the properties of the installation surface. Selecting the appropriate installation method is crucial to ensure the integrity and accuracy of the strain measurement system.

### *2.2.4 STRAIN GAUGE ROSETTES*

Strain gauge rosettes are powerful for engineers, offering precise and versatile strain measurements on materials. These rosettes consist of multiple strain gauges arranged in specific patterns, often resembling a rose (rosette) shape. This configuration allows them to simultaneously measure strain in multiple directions, making them ideal for complex loading scenarios where strain isn't uniform. The rosettes detect changes in electrical resistance caused by the deformation of the attached surface. This deformation can be due to forces, temperature fluctuations, or internal stresses. By analyzing these resistance variations, engineers can accurately determine the strain experienced by the material.

A key benefit of strain gauge rosettes is their ability to capture strain in multiple directions at once. This is particularly valuable when the strain distribution across the material's surface is uneven. With strategically placed gauges in the rosette configuration, engineers gain a comprehensive understanding of how the material behaves under load by measuring strain variations along different axes. The applications of strain gauge rosettes extend across various industries. In aerospace engineering, they monitor the structural integrity of aircraft components under dynamic flight forces. In automotive engineering, they assess the performance of vehicle chassis and suspension systems during diverse driving conditions. Similarly, civil engineers use them to evaluate the behaviour of structural elements in buildings, bridges, and other infrastructure projects. In addition to single-element strain gauges, a combination of strain gauges called rosettes is available in many combinations for specific stress analysis.

**Two-element rosettes**

Two-element rosettes are a type of strain gauge rosette consisting of two strain gauges positioned at a 90-degree angle. They are typically used when the principal directions of strain (the highest and lowest strains experienced by the material) are already known. By measuring the strain in each gauge, the normal strains (strains in the direction of the gauge) in the x and y directions can be determined.

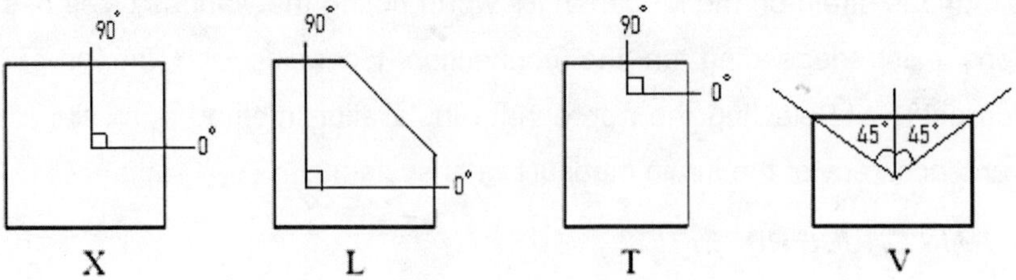


*Figure 2.18 Two-element rosettes*

**Three-element rosettes**

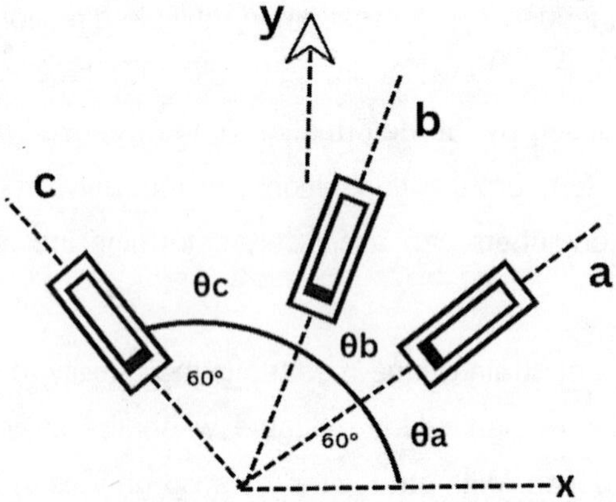


*Figure 2.19 Three-element rosettes*

A three-element rosette is a specialized configuration of strain gauges arranged in a pattern resembling a rosette, comprising three individual strain gauge elements. Each strain gauge within the rosette is strategically positioned at a specific angle relative to the primary axis of strain, allowing for comprehensive strain measurement in multiple directions within the material under test. The three-element rosette is particularly advantageous for analyzing complex strain states in materials where the principal strain directions may vary or are not readily identifiable. By utilizing three strain gauges arranged at different orientations, engineers can accurately capture variations in strain along multiple axes, providing a more complete understanding of the material's mechanical behaviour. Typically, the strain gauges in a three-element rosette are positioned at angles of 0 degrees, 45 degrees, and 90 degrees relative to the primary axis of strain. This configuration enables the measurement of both normal strains ($\varepsilon_x$ and $\varepsilon_y$) and the shear strain ($\gamma_{xy}$) experienced by the material under load.

**Strain Gauge Rosette at Arbitrary Angles**

A single strain gauge can only measure strain in one direction, necessitating two gauges to determine both normal strains ($\varepsilon_x$ and $\varepsilon_y$). However, conventional strain gauges lack the capability to measure shear strain. A practical solution involves attaching three strain gauges to the object at arbitrary angles to resolve the limitation. It's important to note that any rotated normal strain is dependent on the coordinate strains ($\varepsilon_x$, $\varepsilon_y$) and the unknown shear strain ($\gamma_{xy}$). A system of equations can be derived by employing three strain gauges oriented at different angles. This system consists of three equations, each relating to a specific gauge orientation, and contains three unknowns: $\varepsilon_x$, $\varepsilon_y$, and $\gamma_{xy}$. Solving this system enables the

$$\varepsilon_a = \frac{\varepsilon_x + \varepsilon_y}{2} + \frac{\varepsilon_x - \varepsilon_y}{2}\cos 2\theta_a + \frac{\gamma_{xy}}{2}\sin 2\theta_a$$

$$\varepsilon_b = \frac{\varepsilon_x + \varepsilon_y}{2} + \frac{\varepsilon_x - \varepsilon_y}{2}\cos 2\theta_b + \frac{\gamma_{xy}}{2}\sin 2\theta_b$$

$$\varepsilon_c = \frac{\varepsilon_x + \varepsilon_y}{2} + \frac{\varepsilon_x - \varepsilon_y}{2}\cos 2\theta_c + \frac{\gamma_{xy}}{2}\sin 2\theta_c$$

determination of all three strain components- normal strains along both axes and the shear strain. These equations are,

Any three gages used together at one location on a stressed object is called a strain rosette.

**Strain Rosette - 45°**

Large angles are used to increase the accuracy of a strain rosette. A common rosette of three gauges separates the gages by 45°, or $\theta_a = 0°$, or $\theta_b = 45°$, or $\theta_c = 90°$. The three equations can then be simplified to

$$\varepsilon_a = \frac{\varepsilon_x + \varepsilon_y}{2} + \frac{\varepsilon_x - \varepsilon_y}{2}$$

$$\varepsilon_b = \frac{\varepsilon_x + \varepsilon_y}{2} + \frac{\gamma_{xy}}{2}$$

$$\varepsilon_c = \frac{\varepsilon_x + \varepsilon_y}{2} - \frac{\varepsilon_x - \varepsilon_y}{2}$$

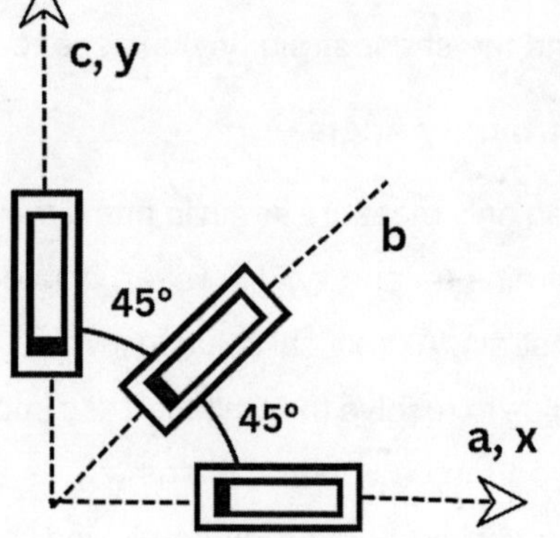


*Figure 2.20 Strain Gauge Rosette at 45°*

Solving for $\varepsilon_x$, $\varepsilon_y$ and $\gamma_{xy}$ gives,

$$\varepsilon_x = \varepsilon_a \qquad \varepsilon_y = \varepsilon_c \qquad \gamma_{xy} = 2\varepsilon_b - (\varepsilon_a + \varepsilon_c)$$

**Strain Rosette - 60°**

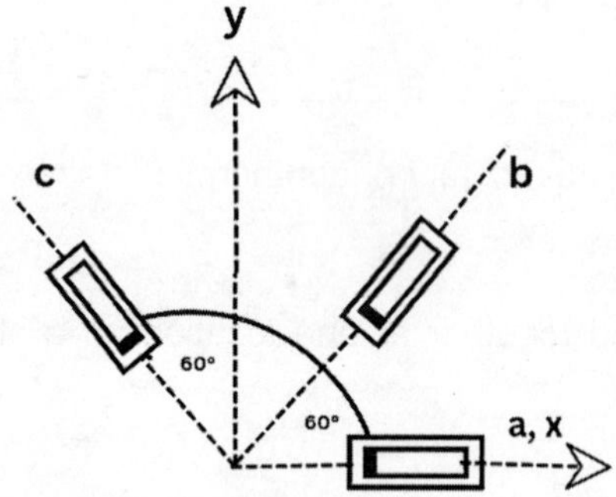


*Figure 2.21 Strain Gage Rosette at 60°*

Similarly, if the angles between the gages are 60°, or $\theta_a$ = 0°, or $\theta_b$ = 60°,or $\theta_c$ = 120°., the unknown strains, for $\varepsilon_x$, $\varepsilon_y$ and $\gamma_{xy}$ will be,

$$\varepsilon_x = \varepsilon_a$$

$$\varepsilon_y = \frac{2\varepsilon_b + 2\varepsilon_c - \varepsilon_a}{3}$$

$$\gamma_{xy} = \frac{2\varepsilon_b - 2\varepsilon_c}{\sqrt{3}}$$

## 2.3 INTRODUCTION TO FORCE, TORQUE, PRESSURE MEASUREMENTS

Force and torque are foundational concepts in mechanics, describing objects' interaction and resulting motion. Force, denoted as a push or pull, induces changes in an object's state of rest or motion. It's represented as a vector with both magnitude and direction. Newton's second law states that force is proportional to the rate of change of an object's velocity, with mass determining the degree of acceleration. Mathematically, force (F) equals mass (m) multiplied by acceleration (a), expressed as $F = ma$. The SI unit of force is the Newton (N), defined as the force required to accelerate a one-kilogram mass at one meter per second squared ($1 \text{ N} = 1 \text{ kg} \times 1 \text{ m/s}^2$). Torque, also called moment of force, refers to the rotational effect of force on an object. It depends on the force's magnitude and the distance from the axis of rotation. Mathematically, torque (T) equals force (F) multiplied by the distance (radius), represented as $T = F \times r$. The SI unit of torque is the Newton-meter (N·m). Pressure, denoted as force applied perpendicular to a surface divided by the area over which it's distributed, is expressed as $p = F / A$. The SI unit of pressure is the pascal (Pa), where 1 Pa equals 1 $N/m^2$. Other pressure units include pounds per square inch (psi) and atmospheres (atm). This chapter covers force, torque, and pressure measurements relevant to instruments employing transducers and strain gauges and the instruments for measuring the force, torque and pressure are as given below:

1) Force Measurement
    i) Spring Balance
    ii) Proving Rings
    iii) Load Cells
2) Torque Measurement
    i) Prony Brake Dynamometer
    ii) Eddy Current Dynamometer
    iii) Hydraulic Dynamometer
3) Pressure Measurement
    i) Mcleod Gauge

### 2.3.1 FORCE MEASUREMENT

Force is a fundamental concept in physics that describes the push or pull that can cause an object to change its state of motion. Measuring force accurately is crucial in various scientific and engineering disciplines. There are two main approaches to force measurement such as direct and indirect.

### Direct Method

Direct methods involve a head-to-head comparison between the unknown and known gravitational forces acting on a standard mass. This leverages the principle that any object with mass experiences an attractive force due to Earth's gravity, also known as weight. The weight (W) can be calculated using the following equation:

$W = mg$

W- Weight of the thing (force due to gravity)

m-Mass of the thing (standard mass)

g-Acceleration due to gravity (constant value, approximately 9.81 $m/s^2$)

### Indirect Method

Indirect methods involve converting the effect of the unknown force into a measurable quantity using various transducers or sensors. These sensors translate the force into a secondary effect, such as deformation or a change in electrical properties, that can be readily measured and correlated back to the force using established principles.

1. **Spring Balances:** Spring balances operate according to Hooke's Law, which dictates that the elongation of an elastic material is directly proportional to the applied force within the material's elastic limit. These devices typically utilize a spring with a known spring constant (k). The spring constant represents the force required to stretch the spring by a specified unit length. The force applied can be calculated by measuring the displacement caused by an unknown force acting on the spring and using the known spring constant. Spring balances are favoured for their simplicity, portability, and capacity to measure a wide range of forces. However, it's important to note that they may exhibit lower accuracy compared to direct measurement methods, especially for highly precise applications.
2. **Strain Gauges:** Strain gauges are electrical resistance-based sensors that are securely attached to a material. When an external force is applied to the material, it undergoes deformation, resulting in a change in the electrical resistance of the strain gauge. This alteration in resistance can be accurately measured and subsequently converted back to the force applied using the gauge's calibration factor. Strain gauges are renowned for their high sensitivity, making them particularly suitable for applications where intricate stress distributions must be measured precisely. By detecting minute changes in resistance, strain gauges provide valuable insights into

the mechanical behaviour of materials under varying loads, facilitating the optimization of structural designs and ensuring the integrity and safety of engineering systems.

3. **Piezoelectric Sensors**: These sensors utilize the piezoelectric effect, where certain materials generate a measurable voltage proportional to the applied force. Piezoelectric sensors are well-suited for dynamic force measurements due to their fast response times.

#### 2.3.1.1 Spring Balance

The spring balance serves as an effective device for measuring force or tension. Comprising a coiled spring enclosed within a metal or plastic shell, it features a hook or loop on one end for attaching the object under measurement and a pointer or scale on the opposite end for reading the applied force.

The core component of the spring balance, the coiled spring, is calibrated with a known spring constant, dictating the extent of expansion or contraction in response to the applied force. These springs are typically crafted from materials like steel with high tensile strength and ensure precise and reliable measurements. The pointer or scale located at the opposite end allows for the direct reading of the applied force. Graduated with force units such as pounds or Newtons, the scale enables straightforward and accurate interpretation of the recorded force. Spring balances offer versatility in force measurement, capable of handling forces ranging from small increments to several kilograms or more. This broad range accommodates various applications, from precision tasks to heavy-duty operations. The working principle of a spring balance is based on Hooke's law, which states that the elongation or compression of a spring is directly proportional to the force or load exerted on it. Consequently, the scale markings on the spring are equally spaced to reflect this proportionality.

Mathematically, Hooke's law is represented as:

$$F = k\ x$$

Where:

F is the load applied,

k is the spring constant, and

x is the elongation or compression of the spring.

According to Hooke's law, if the load applied to the spring is doubled, the deformation of the spring (elongation or compression) and the load attached to it will also double. This direct relationship between the load and the spring deformation forms the basis for the operation of spring balances, allowing for the measurement of forces by observing the extent of spring displacement.

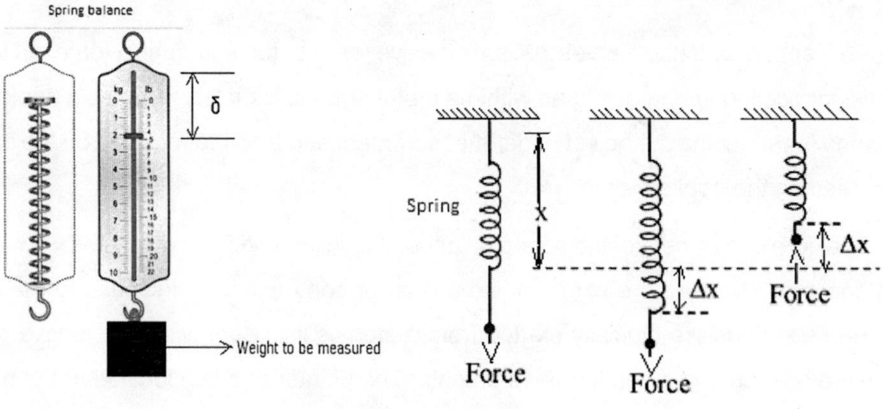


*Figure 2.22 Spring Balance*

**Advantages of Spring Balance**

1. Spring balances are user-friendly and suitable for novices and professionals alike. It offers simple operation, an attachment mechanism, and precise scale readings, enabling quick measurements with minimal training.
2. Calibration to known spring constants ensures accuracy and reliability across diverse applications. Their ability to measure a wide range of forces contributes to their adaptability.
3. Lightweight and portable, spring balances facilitate seamless transfer and usage in field measurements, investigations, and mobile applications.
4. The spring balances exhibit durability and resilience to repeated use, maintaining accuracy over time. They are constructed from high-quality materials like steel.
5. The spring balances are accessible to individuals on a budget or within educational environments, enhancing their value proposition.

#### 2.3.1.2 Proving Rings

The proving ring stands as one of the foremost devices for force measurement. A displacement transducer links the ring's top and bottom to gauge the displacement prompted by applied pressure. Measuring the relative displacement yields the applied force magnitude. Various methods can measure deflection, such as precise micrometers, linear variable differential transformers (LVDTs), or strain gauges. Compared to alternative devices, proving rings exhibit heightened strain due to their construction. Crafted from steel, proving rings find utility in static load measurement and calibration of tensile testing machines. Their load range spans from 1.5 kN to 2 MN. A typical proving ring features a circular ring with a rectangular cross-section, depicted in Fig 2.23 where the thickness (t), radius (R), and axial width (b). Capable of enduring tensile or compressive forces across its diameters, the ring's ends are attached to structures for force measurement. Four strain gauges are affixed to the ring's walls: two on the inner walls and two on the outer walls. Application of force triggers compressive strain (-ε) in gauges 2 and 4, while gauges 1 and 3 undergo tension +ε.

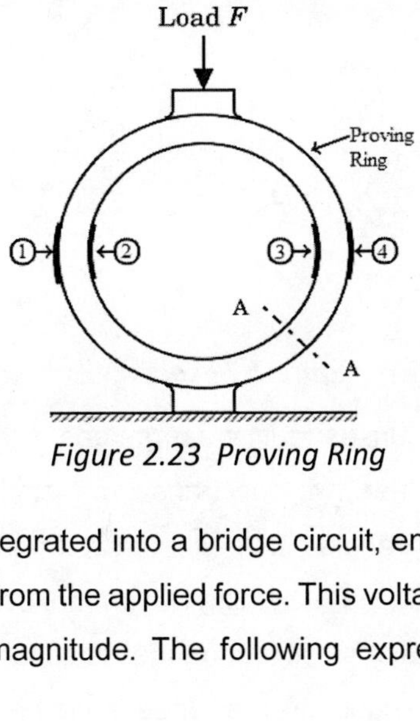


*Figure 2.23 Proving Ring*

The four strain gauges are integrated into a bridge circuit, enabling the measurement of the unbalanced voltage resulting from the applied force. This voltage, calibrated in terms of force, directly indicates the force magnitude. The following expression determines the strain's magnitude:

$$e = 1.08FR/\ Ebt^2$$

The relationship between the applied force and the deflection caused by the applied force is described by the following expression: $\delta_y = \left(\frac{\pi}{2} - \frac{4}{\pi}\right)\frac{Fd^3}{16\ EI}$

where, *E* - Young's modulus, *I* - moment of inertia, *F* - force, *d* - outside diameter of the ring, and *dy* is the deflection.

#### 2.3.1.3 Load Cells

Elastic members play a crucial role in force measurement systems by facilitating displacement assessment. An elastic member transforms into a load cell when integrated with strain gauges to measure force. In load cells, elastic members are primary transducers, while strain gauges are secondary transducers. Load cells adopt an indirect method for force measurement, wherein force or weight is converted into an electrical signal. These devices are extensively utilized across various industries for tasks involving force measurement.

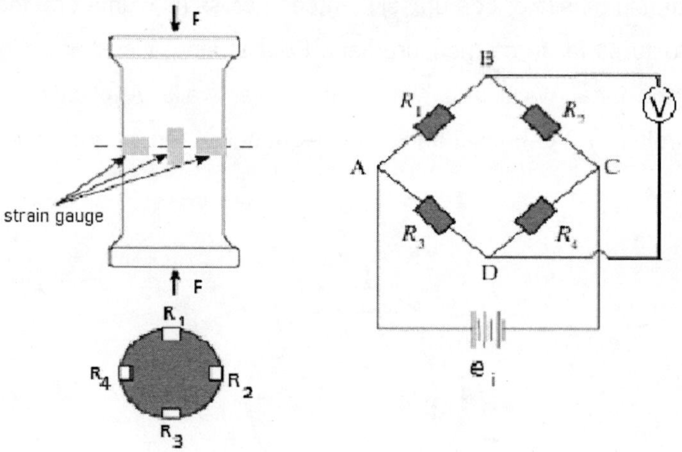


*Figure 2.24 Load Cells*

A load cell typically comprises four strain gauges, with two dedicated to measuring longitudinal strain and the other two for transverse strain. These strain gauges are strategically positioned at 90° angles to each other. In this configuration, two gauges experience tensile stresses while the remaining two endure compressive stresses. Under no-load conditions, the resistance across all four gauges is uniform, resulting in equal potentials across terminals B and D. Consequently, the Wheatstone bridge achieves balance, yielding zero output voltage.

The strain gauges measure the induced strain when the specimen is stressed due to an applied force. Gauges $R_1$ and $R_4$ gauge the longitudinal (compressive) strain, while gauges $R_2$ and $R_3$ assess the transverse (tensile) strain. As a result of this strain, voltage discrepancies arise across terminals B and D, causing the output voltage to fluctuate. This variation serves as an indicator of the applied force after calibration.

The following relation can express the compressive longitudinal strain within the load cell:

$$\varepsilon_1 = -\frac{F}{AE}$$

Strain gauges 1 and 4 undergo this particular strain, while strain gauges 2 and 3 experience a strain described by the subsequent equation:

$$\varepsilon_2 = -\frac{\gamma F}{AE}$$

Here, $\gamma$ is the Poisson's ratio.

This arrangement of mounting gauges effectively compensates for the effects of bending and temperature variations. Symmetric mounting of the gauges ensures complete compensation, providing accurate and reliable measurements across different operating conditions.

## 2.4 TORQUE MEASUREMENT

Torque (T) provides essential load information for analysing mechanical systems' stress or deflection. Torque measurement is crucial in engineering applications, providing essential load information for analyzing stress and deflection in mechanical systems. Torque (T) is calculated by multiplying the applied force (F) by the known radius (r), expressed as T = Fr (in N m). Moreover, torque measurement is vital for determining mechanical power, which denotes the power required to operate or develop a machine. Mechanical power (P) is calculated using the formula P = 2πNT, where N represents the angular speed in revolutions per second. Devices used for torque measurement, known as dynamometers, find widespread application in various machinery, including internal combustion engines, steam turbines, pumps, compressors, and other rotating equipment. The selection of a dynamometer depends on the nature of the machine being tested. Absorption dynamometers are suitable for machines that can absorb the produced power or torque. Conversely, driving dynamometers are used for machines that function as power absorbers and are capable of driving the machine. Transmission dynamometers, positioned within or between machines, sense torque at specific locations and are also known as torque meters. Each type of dynamometer offers distinct advantages tailored to specific torque measurement requirements.

### 2.4.1 PRONY BRAKE DYNAMOMETER

The Prony brake dynamometer, invented in 1821 by French engineer Gaspard de Prony, is a popular choice for measuring engine power. It's known for its simplicity, affordability, and effectiveness among absorption dynamometers.

This mechanical device relies on dry friction to convert the engine's mechanical energy into heat. The Fig shows two wooden blocks mounted on opposite sides of the engine's flywheel. The flywheel is connected to the shaft whose power is being measured. The Prony brake depicted above is composed of several components, including a wooden block, frame, rope, brake shoes, and a flywheel. It functions on the principle of converting power into heat through dry friction. The frictional resistance between the brake shoes and the flywheel amplifies as the rope is tightened, thereby increasing the braking effect. To further augment the frictional force, spring-loaded bolts are integrated to tighten the wooden block against the flywheel. This arrangement enhances the braking performance of the Prony brake by maximizing the contact between the brake components and the flywheel, effectively dissipating the kinetic energy as heat through friction.

All the power absorbed by the Prony brake is converted into heat, necessitating cooling measures. The formula to calculate brake power (Pb) is given by:

$$\textbf{Brake Power } (P_b) = 2\pi NT$$

Where, T=Weight applied (W)×distance (l)

The Prony brake, while cost-effective, suffers from inherent instability, posing challenges in adjusting or maintaining specific loads. Several limitations associated with the Prony brake dynamometer include:

1) Variation in Coefficients of Friction: As the wooden blocks undergo wear over time, the coefficients of friction between the blocks and the flywheel can fluctuate. This necessitates frequent tightening of the clamps to maintain stability, especially during prolonged periods of measuring large powers.
2) Decrease in Coefficients of Friction: Elevated temperatures can lead to a decrease in friction coefficients, posing a risk of brake failure. It is crucial to

implement cooling measures to mitigate temperature rises. One common method involves supplying water into the hollow channel of the flywheel to facilitate cooling and maintain friction coefficients within safe limits.

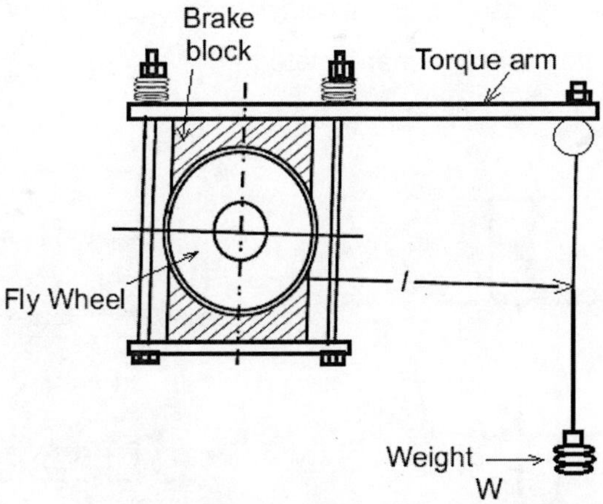


*Figure 2.25 Prony brake dynamometer*

3) Difficulty in observing the Readings: Fluctuations in coefficients of friction can present challenges when taking force (F) readings. Oscillations may occur in the measuring arrangement, particularly in situations where machine torque is not constant. This variability can impact the accuracy and reliability of the measurements, requiring careful consideration and potentially additional calibration procedures to ensure accurate readings.

### 2.4.2 EDDY CURRENT DYNAMOMETER

The eddy current dynamometers are commonly used in various applications such as performance testing of engines and motors, chassis dynamometer testing in automotive engineering, and industrial machinery testing. They work by generating eddy currents within a conductive material, typically a metallic disc or drum, that rotates within a magnetic field. These eddy currents induce an opposing magnetic field, creating a braking effect proportional to the mechanical input. This braking force can be precisely measured and correlated to the mechanical power being applied, providing valuable data for performance analysis and optimization of machinery. It is a specialized device characterized by reduced losses, high efficiency, and enhanced versatility compared to conventional mechanical dynamometers.

Unlike mechanical counterparts, the eddy current dynamometer minimizes losses by eliminating physical contact between windings and excitation.

Its compact size and compatibility render it suitable for a myriad of applications. In certain scenarios, such as testing the performance of internal combustion engines, the eddy current dynamometer serves as a load. This article provides an overview of the functionality and applications of an eddy current dynamometer.

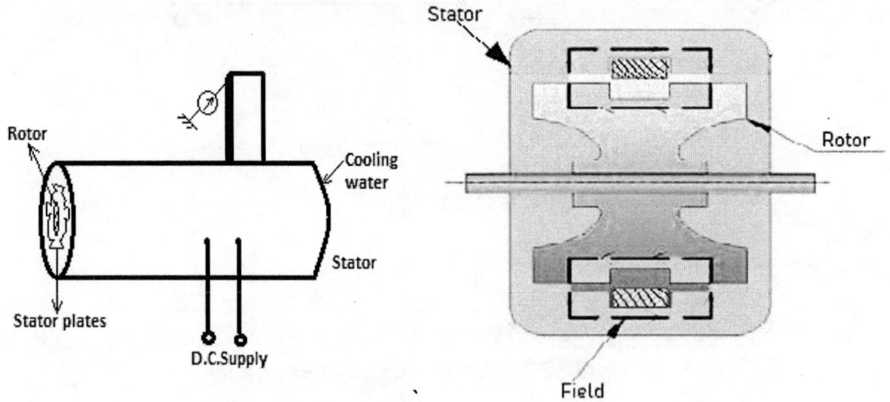


*Figure 2.26 Eddy current dynamometer*

**Construction:**

The eddy current dynamometer comprises an outer frame, known as the stator, which serves as the stationary component of the device. The stator houses windings placed within stator slots. Energizing these stator windings generates a magnetic field within the coils, termed the stator magnetic field. In high-rated machines, three-phase windings are commonly employed in the stator slots. The stator windings, typically composed of copper, are enveloped by a magnetic material like cast iron or silicon steel for delicate applications. Positioned beneath the stator coils is the rotating member, referred to as the rotor, mounted on a shaft to facilitate rotation. Rotor windings are housed within rotor slots, with three-phase configurations utilized in heavy-duty machines.

The rotor must be coupled to the prime mover to receive mechanical input. A DC supply energizes the stator windings, with rectifier units employed for larger machines. Cooling and insulation of the stator windings in heavy machines are accomplished using oil to dissipate heat effectively. A current meter integrated into the system measures the produced current and induced torque. A pointer, linked via an arm to the stator, gauges the torque generated in the rotor. Leveraging this torque value and the known speed, the power generated in the machine can be calculated.

***Working***

The functioning of an eddy current dynamometer hinges on Faraday's Law of electromagnetic induction. As per this principle, when there is movement between conductors and a magnetic field, it induces an electromotive force (emf) in the conductors. This emf, referred to as dynamically induced emf, is utilized within the dynamometer by exciting the stator poles with a direct current (DC) supply.

Upon the activation of the DC supply, the stator coils receive energy, establishing a magnetic field within the stator. In a three-phase setup, this excitation creates a three-phase rotating magnetic field within the stator coils. Meanwhile, as the prime mover rotates, the rotor coils interact with this magnetic field. It's noteworthy that the stator magnetic field remains fixed in this arrangement, as the DC excitation induces a static magnetic field. Consequently, an emf is induced as the rotor coils intersect the static stator magnetic field. This induction arises from the static nature of the magnetic field while the conductors undergo rotation, leading to a relative displacement between the magnetic field and the conductors.

***Features of Eddy Current Dynamometer***

1) The eddy current dynamometer operates on the concept of electromagnetic induction, where the rotor induces an electromotive force (emf) in response to cutting the stator magnetic field. This induces eddy currents within the rotor conductors.
2) Eddy currents generated in the rotor conductors create a force opposing the change in magnetic flux. Despite this opposing force, the rotor continues to rotate due to input from the prime mover.
3) Since there is no physical contact between the magnetic field and the conductors, the losses incurred are minimal compared to conventional generators.
4) The arm's connection to the stator body in the eddy current dynamometer allows for torque measurement and provides a mechanism for transmitting the torque from the rotor to the measuring instrument. This setup ensures accurate and direct torque readings, making eddy current dynamometers highly reliable for torque measurement applications.
5) In addition to measuring torque, the ability to determine the rotor's speed further enhances the versatility of eddy current dynamometers. By combining torque and

speed measurements, engineers and researchers can precisely assess the power output of various machines and systems. This capability is invaluable in performance testing, efficiency optimization, and research and development activities across multiple industries.

***Advantages of Eddy Current Dynamometer:***

1. Eddy current dynamometers boast lower frictional losses than conventional mechanical dynamometers, leading to heightened efficiency.
2. The structure of the dynamometer is simple, facilitating ease of operation and maintenance.
3. Eddy current dynamometers offer greater convenience in operation than traditional dynamometers.
4. The dynamometer exhibits rapid dynamic response owing to its low rotational inertia.
5. The device experiences lower copper losses with fewer windings, enhancing overall efficiency.
6. It can be seamlessly connected to external control units for monitoring and controlling current flow.
7. Eddy current dynamometers deliver high braking torque, contributing to their effectiveness in various applications.
8. These dynamometers are known for their high precision and stability during operation.

### 2.4.3 HYDRAULIC DYNAMOMETER

The hydraulic dynamometer functions as an absorption-type dynamometer, relying on fluid friction for its operation, thereby dissipating mechanical energy. This characteristic leads to its alternative designation as a fluid friction dynamometer. Hydraulic dynamometers feature semicircular vanes positioned within both the rotor and stator components. Water circulation induces a toroidal vortex around these vanes, generating a torque reaction within the dynamometer casing. This reaction is counteracted by the dynamometer and quantified using a load cell. Structurally, hydraulic dynamometers closely resemble fluid flywheels designed to gauge the frictional force between impeller vanes and a moving fluid.

The hydraulic dynamometer comprises a rotating disk connected to the driving shaft of the test machine. The disk features semi-elliptical grooves through which water flows. A stationary casing, mounted on antifriction bearings or trunnions, houses a braking arm and a balance system that allows the casing to revolve freely within limits set by the braking arm.

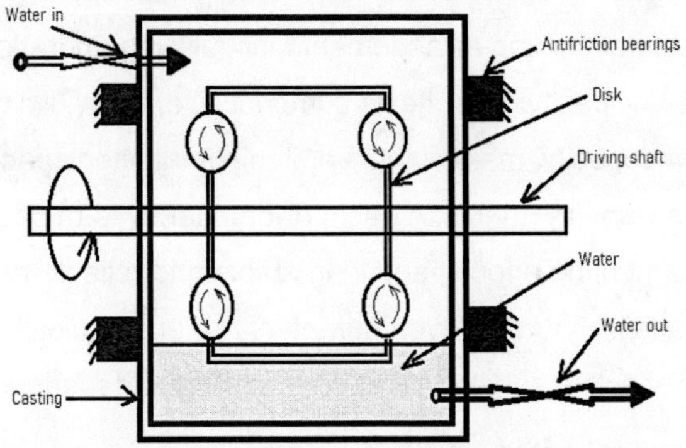


*Figure 2.27 Hydraulic dynamometer*

Similarly, casing also contains semi-elliptical grooves or recesses. These two components are arranged so that the rotating disk rotates within the casing. The schematic of the hydraulic dynamometer is depicted in Fig 2.27. The semi-elliptical grooves on the disk align with corresponding semi-elliptical recesses on the casing, forming a chamber through which liquid flows. As the driving shaft of the prime mover rotates, the liquid follows a helical path in the chamber, creating vortices and eddy currents. These currents cause the casing of the dynamometer to rotate in the direction of the shaft.

The braking action is adjusted and regulated by altering the distance between the casing and disk or by modifying the water amount and pressure. Maximum power absorption occurs when the casing is full, while minimum absorption is achieved with minimal liquid. The total power absorption of this device varies as follows:

1. The cube of the rotational speed
2. The fifth power of the rotating disk diameter

The absorbing element incorporates a force-sensing component, such as a load cell, positioned at the end of the arm with a radius "r". The formula determines the exerted torque:

$$Torque(T)=F\times r$$

Where, F represents the force measured at radius r

The power can then be calculated using the formula: $P=2\pi T$

***Advantages of Hydraulic Dynamometer***

1. Natural Cooling: As water serves as the coolant, hydraulic dynamometers do not necessitate external cooling arrangements, simplifying operation and maintenance.
2. High Absorption Capacity: Despite its compact size, hydraulic dynamometers offer high absorption capacity, making them suitable for limited space applications.
3. Protection from Hunting Effects: A dashpot-damper system can effectively shield the instrument from hunting effects, ensuring stable and reliable performance.
4. Cost-Effectiveness: Hydraulic dynamometers are economically advantageous, offering a cost-effective solution for various testing and measurement needs.

## 2.5 PRESSURE MEASUREMENT

Pressure is a foundational element in numerous facets of daily life, influencing phenomena ranging from atmospheric pressure to blood pressure, gauge pressure, and vacuum conditions. A comprehensive comprehension of pressure and its quantification proves indispensable across diverse domains. At its core, pressure denotes the force exerted by a medium, typically a fluid, per unit area. In instrumentation, pressure measurement often entails assessing differential pressure, commonly known as gauge pressure, which signifies the force exerted per unit area by liquids, gases, or solids.

Expressing mathematically, pressure (P) is derived from the formula:

$$P = F/A$$

A and F signify area and force. Pressure can be quantified using various units such as atmospheres and bars or by referencing the height of a liquid column. Standard atmospheric pressure, typically measured at sea level, is conventionally standardized as 760 mmHg. It is worth noting that atmospheric pressure diminishes with increasing altitude.

Measurement of pressure is significant for several reasons:

1. It is a descriptive quantity of a system.
2. It is a crucial process parameter.
3. Pressure difference is often used to measure fluid flow rate.
4. The range of pressure encountered in practice spans nearly 18 orders of magnitude, from the lowest to the highest pressures.

**Pressure measurement utilizes four primary scales**

1) **Gauge Pressure (Pg)**: Gauge pressure is a measurement scale that quantifies pressure above the prevailing local atmospheric pressure. It is commonly utilized in

various engineering applications where pressure differentials are crucial for operations. Gauge pressure readings disregard atmospheric pressure and solely focus on deviations from this baseline, providing essential data for tasks such as fluid system monitoring, tire pressure assessment, and hydraulic system operation.

2) **Total Absolute Pressure (Pt)**: Total absolute pressure refers to pressure measurement from a zero-pressure reference point. Unlike gauge pressure, which accounts for deviations from atmospheric pressure, total absolute pressure considers the entirety of pressure exerted on a system, including both gauge pressure and atmospheric pressure. Mathematically, it is the summation of atmospheric pressure and gauge pressure. This comprehensive pressure reading serves as a critical parameter in numerous engineering disciplines, aiding in the precise evaluation of system performance, particularly in environments where absolute pressure measurements are paramount for accuracy and safety.

$$Pt = \text{Atmospheric pressure} + Pg$$

3) **Differential Pressure**: Differential pressure is a fundamental concept in fluid mechanics and engineering, denoting the difference in pressure between two distinct points within a system. This measurement scale is pivotal in assessing flow rates, detecting obstructions or blockages, and determining the efficiency of various mechanical systems. Differential pressure sensors are commonly employed in applications such as HVAC systems, filtration processes, and industrial automation, where precise pressure differentials are crucial for optimal performance and safety.

4) **Vacuum Pressure (Pv):** Vacuum pressure refers to a pressure measurement below the local atmospheric pressure level. In practical terms, when the measured pressure falls below atmospheric pressure ($P_{atm}$), it signifies the existence of a vacuum. This phenomenon is often encountered in vacuum systems, where negative gauge pressure readings indicate the absence of atmospheric air within an enclosed space. Vacuum pressure plays a significant role in applications such as vacuum pumps, vacuum chambers, and space simulation environments, where the creation and maintenance of low-pressure conditions are essential for specific industrial processes and scientific experiments.

   Vacuum is defined by the relation:

$$Pv = P_{atm} - P_{abs}$$

1. **Absolute Pressure ($P_{abs}$):** This scale measures pressure above total vacuum or zero absolute, signifying a complete absence of pressure.

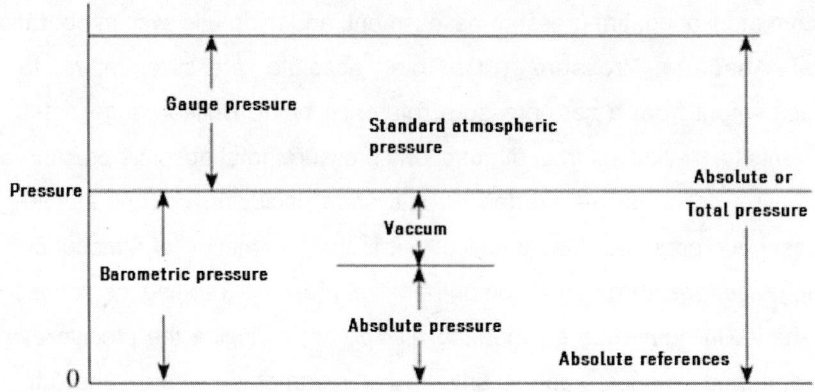


*Figure 2.28 Absolute, gauge, and barometric pressures*

### 2.5.1 MCLEOD GAUGE

Developed by Herbert McLeod in 1874, the McLeod gauge stands as a cornerstone in vacuum measurement, particularly within the pressure range of 10 to 10-4 Torr (1 Torr = 133.322 Pa). Renowned as an absolute standard, this device, also referred to as a compression gauge, operates by compressing the low-pressure gas whose pressure is under assessment. The essence of its operation lies in compressing the gas within a capillary tube, subsequently measuring the resulting height of a mercury column to determine the vacuum level.

Functioning in accordance with Boyle's law, the McLeod gauge underscores the principle that compressing a known volume of low-pressure gas to a higher pressure facilitates the calculation of the initial pressure by quantifying the resultant volume and pressure relationship. This foundational technique has positioned the McLeod gauge as an indispensable tool in various scientific and industrial applications requiring precise vacuum measurements.

The following fundamental relation represents Boyle's law:

$$P_1 = \frac{P_2 V_2}{V_1}$$

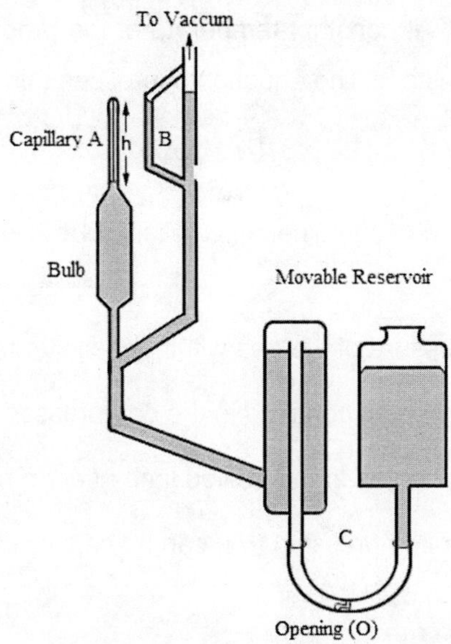


*Figure 2.29 Layout of McLeod Gauge*

The McLeod gauge, a fundamental instrument in vacuum measurement, features a distinctive structural design comprising a capillary tube A, sealed at its upper end, and two interconnected limbs B and C that are integrated into the vacuum system. Limbs A and B are characterized by capillary tubes of identical diameters, ensuring uniformity, while limb C possesses a wider diameter to mitigate capillary errors and enhance accuracy. During operation, the movable reservoir is initially lowered, allowing the mercury column to descend below the opening level O, establishing a connection between all capillaries and limbs with the unknown pressure source. Subsequent elevation of the movable reservoir results in mercury filling the bulb, causing an upward displacement of the mercury level within capillary tube A. This action compresses the gas confined within the system, adhering to Boyle's law. Practically, the mercury level in capillary tube B is adjusted to align with that of limb C, serving as the zero level reference on the scale. The disparity in levels between the two mercury columns in limbs A and B directly reflects the trapped pressure, facilitating straightforward readings from the scale. Through this meticulously designed mechanism, the McLeod gauge provides precise and reliable measurements of vacuum pressures essential for various scientific and industrial applications.

This experiment leverages Boyle's Law to ascertain the unknown pressure (P1) of a gas within a sealed system. At constant temperature, the produc-t of pressure and volume for an ideal gas remains constant. The equation expresses this relationship:

$$P1V1 = P2V2$$

$V_1$ represents the volume of gas contained in capillary tube A above level O before compression.

$P_1$ signifies the unknown pressure of the gas within the system.

$P_2$ denotes the pressure of the gas confined in the compressed limb, typically limb B.

$V_2$ stands for the volume of the gas in the sealed limb after compression.

The volume of the gas after compression ($V_2$) can be calculated using the following equation:

$$V_2 = ah$$

a: Cross-sectional area of the capillary tube

h: Difference in levels of the two columns (representing pressure difference)

This equation states that $V_2$ is equal to the product of the capillary's cross-sectional area (a) and the difference in pressure levels (h).

The pressure difference (h) is equivalent to the difference between the final pressure ($P_2$) and the unknown pressure ($P_1$) of the gas:

$$h = P2 - P1$$

By substituting the expression for h into the equation for $V_2$, we can establish a relationship between the known variables (a, $V_1$, $P_2$) and the unknown pressure ($P_1$). This will lead to the final equation(s) used to solve for $P_1$.

$$P_1V_1 = P_2ah$$

$$P_1V_1 = (h + P_1)ah$$

$$P_1V_1 = ah^2 + ahP_1$$

$$P_1(V_1 - ah) = ah^2$$

*Hence*

$$P_1 = \frac{ah^2}{V_1 - ah}$$

$$P_1 = \frac{ah^2}{V_1} \text{ when } ah \ll V_1$$

McLeod gauges excel at measuring low pressures. This is achieved by designing them with a large bulb volume ($V_1$) compared to the cross-sectional area (a) of the capillary tube. The ratio of $V_1$ to a is called the compression ratio. However, there are trade-offs to consider:

1. Capillary Diameter: A minimal capillary diameter (a) can lead to mercury sticking to the walls, limiting the achievable compression ratio.
2. Bulb Size: While a larger bulb ($V_1$) allows for measuring lower pressures, it also increases the weight of the mercury column, potentially limiting the compression ratio as well.

Despite their usefulness in calibrating other high-vacuum gauges, McLeod gauges have significant limitations. The presence of condensable vapours in the gas being measured can introduce errors. This is because Boyle's Law, which forms the basis of the gauge's operation, may not apply accurately to these vapours.

## 2.6 APPLICATIONS

Transducers and strain gauges are integral to force, torque, and pressure-measuring instruments across industries. Capacitive transducers find extensive application in touchscreens integrated into electronic devices such as smartphones, tablets, and touch-sensitive displays. These transducers detect alterations in capacitance induced by user touch, facilitating precise and responsive interaction with the device interface. In proximity sensing applications, capacitive transducers play a vital role in detecting the presence or absence of objects without physical contact. They are deployed in various devices, including automatic faucets, motion-activated lighting systems, and proximi-ty switches, which are utilized in industrial automation setups. Utilizing capacitive transducers, humidity sensors accurately measure relative humidity levels in diverse environments. Fluctuations in humidity induce variations in capacitance, enabling precise determination of humidity levels crucial for applications such as weather monitoring, HVAC systems, and industrial process control.

Inductance transducers are prominently employed in non-destructive testing methodologies like eddy current testing. They gauge alterations in inductance triggered by the interaction between electromagnetic fields and conductive materials, facilitating the detection of surface defects, cracks, or material thickness variations in metal components.In position and displacement measurement applications, inductance transducers are utilized, notably in linear and rotary encoders. They detect changes in inductance stemming from the movement of a conductive target, providing precise and dependable position feedback essential for machinery, robotics, and automotive systems.Inductance transducers are integral components of metal detectors utilized across various sectors including security screening, mining operations, and manufacturing quality control processes. They enable the detection of metal objects by analyzing variations in inductance.

Resistive transducers, such as resistance temperature detectors (RTDs) and thermistors, are extensively utilized for temperature sensing in industrial, automotive, and consumer electronics domains. Temperature-induced changes in resistance allow accurate measurement of temperature levels, which is critical for applications like HVAC systems, automotive engine monitoring, and food processing. In pressure sensing applications, resistive transducers, notably strain gauges, are employed in pressure sensors to measure alterations in pressure across automotive, aerospace, and industrial systems. Mechanical deformation in the strain gauge, caused by changes in pressure, results in variations in resistance, enabling precise pressure level determination. Resistive transducers, including load cells equipped with strain gauges, are utilized for force and load measurement in diverse applications such as weighing scales, material testing, and industrial automation. Deformation in the strain gauge, induced by changes in force or load, leads to variations in resistance, facilitating accurate measurement of force or load levels.

The load cells are essential in weighing systems from labs to factories, converting force into electrical signals for accurate measurement. Materials testing machines utilize them to assess mechanical properties precisely, aiding quality control and R&D. Additionally, force feedback systems in robotics rely on them for precise environmental interaction.Torque-measuring instruments employ transducers and strain gauges for rotational force measurement. In automotive engineering, dynamometers use them for engine torque measurement, while industrial machinery benefits for monitoring and adjusting rotational forces. Prony brake dynamometers measure engine torque output by applying resistance to the engine's rotating shaft. They are used in the automotive and aerospace industries to assess brake performance metrics. Eddy Current Dynamometer measures torque, speed, and power output in high-speed electric motors. It is used to characterize material properties like strength and stiffness. Hydraulic dynamometers simulate road loads to evaluate vehicle performance. They assess torque, speed, and power output in hydraulic machinery.

McLeod gauges measure ultra-low pressures in scientific research and semiconductor manufacturing. They monitor gas pressures in applications like gas chromatography and semiconductor processing.

## 2.7 UNIT SUMMARY

This unit comprehensively examines transducers and their crucial role in strain measurement, covering a wide range of topics necessary for understanding and effectively applying these devices. The exploration commences with an exhaustive analysis of the characteristics and classifications of transducers, delving into the intricacies of various types, such as two-coil self-inductance and piezoelectric transducers. Through detailed discussions and illustrative examples, learners gain comprehensive insights into the principles, functionalities, and applications of transducer variants. Following the exploration of transducers, the unit delves into strain measurement, offering an extensive overview of strain gauges. Topics covered include the classification of strain gauges, mounting techniques, and the configuration of two-element and three-element rosettes. The learners thoroughly understand the principles and methodologies underlying strain measurement, empowering them to effectively utilize strain gauges in various applications. The unit progresses to explore the applications of transducers in measuring force, torque, and pressure. Engaging discussions encompass common instruments such as spring balances, proving rings, load cells, prony brakes, eddy current dynamometers, hydraulic dynamometers, and McLeod gauges that helps the learners in gaining valuable insights into the principles, operation, and applications of these instruments in diverse engineering contexts.

## 2.8 EXERCISE

### 2.8.1 MULTIPLE CHOICE QUESTIONS

1. What is the primary function of a transducer in metrology?

   a) To amplify electrical signals

   b) To convert physical quantities into electrical signals

   c) To measure distances accurately

   d) To regulate the flow of current

2. In a capacitive transducer, what changes to produce a variation in capacitance?
   a) Voltage
   b) Resistance
   c) Dielectric constant
   d) Distance between plates
3. Capacitive transducers are commonly used in applications requiring:
   a) High accuracy and precision
   b) Low sensitivity
   c) Fast response time
   d) High power consumption
4. In an inductive transducer, what changes to produce a variation in inductance?
   a) Voltage
   b) Resistance
   c) Capacitance
   d) Position of the core or coil
5. Which of the following physical quantities can be measured using an inductive transducer?
   a) Temperature
   b) Pressure
   c) Displacement
   d) Voltage
6. In a two-coil self-inductance transducer, what changes to produce a variation in inductance?
   a) Voltage applied
   b) Resistance of the coils
   c) Distance between the coils
   d) Temperature of the coils
7. Which of the following is an example of a primary transducer?
   a) Strain gauge
   b) Thermocouple
   c) LVDT (Linear Variable Differential Transformer)
   d) Piezoelectric sensor
8. Which of the following is an example of a secondary transducer?
   a) Thermocouple

b) Potentiometer

c) Strain gauge

d) LVDT (Linear Variable Differential Transformer)

9. Which of the following is an example of an active transducer?

a) Thermocouple

b) Photovoltaic cell

c) Piezoelectric sensor

d) Strain gauge

10. How do piezoelectric transducers generate an electrical signal?

a) By changing the capacitance of a material

b) By inducing a magnetic field

c) By converting mechanical stress into electrical charge

d) By altering the inductance of a coil

11. Which material is commonly used in the construction of electrical strain gauges?

a) Copper

b) Aluminum

c) Silicon

d) Nichrome or Constantan

12. What is the purpose of using a quarter-bridge strain gauge configuration?

a) To measure strain in all directions

b) To achieve higher sensitivity

c) To minimize temperature effects

d) To simplify the wiring and circuitry

13. What type of electrical bridge circuit is commonly used with a half-bridge strain gauge configuration?

a) Wheatstone bridge

b) Maxwell bridge

c) Kelvin bridge

d) Schering bridge

14. What is the primary advantage of using a full-bridge configuration over half-bridge or quarter-bridge configurations?

a) Higher sensitivity

b) Better compensation for temperature effects

c) Simpler wiring and circuitry

d) Lower cost

15. In a strain gauge rosette, how are the strain gauges oriented with respect to each other?

    a) They are oriented parallel to each other

    b) They are oriented perpendicular to each other

    c) They are oriented at 45-degree angles to each other

    d) They are oriented randomly

16. What type of spring is commonly used in a spring balance?

    a) Torsion spring

    b) Helical spring

    c) Leaf spring

    d) Extension spring

17. Proving rings are often calibrated in units of:

    a) Pressure

    b) Length

    c) Force or weight

    d) Voltage

18. What is the primary function of a load cell?

    a) To measure temperature

    b) To measure pressure

    c) To measure force or weight

    d) To measure displacement

19. Which principle does a strain gauge load cell commonly operate on?

    a) Capacitive effect

    b) Inductive effect

    c) Piezoelectric effect

    d) Resistance change due to mechanical strain

20. What is the primary function of a Prony brake dynamometer?

    a) To measure temperature

    b) To measure pressure

    c) To measure torque or power

    d) To measure displacement

21. How does an eddy current dynamometer operate?

    a) By converting torque into electrical signals

b) By measuring the deformation of a spring

c) By using magnetic fields to generate resistive forces

d) By using a piezoelectric effect

22. How does a hydraulic dynamometer operate?

a) By converting torque into electrical signals

b) By using fluid flow to generate resistive forces

c) By measuring the deformation of a spring

d) By using a piezoelectric effect

23. Which of the following statements is true regarding these pressure measurements?

a) Absolute pressure can be negative.

b) Atmospheric pressure is always zero at sea level.

c) Gauge pressure is the difference between absolute and atmospheric pressure.

d) Atmospheric pressure is equivalent to gauge pressure.

24. What is gauge pressure?

a) Pressure measured above sea level

b) Pressure measured relative to atmospheric pressure

c) Pressure measured within a confined space

d) Pressure measured by a gauge instrument

25. What is the primary function of a McLeod gauge?

a) To measure temperature

b) To measure pressure in high-vacuum systems

c) To measure atmospheric pressure

d) To measure pressure in hydraulic systems

**Answers: 1)B, 2)d, 3)a, 4)d, 5)c, 6)c, 7)b, 8)b, 9)b, 10)c, 11)d, 12)c, 13)a, 14)b, 15)c, 16)b, 17)c, 18)c, 19)d, 20)c, 21)c, 22)b, 23)c, 24)b, 25)b**

2.8.2. SUBJECTIVE TYPE QUESTIONS

**Short Answer Questions:**

1. Define a transducer and explain its role in measurements.
2. What are the different types of transducers based on their operating principles?
3. How does a strain gauge work to measure strain?
4. Describe the construction and working principle of a resistive strain gauge.
5. What are the factors influencing the sensitivity of a strain gauge?

6. Explain the Wheatstone bridge circuit and its application in strain gauge measurements.
7. What is the significance of temperature compensation in strain gauge measurements?
8. Discuss the advantages and limitations of using strain gauges in measurement applications.
9. How can you calibrate a strain gauge-based measurement system?
10. Explain the concept of gauge factor and its importance in strain gauge measurements.

**Long Answer Questions:**

1. Compare and contrast the working principles of capacitive and resistive transducers.
2. Discuss the types of strain gauges available in the market, highlighting their differences in construction and application.
3. Explain the procedure to install and bond a strain gauge on a specimen for strain measurement.
4. Elaborate on the various sources of error in strain gauge measurements and methods to minimize them.
5. Describe the working principle of a piezoelectric transducer and its applications in measurements.
6. Discuss the role of signal conditioning in enhancing the performance of strain gauge-based measurement systems.
7. Compare the advantages and disadvantages of using strain gauge-based measurements versus optical methods for strain analysis.
8. Explain the concept of hysteresis in transducers and its impact on measurement accuracy.
9. Discuss the challenges associated with dynamic strain measurement and methods to overcome them.
10. Describe a real-world application where strain gauges are used extensively, outlining the measurement setup and potential challenges encountered.

## 2.8 PRACTICAL

### Practical Statement

**PS1.** Construct a load cell using a strain gauge on a metal beam, apply known weights, and plot a calibration curve relating force to output signal.

**PS2.** Measure the Stress and Strain using Strain Gauge on a Cantilever Beam and measure the relationship between stress and strain using a strain gauge mounted on a cantilever beam.

**PS3.** Measuring Pressure of a Fluid in a Pipe using a Pressure Transducer.

**PS4.** Measurement of Force using a Load Cell, Spring Balance and Proving Ring; and compare the results.

**PS5.** Compare the Torque values measured using Prony Brake Dynamometer and Eddy Current Dynamometer.

**PS6.** Pressure Measurement using Bourdon Tube Gauge and Mcleod Gauge.

## 2.9 KNOW MORE

1. **Advanced Technologies:** Introduce readers to cutting-edge advancements in transducer and strain gauge technology, such as microelectromechanical systems (MEMS), fibre-optic sensors, and nanotechnology-based sensors. Explain how these innovations are pushing the boundaries of measurement capabilities and opening up new possibilities for precision sensing.
2. **Environmental Considerations**: Examine the challenges and considerations involved in designing transducers and strain gauges for harsh or specialized environments, such as high temperatures, corrosive substances, or extreme pressures. Discuss strategies for mitigating these challenges and ensuring reliable performance in challenging conditions.
3. **Calibration and Maintenance:** Provide insights into the importance of calibration and maintenance procedures for transducers and strain gauges to ensure accuracy and reliability over time. Discuss best practices for calibration, including traceability to national standards, and regular maintenance routines to prevent sensor drift or degradation.
4. **Emerging Trends:** Highlight emerging trends and future directions in transducer and strain gauge technology, such as wireless sensor networks, internet of things (IoT) integration, and machine learning-based data analytics. Discuss how these trends are shaping the next generation of measurement systems and driving innovation in the field.

## 2.10 REFERENCES AND SUGGESTED READINGS

1. "Strain Gauge Transducers" by S. Timoshenko, Dover Publications, 2013.
2. "Transducers and Their Elements: Design and Application" by A. D. S. J. G. M. Van Holten, Wiley, 2004.
3. "Strain Gauge Technology" by A. Hingston, Wiley, 2010.
4. "Introduction to Sensors and Actuators" by Manifold Calibration and Gauge Testing Society, CRC Press, 2005.
5. "Measurement and Instrumentation: Theory and Application" by Alan S. Morris, Butterworth-Heinemann, 2009.

***SUGGESTED READINGS***

1. "Measurement Systems: Application and Design" by Ernest O. Doebelin - Covers transducers and strain gauges with practical examples.
2. "Sensor Technology Handbook" by Jon S. Wilson - Offers detailed insights into strain gauges and other sensor technologies.
3. "Sensor and Transducer Handbook" edited by Jon S. Wilson - Provides comprehensive information on strain gauges and other transducers.
4. "Practical Stress Analysis with Finite Elements" by Bryan J. Mac Donald - Focuses on practical applications of strain gauges in stress analysis.
5. "Applied Mechatronics" by A. Smaili, F. Mrad, and H. F. Dakhli - Explores the integration of strain gauges in mechatronic systems for feedback control.
6. "Strain Measurement in Experimental Mechanics" by R. S. Lakes - Covers advanced techniques in strain measurement, including strain gauge installation and data analysis.

**Dynamic QR Code for Further Reading**

Strain Gauges

LVDT Transducer

# 3 Applied Mechanical Measurements

## UNIT SPECIFICS

*This unit presents information related to the following topics:*

- *Speed measurement: Classification of tachometers, Revolution counters, Eddy current tachometers*
- *Displacement measurement: Linear Variable Differential Transformers (LVDT)*
- *Flow measurement: Rotometers, Turbine meter*
- *Temperature measurement: Resistance thermometers, Optical Pyrometer*
- *Miscellaneous measurements:*
- *Humidity measurement: hair hygrometer*
- *Density measurement: hydrometer*
- *Liquid level measurement: sight glass Float gauge*
- *Biomedical measurement: Sphygmomanometer*

### *Applications*

*This unit is designed to provide an in-depth understanding of various mechanical measurements applied in engineering. It begins with methods for measuring speed, introducing different types of tachometers, revolution counters, and Eddy current tachometers.*

*The unit then covers displacement measurement techniques, focusing on Linear Variable Differential Transformers (LVDT), which are crucial for accurate linear displacement measurements. Flow measurement is another key topic, with explanations of rotometers and turbine meters.*

*Additionally, the unit includes temperature measurement methods, detailing the use of resistance thermometers and optical pyrometers. Various miscellaneous measurements are also discussed, such as humidity measurement using hair hygrometers, density measurement with hydrometers, and liquid level measurement using sight glass float gauges.*

*Finally, the unit explores biomedical measurement techniques with a focus on the sphygmomanometer.*

*Apart from this, at the end of the unit, the overall broad concepts are provided as a unit summary. Besides, a large number of multiple-choice questions as well as descriptive-type questions with Bloom's taxonomy action verbs are included. A list of references and suggested readings is given in the unit so that one can go through them for practice. It is important to note that for getting more information on various topics of interest, some QR codes have been provided in different sections which can be scanned for relevant supportive knowledge. Video resources along with QR codes are mentioned for getting more information on various topics of interest which can be surfed or scanned through mobile phones for viewing.*

## RATIONALE

*Mechanical measurements are essential in various engineering fields to ensure precision and reliability in processes and products. Understanding the principles and methods of measuring speed, displacement, flow, temperature, and other physical quantities is crucial for engineers to design and maintain efficient systems. This unit provides comprehensive coverage of these measurement techniques, equipping students and professionals with the necessary skills and knowledge to perform accurate mechanical measurements.*

## PRE-REQUISITES

*Before reading this unit, the students are advised to revisit the following:*

- *Basic Physics: Principles of motion, thermodynamics, and fluid mechanics*
- *Basic Electrical Engineering: Understanding of electrical circuits and sensors*
- *Basic Engineering Mechanics*

## UNIT OUTCOMES

*After studying this unit, students will be able to:*

- *U3-O1: Understand the classification and working principles of various tachometers.*
- *U3-O2: Explain the operation and applications of Linear Variable Differential Transformers (LVDT).*
- *U3-O3: Demonstrate the methods of flow measurement using rotometers and turbine meters.*

- *U3-O4: Apply techniques for measuring temperature using resistance thermometers and optical pyrometers.*
- *U3-O5: Perform miscellaneous measurements such as humidity, density, liquid level, and biomedical measurements accurately.*

## EXPECTED MAPPING WITH COURSE OUTCOMES

*(1- Weak Correlation; 2- Medium correlation; 3- Strong Correlation)*

| Unit Outcomes (U3) | CO-1 | CO-2 | CO-3 | CO-4 | CO-5 |
|---|---|---|---|---|---|
| **U3-O1** | 3 | 2 | 3 | 2 | 1 |
| **U3-O2** | 3 | 3 | 2 | 2 | 1 |
| **U3-O3** | 2 | 2 | 3 | 1 | 1 |
| **U3-O4** | 3 | 3 | 2 | 3 | 1 |
| **U3-O5** | 2 | 3 | 3 | 2 | 2 |

## 3.1 SPEED MEASUREMENT

Speed, a fundamental aspect of motion, represents the pace at which an object shifts its position over time. Notably, the assessment of rotational speed has gained prominence over linear speed measurement. It is measured in a variety of ways. Common formats include linear speed, which is commonly represented in meters per second (m/s), and angular speed, which is commonly expressed in radians per second (rad/s) or, for rotating systems, rotations per minute (rpm).

Continuous linear speed measurement mostly depends on angular speed measurement. Determining the linear speed of the reciprocating components in mechanical systems is made possible by having a thorough understanding of rotational velocity. Rotational speed measurement is important in engineering and related industries because of the angular and linear speed interdependence.

### 3.1.1. TACHOMETER

Angular measurements are facilitated by a tool known as a tachometer. The definitions attributed to a tachometer encompass its pivotal role in measurement:

i. A device for measuring angular velocity, usually of a shaft, measures the number of revolutions in a specified amount of time or shows the number of rotations per minute.
ii. A device that shows rotational speed constantly or gives a consistent average speed reading at quickly repeated intervals of time.

**Classification:** Tachometers are broadly categorized into two main types: Mechanical and Electrical variants. The selection of the appropriate tachometer hinges on several factors including cost considerations, the necessity for portability, desired accuracy levels, the range of speeds to be measured, and the dimensions of the rotating component.

1) **Mechanical Tachometer**

Mechanical Tachometers rely solely on mechanical components and movements to gauge speed. These devices, often known as revolution counters or speed counters as shown in figure 3.1, operate with a simple yet effective mechanism. They utilize a worm gear, serving as both the connection to the shaft and the conduit for speed transmission.

When the shaft rotates, it drives the worm gear, which in turn moves a spur gear. This spur gear is connected to a pointer on a meticulously calibrated dial. As the gears rotate, the pointer indicates the number of revolutions the input shaft completes within a specific time frame.

It's important to note that this method requires a separate timer to precisely measure time intervals. Consequently, the revolution counter provides an average rotating speed rather than real-time updates. However, with proper design and manufacturing, these counters can offer satisfactory speed measurements, typically accurate up to speeds of 2000-3000 revolutions per minute (rpm).

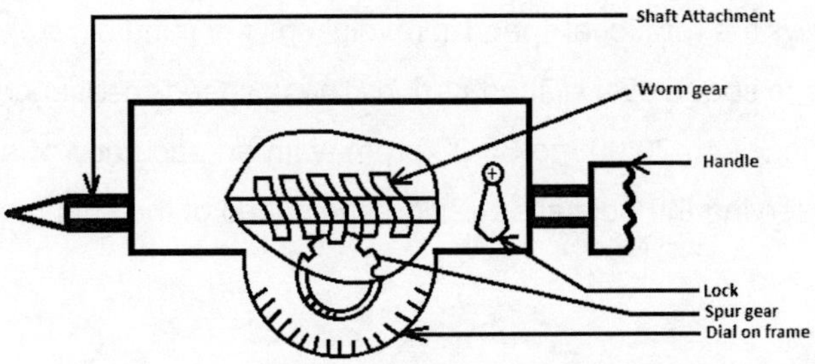


*Figure 3.1 Revolution Counter*

## a. Tachoscope

The need to synchronize the starting of a watch and a counter gave rise to the invention of the tachoscope as shown in Figure 3.2. This device combines a revolution counter with a timing mechanism, allowing both to start together. As the contact point makes contact with the rotating shaft, both parts move simultaneously. As long as the contact point is attached to the shaft, the tachoscope will continue to function. The rotation speed can be ascertained by examining the counter and timer readings. Even at 5000 revolutions per minute (rpm), the tachoscope can measure speeds with accuracy.

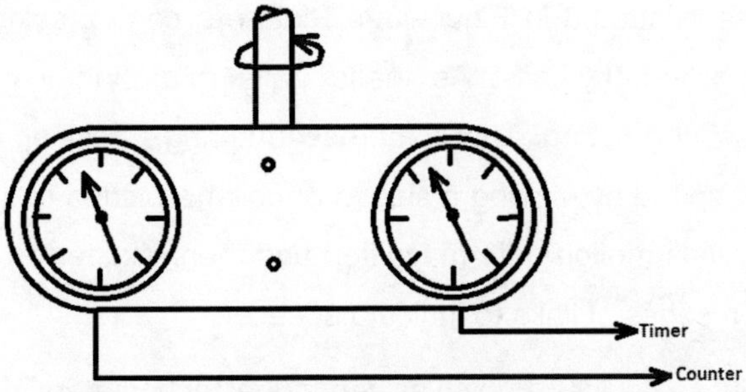


*Figure 3.2 Tachoscope*

### b. Hand Speed Indicators

The indicator comes with a stopwatch and counter built-in, which disconnects automatically. When the spindle touches the shaft, it begins working. However, the counter only starts when you press the start and wind button. This button also activates the automatic clutch and starts the stopwatch as depicted in Figure 3.3.

A stopwatch can also start by pressing the starting button. The revolution counter stops automatically after a set time, typically three or six seconds. The dial accurately displays the rotational speed in revolutions per minute (rpm), and the device shows the average speed over a short period. These speed-measuring tools are used for speeds ranging from 20,000 to 30,000 rpm, with an accuracy of about 1% of the full scale. By observing the pointer's position, the speed of the shaft can be measured with ease.

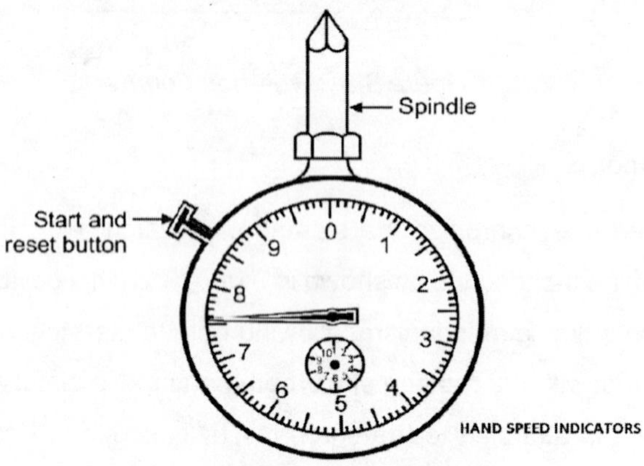


*Figure 3.3 Hand Speed Indicators*

### c. Centrifugal Force Tachometers

Centrifugal force, proportional to the rotational speed, drives the operation of this device as illustrated in Figure 3.4. Picture a central spindle encircled by two small weights called fly balls. As these balls rotate, they generate centrifugal force, compressing a spring. The compressed spring's position can be altered concerning the shaft speed by moving a sleeve or collar attached to its free end along the shaft. Typically, this motion gets magnified and then transferred to the instrument's pointer through a series of links to indicate speed.

These devices, known as centrifugal tachometers, can also gauge linear speed by adding specific attachments to the spindle. To cover a wide range of speeds, manufacturers often produce them with multiple range options. The device can smoothly switch between these ranges by utilizing a gear train between the fly ball shaft and the spindle. However, it's crucial to select the appropriate speed range carefully, as exceeding the device's capacity can result in significant damage. It's also important to note that altering the range while the instrument is in use is not advisable.

Centrifugal tachometers are highly favored for their accuracy, typically around ±1%, and are commonly used to monitor rotational speeds of up to 40,000 rpm. Centrifugal tachometers surpass revolution-counter-stopwatch mechanisms in this regard, as the latter cannot provide real-time speed information.

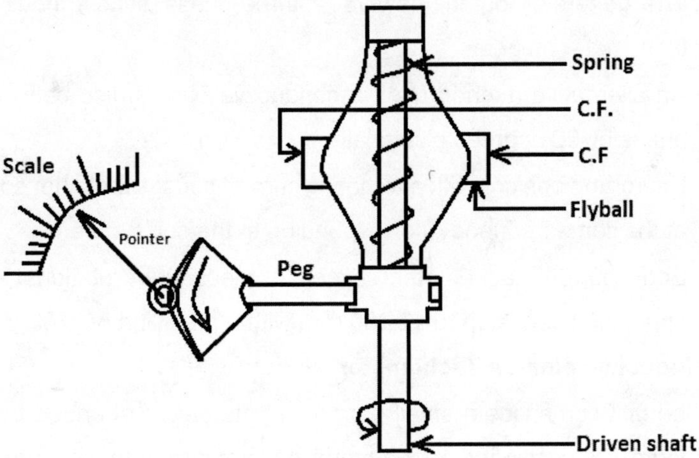


*Figure 3.4 Centrifugal Tachometer*

**2) Electrical Tachometers**

An electrical tachometer works by producing an electric signal that corresponds to how fast a shaft is rotating. These tachometers come in various designs, depending on the type of sensor used.

**a. Eddy Current Tachometer**

- In an eddy current tachometer, a permanent magnet is affixed to a shaft and rotated.
- Rotation of the magnet induces eddy currents in a nearby drag cup or disc.
- These eddy currents produce a torque that opposes the cup's rotation, counteracted by a spiral spring's torque.
- When the torque from the eddy currents balances the spring's torque, the cup aligns with the magnetic field and begins rotating.

- The rotational speed is indicated on a scale by a pointer fixed to the cup, similar to how car speedometers function.
- Car speedometers determine wheel speed, converting it into linear speed using an assumed average wheel diameter and adjusting the scale accordingly.
- In locomotive tachometers, a fixed magnet and rotating soft iron rotor generate a magnetic field.
- Aviation tachometry employs an electrical system, replacing the mechanical setup with a three-phase alternating current (a-c) generator powered by the tested machinery.
- The generator output powers a three-phase synchronous motor, driving the tachometer magnet.
- An alternative method uses a conductive cup or disc between two coils, out of phase by 90 degrees electrically.
- Energizing one coil with alternating current causes the other coil to register a signal at the same frequency, corresponding to the cup's speed.
- Eddy current tachometers excel in measuring rotational speeds, accurately capturing speeds up to 12,000 rpm with a precision of ±3%.

**b. Inductive pick-up Tachometer**

- The unit comprises a small permanent magnet surrounded by a coil as shown in Figure 3.5, positioned near a metallic toothed rotor to measure its speed.
- As the rotor shaft rotates, its teeth pass by the magnetic pickup, altering the magnetic circuit's reluctance and inducing a voltage in the coil.
- The frequency of these voltage pulses is directly proportional to the rotor's speed and the number of teeth on the rotor.
- These pulses are then amplified, squared, and directed into a frequency-measuring unit or digital counter for analysis.
- Speed = (pulses per second / number of teeth)  60 RPM, the speed in revolutions per minute can be calculated.
- For example, with a rotor possessing 60 teeth and the counter tallying pulses within one second, the counter will display the speed in revolutions per minute.
- Additionally, the system incorporates a vane attached to one end of the rotating shaft, causing changes in capacitance as it rotates amidst fixed capacitive plates.

- The capacitor, part of an oscillator tank, experiences frequency fluctuations per unit time, reflecting the shaft's velocity.
- These frequency-modulated pulses are then amplified, converted into square waves, and can be fed into a frequency-measuring unit or digital counter to provide a digital representation of the shaft's rotation.

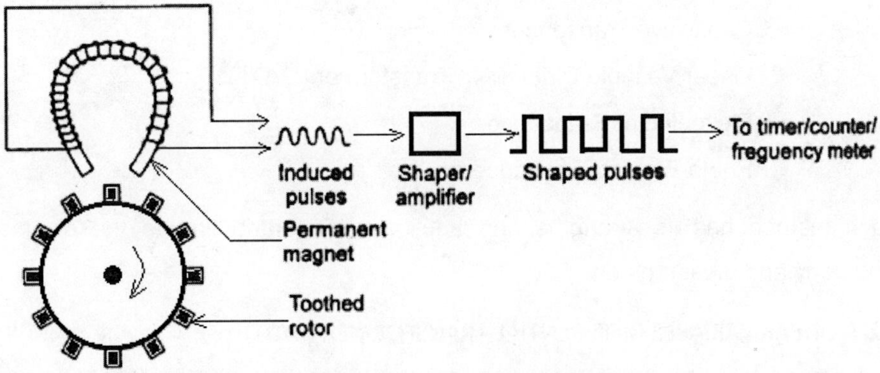


*Figure 3.5 Inductive Pick-Up Tachometer*

## 3.2. DISPLACEMENT MEASUREMENT

In the world of measurements, a key tool for figuring out how far something moves in a straight line is called a displacement transducer, or DT. Picture following an object as it moves along a straight path—that's what we mean by linear displacement.

The main job of a displacement sensor, also called a displacement gauge, is to tell us how far something moves compared to a fixed point. These sensors are used for measuring dimensions like width, height, and thickness.

Displacement is a really important thing because it affects force, acceleration, torque, and speed. To measure displacement, transducers is used, which come in different types like electrical, optical, pneumatic, and mechanical. Sometimes, combined techniques are used together to get an electrical output.

For instance, optical methods utilize photo-detectors to convert what they observe into electrical signals, such as voltage or current. This is a reason for the combination of mechanical and optical techniques is common. Displacement measurement can be done directly or indirectly, but the indirect method is used widely, especially when seeking related factors like force or acceleration.

Various methods exist for displacement measurement, though electrical signals from these transducers typically rely on displacement as a fundamental parameter. Some commonly utilized methods include:

- Linear Potentiometer Transducer
- Linear Motion Variable Inductance Transducer
- Proximity Inductance Transducer
- Capacitive Transducer
- Linear Variable Differential Transformer (LVDT)
- Piezoelectric Transducer
- Photo-Electric Transducers

Each method has its strengths and applications, contributing to the diverse toolkit of metrology and measurement.

### 3.2.1. LINEAR VARIABLE DIFFERENTIAL TRANSFORMER (LVDT)

**Definition:** The Linear Variable Differential Transformer (LVDT) is a key device in Measurements and Metrology, often abbreviated as LVDT. It's a type of inductive transducer that converts linear motion into an electrical signal, widely recognized for its efficiency and accuracy.

Its name, LVDT, highlights its unique function: it measures the variation or difference in output across its secondary coil. Compared to other types of inductive transducers, the LVDT stands out for its exceptional precision and reliability.

**Construction of LVDT**

- The transformer consists of a primary winding (P) and two secondary windings (S1 and S2) wound around a hollow cylindrical former containing a core as illustrate in Figure 3.6.
- Both secondary windings, S1 and S2, are positioned on either side of the primary winding and contain an equal number of turns.
- When an alternating current (AC) source is connected to the primary winding, it generates a flux in the air gap, inducing voltages in the secondary windings.
- A movable soft iron core is placed within the former, and the displacement to be measured is linked to this core. Typically, the iron core possesses high

permeability, aiding in reducing harmonics and enhancing the LVDT's sensitivity.

- To shield from electromagnetic and electrostatic interference, the LVDT is often housed within a material like stainless steel.
- The output of the LVDT is obtained by measuring the voltage difference between the two secondary windings.

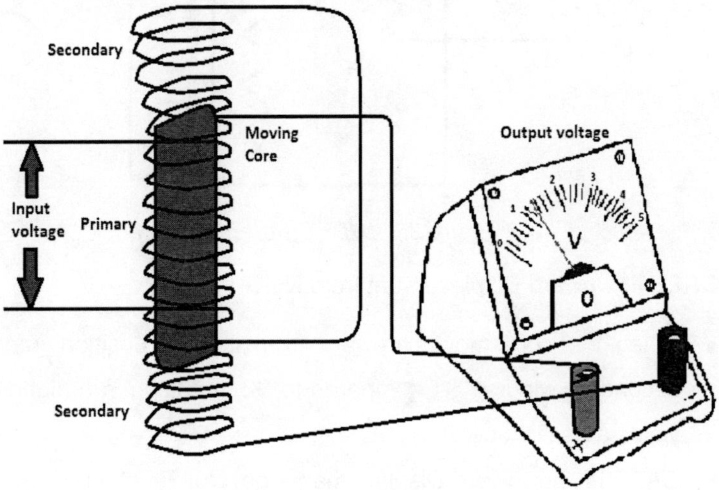


*Figure 3.6 Linear Voltage Differential Transformer*

**Working Principle**

- The primary of an LVDT is linked to an AC power source, resulting in the generation of alternating currents and voltages in its secondary coils.
- Two secondary coils, S1 and S2, produce voltages e1 and e2 respectively. The differential output, $e_{out}$, is calculated as the difference between e1 and e2, expressing the LVDT's operational principle (Figure 3.7).
- Three distinct cases elucidate the functioning of the LVDT based on the position of its core:

**CASE I:** Null Position (No Displacement)

- When the core is in its null position, equal flux links both secondary windings, inducing equal emf in both coils. Consequently, $e_{out}$ equals zero, signifying no displacement.

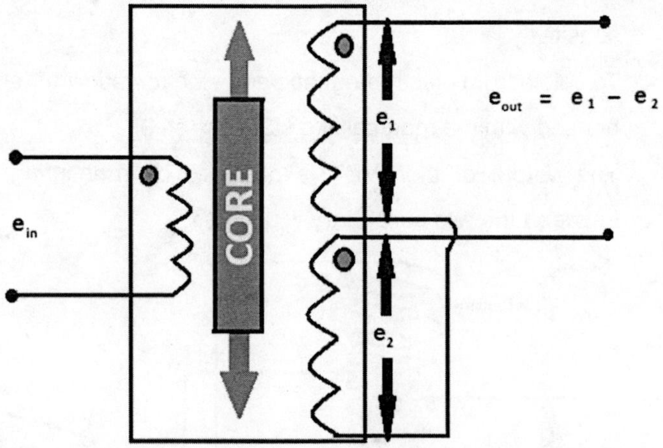


*Figure 3.7 LVDT Differential Output*

**CASE II:** Upward Displacement from Null Position

- When the core moves upward from its null position, more flux links with secondary winding S1 compared to S2, resulting in a higher e1 than e2. This yields a positive $e_{out}$.
- CASE III: Downward Displacement from Null Position
- Conversely, when the core moves downward from its null position, e2 becomes greater than e1 due to increased flux linkage with S2. This leads to a negative $e_{out}$, indicating displacement below the reference point.
- The relationship between output voltage and core displacement follows a linear curve, demonstrating that the output voltage varies proportionally with the core's movement.

Noteworthy points regarding the magnitude and polarity of induced voltage in an LVDT:

- The voltage change, whether positive or negative, correlates directly with the core's linear motion.
- Monitoring the output voltage's increase or decrease enables the determination of the direction of motion.
- The output voltage of an LVDT maintains a linear relationship with core displacement.

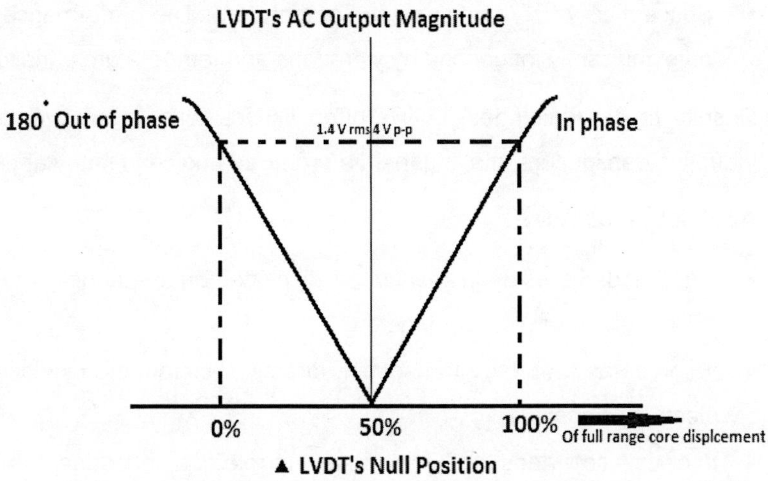


*Figure 3.8 AC Output of Conventional LVDT vs Core Displacement*

**Advantages**

- Extensive Measurement Range: LVDTs boast an impressive range for displacement measurement, spanning from 1.25 mm to 250 mm, making them versatile for various applications.
- Friction-Free Operation: Due to the core's movement within a hollow former, LVDTs experience minimal frictional losses, ensuring accurate displacement measurement.
- High Input and Sensitivity: LVDTs deliver a robust output without requiring additional amplification, thanks to their high sensitivity, typically around 40V/mm.
- Minimal Hysteresis: LVDTs exhibit low hysteresis, resulting in excellent repeatability across different operating conditions.
- Efficient Power Usage: With power consumption around 1W, LVDTs are notably energy-efficient compared to other transducers.
- Seamless Electrical Signal Conversion: LVDTs effortlessly convert linear displacement into electrical voltage, simplifying signal processing.

**Disadvantages**

- Shielding Against Stray Magnetic Fields: LVDT (Linear Variable Differential Transformer) is highly sensitive to stray magnetic fields, necessitating the implementation of a protective setup to shield it from such interference.

- Susceptibility to Vibrations and Temperature: The performance of LVDT can be significantly influenced by vibrations and temperature variations.

Despite these challenges, LVDTs offer distinct advantages over other types of inductive transducers, making them a preferred choice in many applications.

**Application of LVDT**

- LVDT finds its utility in measuring displacements spanning from fractions of millimeters to several centimeters.
- It serves as a primary transducer, directly transforming displacement into an electrical signal.
- In certain scenarios, LVDT assumes the role of a secondary transducer.
- For instance, consider the Bourdon tube, which initially converts pressure into linear displacement.
- Subsequently, the LVDT translates this displacement into an electrical signal.
- Following calibration, this signal yields accurate readings of the fluid pressure.

## 3.3. FLOW MEASUREMENT

In pressurized pipes, it's important to accurately measure the flow rate of fluids for various purposes such as controlling industrial processes and monitoring the rate of flow within the pipes. One commonly used method for this is through a type of instrument called a differential pressure flow meter. These meters come in different forms like venturi, flow nozzle, and orifice meters.

Each of these meters works by measuring the pressure difference between the natural flow of the fluid and the flow through a narrowed section in the pipe. By detecting this pressure difference, the flow rate of the fluid can be calculated. Essentially, a flow meter is a tool that helps us understand how much or how fast a fluid is moving through a pipe, whether the pipe is open or closed. There are four main types of flow meters that we use to classify these measuring devices.

1) **Mechanical Type Flow Meters:** This group includes devices that employ mechanical mechanisms for measurement. Examples include fixed restriction variable head type flow meters, which utilize sensors such as orifice plates, venturi tubes, flow nozzles, pitot tubes, and dall tubes. Additionally, quantity meters like positive displacement meters and mass flow meters also belong to this category.

2) **Inferential Type Flow Meters:** These meters infer flow rate based on certain characteristics. Examples include variable area flow meters (Rotameters), turbine flow meters, and target flow meters.
3) **Electrical Type Flow Meters:** This group comprises devices that utilize electrical principles for measurement. Examples include electromagnetic flow meters, ultrasonic flow meters, and laser Doppler anemometers.
4) **Other Flow Meters:** This category encompasses a diverse range of flow measurement devices, such as purge flow regulators, flow meters designed for solids flow measurement, cross-correlation flow meters, vortex shedding flow meters, and flow switches.

### 3.3.1. ROTAMETERS

- Orifice meters, venturimeters, and flow nozzles are instruments used for measuring fluid flow. They work by maintaining a constant obstruction area while allowing the pressure drop to change according to the flow rate.
- In simpler terms, these devices keep the blockage size constant while the pressure loss varies based on how fast the fluid is flowing.
- On the other hand, the rotameter(as shown in Figure 3.9) functions differently. It acts as a variable area meter, where the obstruction area changes as the fluid flows through it.
- However, for accurate measurement, rotameters require vertical pipelines.
- The functioning of a rotameter relies on fundamental principles such as buoyancy, drag, and gravity acceleration to measure fluid flow.
- A typical rotameter consists of a tapered glass tube filled with liquid and a floating device.
- When the setup is introduced into a pipeline and fluid starts flowing, two main changes occur: the pressure interval ($\Delta P$) shifts, and the float moves.
- According to the drag equation, $\Delta P$ changes as the square of the fluid flow rate.
- To maintain a constant pressure interval despite this change, the meter's area is adjusted, resulting in the tapered design of the rotameter.
- As the float moves upward, it eventually reaches a point of balance.
- The scale on the glass, which measures the float's displacement, directly correlates with the fluid flow rate, following the equation: ( $Q = K(At - Af)$).

- Some rotameters have flow rate values directly marked on the glass, enabling immediate measurement.

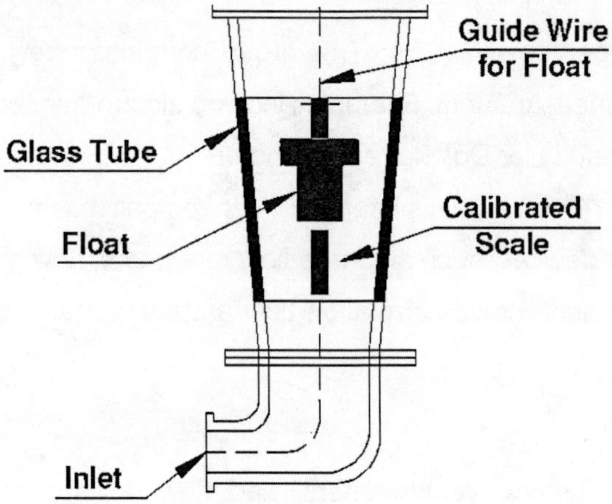


*Figure 3.9 Rotameter*

**Applications:**

1) Measurement of Corrosive Fluid Flow Rates: Useful for determining flow rates of corrosive liquids, gases, or vapors.
2) Ideal for Low Flow Rates: Particularly effective in measuring low flow rates accurately.

**Advantages:**

1) Visual Flow Conditions: Flow conditions are easily observable, aiding in monitoring and assessment.
2) Linear Flow Rate Functionality: Flow rate corresponds directly to the position of the float, facilitating uniform flow scales.
3) Versatile Fluid Measurement: Capable of measuring flow rates of liquids, gases, and vapors with precision.
4) Adjustable Capacity: Modification of the float, tapered tube, or both allows for customization of the rotameter's capacity.

**Limitations:**

1) Vertical Installation Required: Installation must be vertical for accurate measurements.
2) Impractical for Moving Objects: Unsuitable for measuring flow in moving objects or environments.

3) Visibility Issues with Colored Fluids: Float may not be visible when opaque or colored fluids are used.
4) Costly for High Pressure/Temperature Fluids: Expense increases for measurements involving high-pressure or high-temperature fluids.
5) Incapability with Solid-Containing Fluids: Unsuitable for fluids with a high percentage of solids in suspension due to potential obstruction issues

### 3.3.2. TURBINE METER

- Gases with very low flow rates and liquids can be effectively measured using the turbine flow meter principle.
- The turbine flow meter (as shown in figure 3.10) operates based on a simple principle: a turbine wheel, or multibladed rotor, positioned at a 90-degree angle from the flow of liquid or gas.
- A shaft support portion ensures stability within the flow meter housing, while ball or sleeve bearings support the rotor, allowing it to freely spin on its axis.
- As the liquid or gas flows, it hits the turbine blades (rotor), exerting force that drives the rotor's rotation.
- The rotational speed of the rotor is directly proportional to the fluid velocity, hence providing a measure of the volumetric flow rate.
- Monitoring the speed of rotation is achieved through a magnetic pickup fitted on the outside of the meter housing.
- The magnetic pickup consists of a permanent magnet with coil windings, placed close to the rotor within the fluid channel. Each passing rotor blade generates a voltage pulse, proportional to the flow rate.
- Digital techniques allow for manipulation, totalization, and difference of the electrical voltage pulses, ensuring minimal error from pulse generation to final reading.

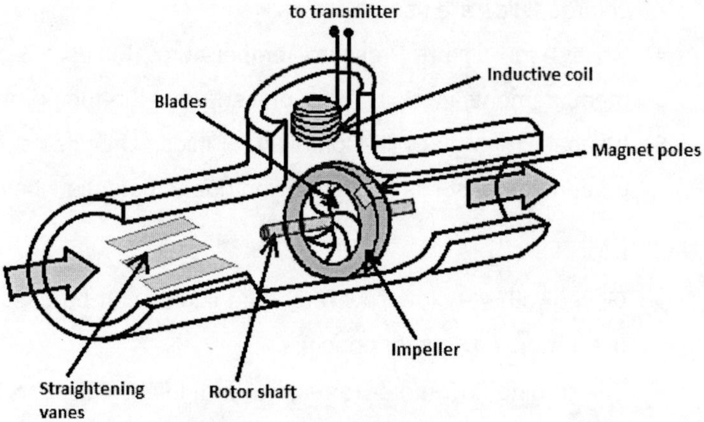


*Figure 3.10 Turbine Meter*

- The K factor, representing the number of pulses per volume unit, along with the time constant (Tk), frequency (f), and volumetric flow rate (Q) are essential parameters for calibration and measurement.
- Turbine flow meters offer exceptional precision and reproducibility, with accuracies ranging from ± 0.25 to ± 0.5%, and precision as fine as ± 0.02%.
- Typically measuring between 10:1 and 20:1, turbine meters can exceed 100:1 range in military applications.
- Available in various sizes, from 6.35 to 650 mm, with liquid flow ranges spanning from 0.1 to 50,000 gallons per minute.
- Primarily utilized in military applications, turbine flow meters also find applications in petroleum blending systems, aerospace, and airborne operations for energy fuel and cryogenic flow measurements.

**Advantages**

1) Precision: Turbine flow meters offer high accuracy in measuring flow rates.
2) Consistency: They provide excellent repeatability and can measure a wide range of flow rates reliably.
3) Low pressure drop: These meters maintain a fairly low pressure drop, minimizing energy loss in the system.
4) Easy installation and maintenance: Turbine flow meters are straightforward to install and require minimal maintenance, reducing operational hassles.

5) Versatility: They exhibit good temperature and pressure tolerance, making them suitable for various operating conditions.
6) Viscosity compensation: Turbine flow meters can be adjusted to account for changes in fluid viscosity, ensuring accurate readings across different fluid types.

**Disadvantages:**

Costly investment: Turbine flow meters come with a higher initial cost, which might be prohibitive for some applications.

1) Limited suitability for slurry: These meters are not ideal for measuring flow rates of slurry applications due to potential accuracy issues.
2) Challenges with non-lubricating fluids: Turbine flow meters may encounter operational problems when used with fluids that lack lubricating properties, potentially affecting accuracy and lifespan.

## 3.4 TEMPERATURE MEASUREMENT

- Temperature stands out as one of the most frequently monitored and controlled variables in industrial processes due to its significance.
- Its importance is highlighted by its involvement in various chemical processes, heat transfer mechanisms, and principles of thermodynamics.
- One straightforward definition of temperature is "the level of heat or coldness of an object or its surroundings, measured using a specific scale."
- Regardless of the scale or scope of a system, temperature remains a crucial parameter to consider.
- Achieving thermodynamic equilibrium between the system and the temperature-measuring device is essential for accurate temperature measurement.
- The physical properties of the sensor are influenced by temperature fluctuations, and these alterations are utilized to determine the temperature accurately.

**Four common types of measurement methods are:**

1) **Mechanical:** This includes tools like liquid-in-glass thermometers and bimetallic strips.
2) **Thermojunctive:** Using thermocouples, which measure temperature differences.
3) **Thermoresistive:** These methods involve Resistance Temperature Detectors (RTDs) and thermistors, which change resistance with temperature.

4) **Radiative:** This category includes infrared and optical pyrometers, which measure temperature by detecting radiation emitted from the object being measured.

### 3.4.1. RESISTANCE THERMOMETERS

A resistance thermometer is a tool utilized for gauging changes in temperature within a control room.

The resistance of metal conductors changes with temperature fluctuations. By observing these resistance changes, it is possible to determine temperature changes. Instruments that utilize this principle are known as resistance thermometers.

**Construction**

- The diagram illustrates the structure of a resistance thermometer detector (RTD as illustrate in Figure 3.11), which is commonly used for measuring temperature.
- RTDs utilize materials such as copper, nickel, or platinum as their resistance elements.
- Platinum wire is often wound around a ceramic bobbin to create the resistance element.
- This resistance element is enclosed within a protective tube, typically made of carbon steel or stainless steel.
- Internal lead wires are used to connect the resistance element to external terminals.
- The lead wires are covered with insulation to prevent short circuits, with fiberglass used for low and medium temperatures and ceramic for high temperatures.
- A protection tube shields the resistance element and internal lead wires from the surrounding environment.
- The protection tube is equipped with mounting attachments for installing the RTD at the measurement point.

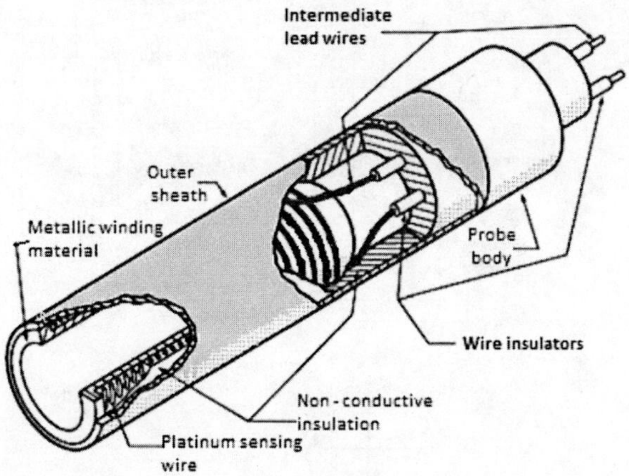


*Figure 3.11 Construction of Resistance Thermometers*

## Operation

In the process of measuring temperature, we start by using a tool called the Wheatstone bridge to find the initial resistance. We position the probe tip of the RTD (Resistance Temperature Detector) near the heat source, and the outer cover evenly spreads the heat to the sensing resistance element. As the temperature changes, so does the resistance of the material. After this initial measurement, we measure the final resistance again. By comparing these two resistances, we can determine how much the temperature has changed.

To calculate the temperature difference, we use the following formula:

*[ Rt = R0 (1 + Dt)]*

Where:

( Rt ) is the resistance at a certain temperature ( C ).

( R0) is the resistance at room temperature.

( Dt ) is the temperature difference.

( x ) is the temperature coefficient of the RTD material.

*[ Dt = frac{{(Rt/R0) - 1}}{x} ]*

By plugging in the values of ( Rt ), ( R0 ), and ( x ), we can easily calculate the temperature difference. This allows us to accurately measure changes in temperature using the RTD.

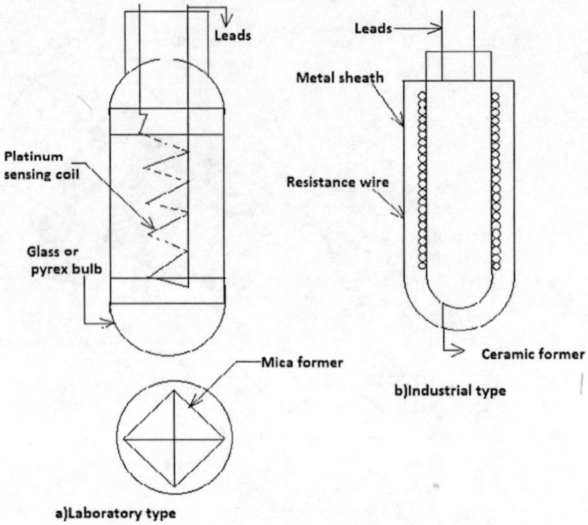


*Figure 3.12 Resistance Thermometers*

**Advantages:**

- Higher Accuracy: Provides more precise measurements.
- Linear Output: Shows a smoother, more predictable response compared to thermocouples.
- No Need for Temperature Compensation: Eliminates the requirement for additional adjustments based on temperature changes.
- Long-Term Stability: Maintains consistent performance over extended periods.

**Disadvantages:**

- Costly: Generally, these instruments are expensive to procure.
- Limited Temperature Change Sensitivity: Even significant changes in input temperature result in only minor alterations.
- External Power Requirement: Requires an external power source for operation.
- Low Sensitivity: Exhibits a reduced ability to detect subtle changes.

### 3.4.2. OPTICAL PYROMETER

**Working Principle**

In optical pyrometry, the principle of temperature measurement through brightness comparison is used. This method relies on observing changes in color as temperature increases, which serves as an indicator of temperature.

An optical pyrometer compares the brightness of an image generated by a heat source with that of a reference lamp set at a known temperature. By adjusting the current flowing through the lamp until its brightness matches that of the image produced by the heat source, we effectively gauge the temperature of the source.

This process hinges on the fact that the intensity of light emitted at any wavelength is contingent upon the temperature of the object emitting it. Consequently, once calibrated, the current passing through the lamp provides a reliable measure of the temperature of the heat source.

**Construction**

In one end of the instrument, as depicted in Figure 3.13, there's an eyepiece, and on the other end, there's an objective lens. It's powered by a battery, and there's a rheostat and a millivoltmeter connected to a reference temperature bulb to measure current. Between the objective lens and the reference temperature lamp, there's an absorption screen. This screen helps widen the temperature range that the instrument can measure. Additionally, there's a red filter between the eyepiece and the lamp, which only allows a specific narrow range of light wavelengths, around 0.65 micrometers.

**Operation**

- To measure the temperature of a source, its radiation is directed onto a filament of a reference temperature lamp using an objective lens.
- The eyepiece is adjusted until the filament of the reference temperature lamp is in clear focus and appears superimposed on the image of the temperature source.
- The observer adjusts the lamp current. If the filament appears dark (as in Figure A), it means it's cooler than the temperature source. If it appears bright (as in Figure B), it's hotter than the source. If it's not visible (as in Figure 3.13), it's at the same temperature as the source.
- The observer adjusts the lamp current until the filament and the temperature source have the same brightness, indicated by the filament disappearing in the superimposed image.
- At this point, the current flowing through the lamp, indicated by the mill voltmeter connected to it, becomes a measure of the temperature of the source, once calibrated.

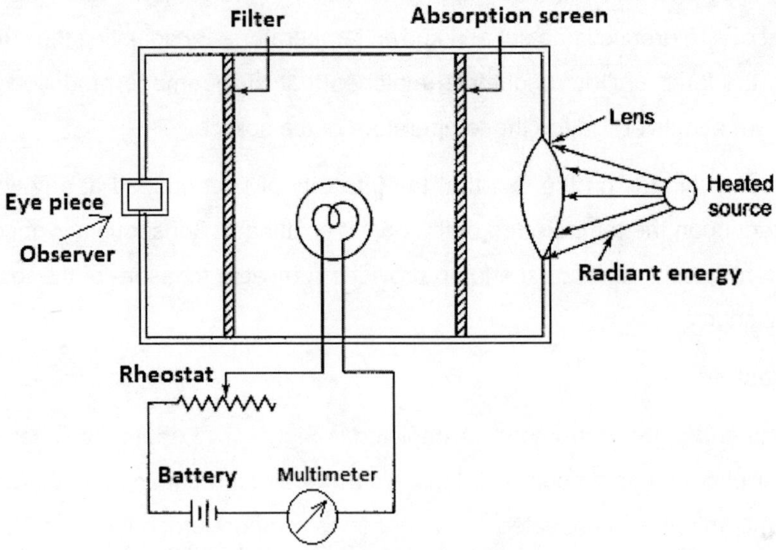


*Figure 3.13 Optical Pyrometer*

### Applications of Optical Pyrometers

- Optical pyrometers serve to gauge the temperature of molten metal or heated materials.
- They are employed to measure the temperature of furnaces and hot bodies.

### Advantages of Optical Pyrometers

- No physical contact with the temperature source is necessary for measurement.
- They offer a high level of accuracy, typically within a range of ±5°C.
- As long as the instrument captures a properly sized image of the temperature source, the distance between the instrument and the source becomes inconsequential.
- Operating the instrument is straightforward and user-friendly.

### Limitations of Optical Pyrometers

- They can only measure temperatures exceeding 700°C, as illuminating the temperature source is crucial for accurate readings.
- Optical pyrometers are manually operated, which limits their utility for continuous monitoring and control purposes.

## 3.5 . MISCELLANEOUS MEASUREMENTS

### 3.5.1. HUMIDITY MEASUREMENT

- Humidity measurements trace back over 2000 years to ancient China, where the first attempts were made.
- The 15th century saw significant advancements, culminating in Leonardo Da Vinci's gravimeter hygrometer design.
- By the late 17th century, dew-point meters emerged, utilizing ice cooling to condense water vapor for measurement.
- The late 18th century marked progress towards understanding relative humidity, with the development of hygrometers employing hair.
- In 1803, L.W. Gilbert established the concept of relative humidity as a ratio of present water vapor to maximum water vapor at the same temperature.
- Mechanical hygrometers, relying on hair stretching, and psychrometers were commonly used before electronic innovations.
- Finland's Prof. Vilho Väisälä pioneered the first electronic humidity sensor and radiosonde in 1934, followed by Dr. Dunnmore's resistive hygrometer in 1938.
- Post-World War II, sensor technology surged, introducing advanced sensors and new measurement methods like chilled mirror dew-point meters and optical hygrometers by the late 20th century.
- Initiatives for a national humidity standard began in 1991, with the establishment of the Technical Inspection Centre and later the Centre for Metrology and Accreditation.
- The first primary standard for humidity debuted in 1993 after international comparisons.

**Important Definitions and Units**

1. Vapor Pressure:

    - Vapor pressure is the pressure exerted by water vapor molecules in the air. It's measured in hPa (hectopascals), a unit of pressure.

2. Saturation Vapor Pressure:

    - Saturation vapor pressure refers to the maximum pressure of water vapor that can exist in equilibrium with water or ice surfaces. It's also measured in hPa.

3. Dewpoint Temperature:

- Dewpoint temperature indicates the temperature at which moist air becomes saturated with water vapor at a specific pressure. It's usually equal to or lower than the actual air temperature. When moist air saturates with respect to ice, it's called the frost point temperature. Both temperatures are measured in degrees Celsius (℃).

4. Relative Humidity:

- Relative humidity (RH) represents the amount of moisture in the air compared to the maximum moisture it can hold at a given temperature. It's expressed as a percentage.

- The formula for calculating relative humidity is:

  *RH = (Actual vapor pressure / Saturation vapor pressure) × 100%*

- The saturation vapor pressure can vary depending on whether it's with respect to water or ice. So, the formula can be:

**For water: RH = (Actual vapor pressure / Saturation vapor pressure with respect to water) × 100%**

**For ice: RH = (Actual vapor pressure / Saturation vapor pressure with respect to ice) × 100%**

#### *3.5.1.1. Hair Hygrometer*

The hair hydrometer (Figure 3.14), a specific variant of absorption hydrometers, employs the principle of mechanical moisture detection. This device utilizes the unique properties of human or animal hair to gauge atmospheric moisture levels with precision.

***Principle of Measurement***

The hair hygrometer (as shown in Figure 3.15) capitalizes on the unique property of hair, which expands or contracts in response to changes in relative humidity. This principle stems from the fact that the dimensions of organic materials, including human hair, fluctuate with variations in moisture content. As humidity levels shift, so does the moisture content within these materials, consequently affecting their length.

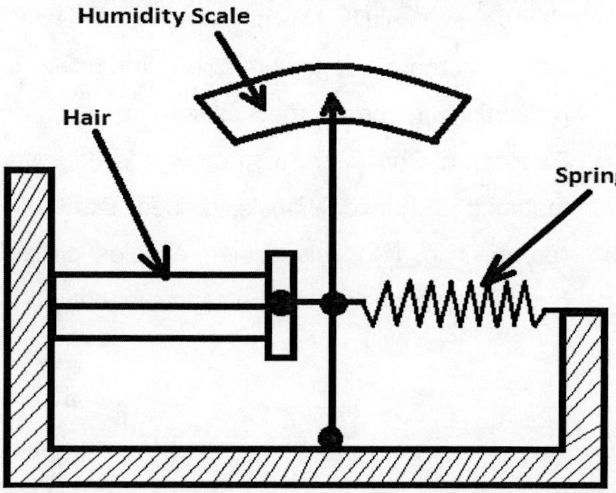


*Figure 3.14 Hair Hygrometer for Humidity Measurement*

When subjected to varying relative humidity levels ranging from 0 to 100%, the length of human hair, after moisture removal, typically increases by 2 to 2.5%. It's important to note that different types of human hair exhibit distinct responses, yet there remains a consistent correlation between hair length and relative humidity.

The hair hygrograph, a type of hair hygrometer, incorporates a clock-driven drum mechanism to record humidity levels on a chart accurately. Here's how it operates:

1. **Hair Bundle Response:** As atmospheric humidity fluctuates, a hair bundle expands or contracts accordingly. This movement is translated through a metal attachment on the hair joint lever, initiating the rotation of a main cam.
2. **Pen Arm Movement:** The weight of a pen arm affixed to the shaft applies a downward force to a sub cam. This force is crucial for magnifying even slight variations in the hair bundle's movement.
3. **Cam Interaction:** Two specialized cams, intricately designed and jointed by a spring mechanism, play a pivotal role in the hygrometer's precision.

The interaction between the main and sub cams determines the extent of movement exhibited by the pen arm.

4. **Proportional Measurement:** By carefully calibrating the cams, the hair hygrometer ensures that the pen arm's movement accurately reflects changes in humidity. This calibration is essential, particularly because hair length increases logarithmically with rising humidity, necessitating a proportional recording mechanism.
5. **Recording Chart:** The hygrometer is equipped with a recording chart featuring a humidity scale divided into 100 equal segments, each representing 1%. This design enables direct and precise reading of humidity levels based on the chart's markings.

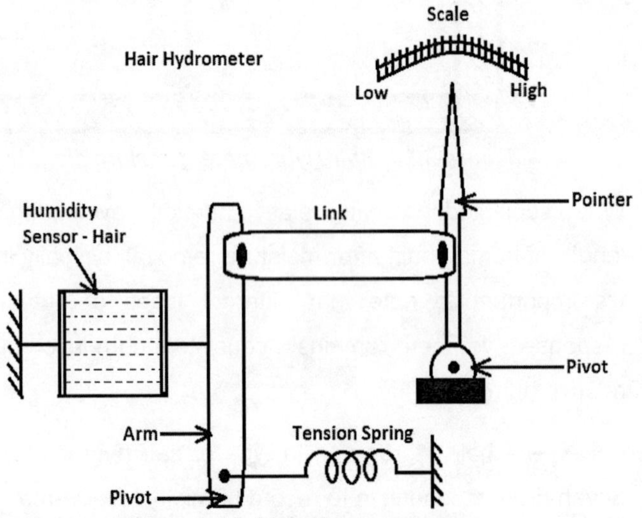


*Figure 3.15 Hair Hygrometer*

The hair hygrometer leverages the unique characteristics of human hair to provide accurate and proportional measurements of relative humidity. Its intricate design, incorporating specialized cams and a recording chart, ensures reliable performance across a range of humidity levels.

### Applications

- Hair hygrometers are employed within the temperature spectrum of 0°C to 75°C.
- They are effective within a relative humidity range of 30% to 95%.

**Limitations**

- Slow response time is a characteristic drawback of these hygrometers.
- Continuous usage may lead to calibration drift in hair hygrometers.

## 3.5.2. DENSITY MEASUREMENT

- Density is a crucial aspect of measurement and instrumentation, serving two key purposes:
  i. Determining the mass and volume of products.
  ii. Assessing the quality of the product, particularly in industrial applications where density measurement indicates product value.
- Density is defined as the mass of a substance per unit volume under specific conditions, but it varies with pressure and temperature, especially noticeable in gases.
- Modern density measurement often relies on sampling techniques, employing two primary approaches:
  I. Static density measurement.
  II. Dynamic (on-line) density measurement, each utilizing various methods based on distinct physical principles.
- Selection of the most suitable method depends on the application and process characteristics. Static methods are typically cost-effective and accurate, while dynamic methods offer automation and advanced signal processing.
- Despite advancements, there's no universal density measurement technique. Different methods are used based on the product and material, often normalizing density under reference conditions.
- Specific gravity (SG) is a vital indicator, calculated by dividing the density of a substance by that of a standard substance under identical conditions. For liquids and gases, specific gravities under reference conditions are expressed as ratios to the density of water and air, respectively.

### 3.5.2.1 Hydrometers

- Hydrometers (as shown in Figure 3.16) are widely utilized tools for measuring the density of liquids and are governed by national and international standards like ISO 387.

- These devices operate on the buoyancy principle, where the volume of a fixed mass is converted into a linear distance using a sealed bulb-shaped glass tube with a measurement scale.
- The bulb contains lead shot and pitch for ballast, with the mass varying depending on the density range of the liquid being measured.
- To measure density, the hydrometer is simply immersed in the liquid, and the density reading is obtained from the scale, typically calibrated in units such as kg m–3.
- Manufacturers often provide alternative scales including specific gravity, API gravity, Brix, Brine, etc., catering to various industries and applications.
- Hydrometers can be calibrated for different ranges of surface tensions and temperatures, with temperature corrections available for standard temperatures like 15°C, 20°C, or 25°C.
- ISO 387 standardizes hydrometers for a density range of 600 kg m–3 to 2000 kg $m^{-3}$, ensuring consistency and accuracy in measurements.

While hydrometers offer advantages such as ease of use and versatility, they also have limitations and drawbacks that should be considered in their application.

**Advantages:**

- Cost-effective and user-friendly
- Provides good resolution within a small range
- Traceable to both national and international standard

**Disadvantages:**

- Limited span necessitates multiple meters to cover a significant range
- Fragility due to glass construction; metal and plastic versions sacrifice accuracy
- Requires an offline sample of the fluid, which may not accurately represent process conditions
- Pressure hydrometers for low vapor pressure hydrocarbons require precise pressure determination

- Achieving high precision can be challenging, requiring corrections for surface tension and temperature
- Additional corrections may be needed for opaque fluids.

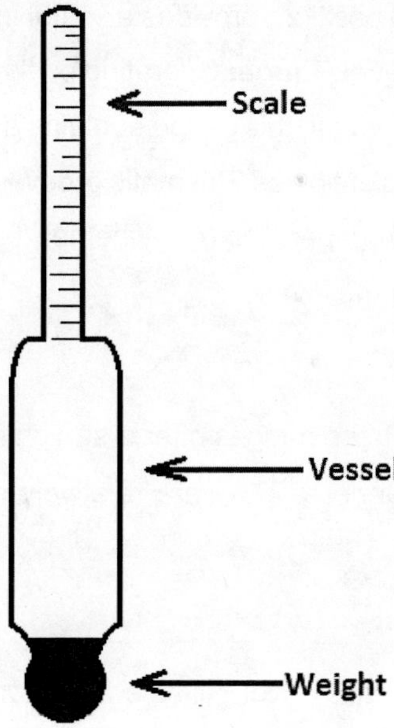


*Figure 3.16 Hydrometer*

### 3.5.3. LIQUID LEVEL MEASUREMENT SIGHT GLASS FLOAT GAUGE

- When it comes to measuring the level of liquid in a tank or vessel, simplicity is often key. One of the most direct methods is through the use of a sight glass. This transparent apparatus is affixed to the exterior of the tank, offering a clear view of the liquid level inside. Graduations marked on the sight glass aid in precise measurement. However, it's important to note that this method provides a localized indication only, limited to the inspection of the vessel.

**Types of Level Gauges**

1) ***Transparent Level Gauge:*** This type employs two transparent glasses, each with a liquid chamber. The difference in transparency between the liquids on either side indicates the level. In applications involving water or steam, an illuminator is positioned behind the gauge, illuminating the water surface for easy observation.

2) ***Magnetic Level Gauge:*** Equipped with a float containing a magnet, this gauge tracks the liquid level within the chamber, corresponding to the tank's level. Outside the chamber, a bi-colored flapper, rotated by 180 degrees according to the float's position, provides a visual indication.
3) ***Reflex Level Gauge:*** Operating on the principle of differing refractive indices of liquid and vapor, this gauge contains a liquid column within a recessed chamber behind a sight glass. Prismatic grooves on the glass interact with light, reflecting differently depending on whether they encounter liquid or vapor, thereby indicating the level.

**Advantages:**

- Simplicity: These gauges offer a straightforward solution for level measurement.
- Cost-effectiveness: They are relatively inexpensive compared to more complex methods.

**Disadvantages:**

- Manual Operation: Not suitable for automated control systems, requiring manual monitoring.
- Maintenance Needs: Regular cleaning is necessary for optimal performance.
- Fragility: These gauges can be easily damaged, requiring careful handling.

**Applications**

- While these gauges may not be ideal for industrial automation due to their manual operation, they find utility in various settings. Common applications include tanks for storing lubricating oils or water. They provide a simple means of obtaining level information, streamlining the process of visually inspecting or dipping a tank. However, their use is typically limited to operator inspection.
- In conclusion, while sight glasses and similar level gauges offer simplicity and affordability, they require manual oversight and maintenance. Understanding their principles and limitations is crucial for selecting the appropriate method for liquid-level measurement in different applications.

### 3.5.4. BIOMEDICAL MEASUREMENT

- Biomedical measurement refers to the process of quantitatively assessing various physiological parameters and phenomena within the human body using specialized instruments and techniques.
- It plays a crucial role in clinical diagnosis, patient monitoring, medical research, and the development of therapeutic interventions.
- The field has witnessed significant advancements driven by advancements in technology, leading to the development of highly accurate, reliable, and sophisticated measurement devices.

**Types of Biomedical Instrumentation**

- Biomedical instrumentation can be broadly categorized into two main types: clinical and research.
- Clinical Instrumentation: This category is primarily dedicated to diagnosing, treating, and monitoring patients. It includes devices used in hospitals, clinics, and other healthcare settings for routine patient care.
- Research Instrumentation: Research instrumentation is utilized in scientific research to explore and understand various physiological processes and systems within the human body. It aids researchers in studying diseases, testing hypotheses, and developing new medical technologies.

**Functions of Clinical Instrumentation**

- The primary function of clinical instrumentation is to measure physiological variables.
- Physiological Variables: These are quantities that represent different aspects of the body's physiological state and change over time. Examples include:
- Body Temperature: Measurement of body temperature is essential for detecting fever, hypothermia, and monitoring the effectiveness of treatments.
- Electrocardiogram (ECG): ECG is used to measure the electrical activity of the heart. It provides valuable information about heart rate, rhythm, and abnormalities such as arrhythmias.
- Arterial Blood Pressure: Monitoring blood pressure helps assess cardiovascular health and detect conditions such as hypertension or hypotension.

- Respiratory Airflows: Measurement of respiratory parameters, including airflow rate and volume, aids in diagnosing respiratory disorders such as asthma or chronic obstructive pulmonary disease (COPD).

**Significance of Biomedical Measurement**

- Accurate and precise biomedical measurements are essential for making informed clinical decisions, designing effective treatment strategies, and monitoring patient progress.
- Continuous advancements in biomedical instrumentation enhance healthcare delivery, improve patient outcomes, and contribute to the overall advancement of medical science.
- Biomedical measurement serves as a bridge between theoretical knowledge and practical application, enabling healthcare professionals to translate scientific insights into clinical practice.

#### 3.5.4.1 Sphygmomanometer

**Definition:** A sphygmomanometer, also known as a blood pressure meter or gauge, is a device utilized for measuring blood pressure.

The term "sphygmomanometer" originates from the Greek words "sphygmos" (meaning "heartbeat" or "pulse") and "manometer" (referring to a device for measuring pressure or tension).

Samuel Siegfried Karl Ritter von Basch introduced the sphygmomanometer in 1881, while Scipione Riva-Rocci refined it into a more compact form in 1896.

**Functionality**

- The primary function of a sphygmomanometer is to determine an individual's blood pressure, which is a crucial physiological parameter.
- It operates by temporarily obstructing the flow of blood through an artery, typically the brachial artery in the arm, using an inflatable cuff.
- Pressure within the cuff is gradually released while a stethoscope is used to detect the return of blood flow, indicated by the characteristic sounds known as Korotkoff sounds.

**Components**

- A typical sphygmomanometer consists of three main components: an inflatable cuff, a pressure gauge or manometer, and a mechanism for inflation and deflation.
- The cuff is wrapped around the upper arm and inflated to a pressure exceeding the systolic blood pressure to occlude arterial blood flow temporarily.
- The pressure gauge displays the pressure within the cuff, typically in millimeters of mercury (mmHg), allowing the healthcare provider to accurately read the blood pressure.

**Types**

Sphygmomanometers come in various types, including mercury, aneroid, and digital models.

- Mercury sphygmomanometers utilize a column of mercury to measure pressure, offering high precision but are gradually being replaced due to environmental concerns.
- Aneroid sphygmomanometers use a mechanical gauge with a pointer to display pressure and are often preferred for their portability.
- Digital sphygmomanometers, equipped with electronic pressure sensors, provide easy-to-read digital displays and are suitable for home use.

**Working Mechanism**

- Figure 3.17 showcases a transmission mechanism commonly employed in various measuring instruments. In this setup, a sturdy rod denoted as R is firmly affixed to a toothed sector, labeled as S, positioned at point T. This toothed sector meshes with the pointer pinion, identified as P, establishing a linkage for transmitting motion. It's crucial to note that the precision of this mechanism is vital for accurate measurement outcomes.
- The contact interface between the mechanism and the measurement element is facilitated by the diaphragm capsules, represented by C. These capsules play a pivotal role in translating physical phenomena, such as pressure or displacement, into measurable signals. Ensuring consistent

and reliable contact between the mechanism and the diaphragm capsules is essential for maintaining measurement accuracy and repeatability.

- This transmission mechanism design is widely utilized across various biomedical measurement instruments, where precise and reliable measurement of physiological parameters is paramount.

**Application in Biomedical Measurement**

- Accurate blood pressure measurement is fundamental in diagnosing and managing various cardiovascular conditions, including hypertension and hypotension.
- Sphygmomanometers play a vital role in routine clinical assessments, preventive screenings, and monitoring patient health status in healthcare settings.
- Continuous advancements in sphygmomanometer technology aim to enhance accuracy, reliability, and user-friendliness, contributing to improved patient care and outcomes in biomedical practice.

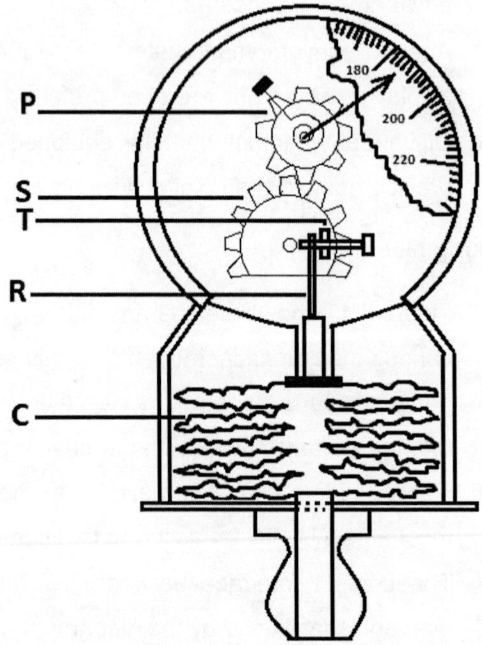


*Figure 3.17 Sphygmomanometer*

## 3.6 APPLICATION OF APPLIED MECHANICAL MEASUREMENTS

Speed Measurement

- Automotive Industry: Tachometers play a crucial role in monitoring engine speed, ensuring optimal performance and fuel efficiency.
- Manufacturing: Revolution counters are utilized in machinery to monitor rotational speed, aiding in quality control and maintenance.
- Aerospace: Eddy current tachometers are employed in aircraft engines for precise speed monitoring, contributing to flight safety and engine efficiency.

Displacement Measurement

- Manufacturing: Linear Variable Differential Transformers (LVDT) are extensively used for quality control in machining processes, ensuring precise positioning and dimensional accuracy.
- Robotics: LVDTs find application in robotic arms for accurate positioning and control, enhancing automation efficiency in industries such as automotive assembly.

Flow Measurement

- Chemical Industry: Rotometers and turbine meters are employed for measuring flow rates of liquids and gases in chemical processing plants, facilitating precise control of ingredient proportions and process efficiency.
- Water Management: Turbine meters are utilized in water treatment plants and distribution networks for monitoring water flow, aiding in conservation efforts and leak detection.

Temperature Measurement

- Food Industry: Resistance thermometers are utilized in food processing to monitor and control temperature during cooking, preserving food quality and safety.
- Energy Sector: Optical pyrometers are used in power plants for measuring high temperatures in boilers and furnaces, ensuring operational safety and efficiency.

Miscellaneous Measurements

- Climate Control: Humidity measurement with hair hygrometers is crucial in HVAC systems for maintaining optimal indoor air quality and comfort.

- Beverage Industry: Hydrometers are utilized in breweries and distilleries for measuring the density of liquids during fermentation and distillation processes, ensuring product consistency and quality.
- Chemical Processing: Sight glass float gauges are employed in tanks and vessels for level measurement, enabling precise monitoring and control of chemical processes.

Biomedical Measurement

- Healthcare: Sphygmomanometers are indispensable devices in healthcare facilities for measuring blood pressure, aiding in the diagnosis and management of cardiovascular diseases.

Applied mechanical measurements find extensive application across various industries and sectors, contributing to enhanced efficiency, safety, and quality in processes ranging from manufacturing to healthcare. By employing precise measurement techniques and instruments, industries can achieve higher levels of productivity, reliability, and regulatory compliance.

### 3.7 UNIT SUMMARY

This unit explores techniques and instruments employed for quantifying key parameters in mechanical systems, facilitating accurate analysis and control. The unit encompasses diverse aspects such as speed measurement, displacement measurement, flow measurement, temperature measurement, and several miscellaneous measurements crucial for engineering and scientific endeavors.

1. Speed Measurement:

- Classification of Tachometers: A comprehensive overview of different types of tachometers used for measuring rotational speed in mechanical systems.
- Revolution Counters: Examination of devices utilized for counting revolutions per unit time, aiding in assessing the performance of rotating machinery.
- Eddy Current Tachometers: Insight into the principle and application of eddy current-based tachometers for high-precision speed measurement.

2. Displacement Measurement:

- Linear Variable Differential Transformers (LVDT): In-depth discussion on LVDTs, which are widely employed for measuring linear displacement with high accuracy and reliability.

3. Flow Measurement:

- Rotometers: Exploration of rotometers as instruments for measuring the flow rate of fluids, providing essential data for process control and optimization.
- Turbine Meter: Analysis of turbine meters utilized for precise measurement of fluid flow based on the rotational motion of a turbine.

4. Temperature Measurement:

- Resistance Thermometers: Examination of resistance thermometers, including their construction, working principle, and applications in temperature sensing across various industries.
- Optical Pyrometer: Overview of optical pyrometers as non-contact devices used for measuring high temperatures by analyzing the thermal radiation emitted by a target object.

5. Miscellaneous Measurements:

- Humidity Measurement: Introduction to hair hygrometers for quantifying atmospheric humidity, essential for various environmental monitoring and control applications.
- Density Measurement: Discussion on hydrometers employed for measuring the density of liquids, aiding in quality control and material characterization.
- Liquid Level Measurement: Examination of sight glass and float gauge techniques utilized for determining the liquid level in tanks and vessels.
- Biomedical Measurement: Insight into the sphygmomanometer, a vital instrument for measuring blood pressure in medical diagnostics and patient care.

## 3.8 EXERCISES

### Multiple Choice Questions

1. Which of the following is NOT a type of tachometer?

a) Revolution counters

b) Eddy current tachometers

c) Rotameters

d) Classification of tachometers

2. What is used in displacement measurement to convert linear motion into an electrical signal?

a) Revolution counters

b) Optical Pyrometer

c) Linear Variable Differential Transformers (LVDT)

d) Turbine meter

3. Which instrument is commonly used for flow measurement in industrial applications?

a) Eddy current tachometers

b) Optical Pyrometer

c) Rotameters

d) Resistance thermometers

4. Which type of thermometer measures temperature by sensing changes in electrical resistance?

a) Optical Pyrometer

b) Resistance thermometers

c) LVDT

d) Hydrometer

5. What is the purpose of a hair hygrometer?

a) Density measurement

b) Humidity measurement

c) Temperature measurement

d) Liquid level measurement

6. Which instrument is used to measure the density of a liquid?

a) Hydrometer

b) Rotameter

c) LVDT

d) Optical Pyrometer

7. What type of measurement does a float gauge assist with?

a) Speed measurement

b) Temperature measurement

c) Liquid level measurement

d) Displacement measuremen

8. Which device is commonly used to measure blood pressure?

a) Sphygmomonometer

b) Rotameter

c) Eddy current tachometer

d) Hydrometer

9. Which type of thermometer uses light radiation to measure temperature?

a) Resistance thermometers

b) Optical Pyrometer

c) Rotameters

d) LVDT

10. Which instrument is NOT used for flow measurement?

a) Turbine meter

b) Rotameters

c) Hydrometer

d) LVDT

11. What is the principle behind the operation of an LVDT?

a) Light radiation

b) Electrical resistance

c) Inductance variation

d) Linear motion

12. Which measurement does a Rotameter provide?

a) Displacement

b) Temperature

c) Flow

d) Density

13. What does an eddy current tachometer measure?

a) Blood pressure

b) Temperature

c) Speed

d) Displacement

14. Which device is suitable for measuring humidity?

a) Sphygmomonometer

b) Optical Pyrometer

c) Hair hygrometer

d) Hydrometer

15. What is the primary purpose of a hydrometer?

a) Measure density

b) Measure flow

c) Measure temperature

d) Measure speed

Answer

**1. c) 2. c) 3. c) 4. b) 5. b) 6. a) 7. c) 8. a) 9. b) 10. c)11. d) 12. c) 13. c) 14. c) 15. a)**

**Subjective Type Questions**

1. Compare and contrast the working principles of revolution counters and eddy current tachometers for speed measurement. How do they differ in their applications and accuracy?
2. Explain the working principle of Linear Variable Differential Transformers (LVDTs) for displacement measurement. Discuss the advantages and limitations of using LVDTs compared to other displacement measurement techniques.

3. Discuss the operational characteristics and applications of rotometers and turbine meters for flow measurement. How do these two types of flow meters differ in their working principles and accuracy?
4. Describe the construction and working principle of resistance thermometers for temperature measurement. Discuss the factors affecting their accuracy and calibration methods.
5. Compare and contrast optical pyrometers with other temperature measurement devices. What are the advantages and limitations of using optical pyrometers in industrial applications?
6. Explain the working principle of a hair hygrometer for humidity measurement. Discuss its sensitivity, range, and factors affecting its accuracy in measuring humidity.
7. Discuss the working principle and applications of hydrometers for density measurement. How does the design of a hydrometer vary based on the density range it is intended to measure?
8. Describe the operation of a sight glass float gauge for liquid level measurement. Discuss its advantages and limitations compared to other liquid level measurement techniques.
9. Explain how a sphygmomanometer is used for biomedical measurement. Discuss the different types of sphygmomanometers and their applications in clinical settings.
10. Choose two miscellaneous measurements (e.g., humidity, density, liquid level) and compare the methods used for their measurement. Discuss the factors influencing the choice of measurement technique in each case, considering accuracy, cost, and environmental conditions.

## 3.9 PRACTICAL

### Practical Statement

PS1. Measurement & Calibration of Displacement using LVDT

PS2. Measurements and Calibration of Temperature using Resistance Temperature Detector

PS3. Measurements and Calibration of Level using Sight Glass Technique

**Relevant Theory**

Refer to the topic of 3.2 displacement measurement , 3.4 temperature measurement, and 3.5.3 level measurement.

**Practical Outcome**

**PO1.** Students will gain proficiency in the measurement and calibration of displacement, temperature, and level using advanced techniques such as LVDT, RTD, and Sight Glass Technique.

**PO2.** Students will develop the ability to analyze experimental data, troubleshoot measurement errors, and effectively communicate findings, preparing them for real-world applications in engineering and related fields.

### 3.10 KNOW MORE

1. **Tachometers:** While the content discusses classification and types of tachometers, it's worth delving into more advanced techniques like digital tachometers and their applications in modern industries such as automotive, aerospace, and robotics. Additionally, exploring the integration of tachometers with control systems for real-time monitoring and feedback can enhance understanding.

2. **Advanced Displacement Sensors**: Apart from Linear Variable Differential Transformers (LVDTs), exploring other displacement measurement sensors like capacitive sensors, inductive sensors, and potentiometers can provide a comprehensive understanding of displacement measurement techniques. Applications of these sensors in precision engineering, robotics, and automation can be intriguing to readers.

3. **Cutting-edge Flow Measurement Technologies**: While Rotameters and Turbine meters are covered, emerging technologies such as ultrasonic flow meters, Coriolis flow meters, and electromagnetic flow meters are gaining prominence for their accuracy and versatility. Understanding their principles of operation and applications in industries like oil and gas, chemical processing, and water management adds depth to the topic.

4. **Innovations in Temperature Measurement**: While Resistance thermometers and Optical Pyrometers are discussed, exploring recent developments such as infrared thermometers, thermocouples, and thermal imaging cameras provides insight into non-

contact temperature measurement techniques. Applications in fields like manufacturing, healthcare, and energy highlight their significance in diverse industries.

5. **Exploring Miscellaneous Measurements**: Beyond the mentioned humidity, density, and liquid level measurements, readers can benefit from learning about other miscellaneous measurements such as pressure measurement (using manometers, pressure transducers), force measurement (using load cells, strain gauges), and vibration measurement (using accelerometers, piezoelectric sensors). Understanding these measurements broadens the scope of applications in various industries including automotive, aerospace, and civil engineering.
6. **Biomedical Measurement Advancements**: While the Sphygmomanometer is discussed, exploring other biomedical measurement devices such as electrocardiograms (ECG), pulse oximeters, and glucose monitors sheds light on the intersection of engineering and healthcare. Understanding these devices and their role in diagnosing and monitoring medical conditions contributes to a holistic view of applied mechanical measurements in biomedical engineering.
7. **Integration of Sensors with Data Acquisition Systems**: Understanding how sensors are integrated with data acquisition systems, such as microcontrollers, PLCs (Programmable Logic Controllers), and SCADA (Supervisory Control and Data Acquisition) systems, is crucial for real-time monitoring, control, and analysis in industrial applications. Exploring communication pRotacols like Modbus, Profibus, and Ethernet further enhances comprehension of sensor networks and data management.
8. **Industry 4.0 and Smart Sensors**: With the advent of Industry 4.0, the integration of sensors with IoT (Internet of Things) platforms and cloud-based analytics has revolutionized industrial processes. Exploring concepts like predictive maintenance, digital twins, and remote monitoring using smart sensors provides insights into the future of applied mechanical measurements in the era of digital transformation.

## 3.11 REFERENCE AND SUGGESTED READINGS

### Reference

1. Doebelin, E. O. (2010). Measurement Systems: Application and Design. New York: McGraw-Hill Education.

2. Figliola, R. S., & Beasley, D. E. (2015). Theory and Design for Mechanical Measurements. Hoboken, NJ: John Wiley & Sons.
3. Sirohi, R. S., & Shao, Y. (Eds.). (2016). Mechanical Measurement Systems. Boca Raton, FL: CRC Press.
4. Thomas, D. E., & White, R. E. (2015). Introduction to the Electronic Properties of Materials. Cambridge University Press.

**Suggested Readings**

1. Morris, A. S., Langari, R., & Çamci, F. (2005). Measurement and Instrumentation: Theory and Application. Burlington, MA: Academic Press.
2. Bentley, J. P. (2011). Principles of Measurement Systems. Harlow, England: Pearson Education Limited.
3. Ramakrishnan, T. V. (2017). Sensors and Transducers. New Delhi, India: Pearson Education India.
4. Bishop, R. H. (2014). Understanding Engineering Mathematics. Oxford, England: Butterworth-Heinemann.
5. Hearn, E. J. (2013). Mechanics of Materials 2: The Mechanics of Elastic and Plastic Deformation of Solids and Structural Materials. Oxford, England: Butterworth-Heinemann.
6. Tariq, A., & Memon, N. (Eds.). (2019). Advances in Mechatronics and Mechanical Engineering: Select Proceedings of ICRMM 2019. Singapore: Springer.

**Additional Materials**

1. "**Introduction to Mechanical Measurements**" by MIT Open Courseware - This video series provides a comprehensive overview of mechanical measurements, covering topics such as sensors, data acquisition, and calibration techniques.
2. "**Practical Applications of Measurement Systems**" by National Instruments - This video series explores real-world applications of measurement systems in industries such as automotive, aerospace, and manufacturing, demonstrating how theoretical concepts are applied in practice.
3. "**Instrumentation and Measurement Techniques**" by NPTEL - This video course delves into instrumentation and measurement techniques used in engineering applications, including sensors, signal conditioning, and measurement uncertainty analysis.

4. "**Metrology: The Science of Measurement**" by EngineerGuy - This video explains the importance of metrology in various industries and demonstrates the precision and accuracy involved in measurement processes.

**Dynamic QR Code for Further Reading**

Mechanical Measurement Systems

Humidity Measurement

Use of Sphygmomanometer

# 4 Limits, Fits and Tolerances

**UNIT SPECIFICS**

*This unit presents information related to the following topics:*

- *Concept of Limits, Fits, and Tolerances*
- *Selective Assembly; Interchangeability*
- *Hole and Shaft Basis System*
- *Taylor's Principle; Design of Plug; Ring Gauges; IS 919-1993 (Limits, Fits & Tolerances, Gauges} IS 3477-1973*
- *Concept of multi-gauging and inspection*
- *Angular Measurement: Instruments for Angular Measurements; Working and Use of Universal Bevel Protractor, Sine Bar, Spirit Level; Principle of Working of Clinometers; Angle Gauges (With Numerical on Setting of Angle Gauges)*
- *Screw thread Measurements: ISO grade and fits of thread; Errors in threads; Pitch errors; Measurement of different elements such as major diameter, minor diameter, effective diameter, pitch; Two wire method; Thread gauge micrometer; Working principle of floating carriage dial micrometer*

***Applications***

*This unit is designed to provide an in-depth understanding of limits, fits, and tolerances which are fundamental in manufacturing and mechanical design. It starts with the basic concepts of limits, fits, and tolerances and their importance in ensuring the interchangeability of parts and assemblies.*

*The unit then covers the selective assembly process and the principles of interchangeability, as well as the difference between hole and shaft basis systems. Taylor's Principle is introduced, along with the design and use of plug and ring gauges, adhering to IS 919-1993 and IS 3477-1973 standards.*

*Further, the unit delves into multi-gauging and inspection methods, and the instruments used for angular measurements. It provides detailed explanations of the working and use of universal bevel protractors, sine bars, and spirit levels, along with the principles of clinometers and angle gauges.*

*Screw thread measurements are also discussed, covering ISO grades and fits of threads, common thread errors, and various measurement methods including the two-wire method and the use of thread gauge micrometers and floating carriage dial micrometers. Apart from this, at the end of the unit, the overall broad concepts are provided as a unit summary. Besides, a large number of multiple-choice questions as well as descriptive-type questions with Bloom's taxonomy action verbs are included. A list of references and suggested readings is given in the unit so that one can go through them for practice. It is important to note that for getting more information on various topics of interest, some QR codes have been provided in different sections which can be scanned for relevant supportive knowledge. Video resources along with QR codes are mentioned for getting more information on various topics of interest which can be surfed or scanned through mobile phones for viewing.*

## RATIONALE

*Understanding limits, fits, and tolerances is critical for engineers and designers to ensure that manufactured parts fit together properly and function as intended. These concepts are fundamental in precision engineering and manufacturing, affecting the quality, performance, and interchangeability of components. This unit provides comprehensive knowledge on these topics, preparing students and professionals to apply these principles effectively in real-world applications.*

## PRE-REQUISITES

*Before reading this unit, the students are advised to revisit the following:*

- *Basic Mathematics: Concepts of measurement and geometry*
- *Basic Engineering Drawing: Familiarity with engineering drawings and symbols*
- *Introduction to Manufacturing Processes*

## UNIT OUTCOMES

*After studying this unit, students will be able to:*

- *U4-O1: Understand the concepts of limits, fits, and tolerances and their significance in manufacturing.*

- *U4-O2: Explain the principles of selective assembly and interchangeability.*
- *U4-O3: Apply the hole and shaft basis systems in design.*
- *U4-O4: Utilize Taylor's Principle and design plug and ring gauges according to relevant standards.*
- *U4-O5: Perform angular and screw thread measurements using appropriate instruments and techniques.*

## *EXPECTED MAPPING WITH COURSE OUTCOMES*

*(1- Weak Correlation;* ***2- Medium correlation; 3- Strong Correlation)***

| Unit Outcomes (U4) | CO-1 | CO-2 | CO-3 | CO-4 | CO-5 |
|---|---|---|---|---|---|
| **U4-O1** | 3 | 2 | 3 | 2 | 1 |
| **U4-O2** | 3 | 3 | 2 | 2 | 1 |
| **U4-O3** | 2 | 2 | 3 | 1 | 1 |
| **U4-O4** | 3 | 3 | 2 | 3 | 1 |
| **U4-O5** | 2 | 3 | 3 | 2 | 1 |

## 4.1 CONCEPTS OF LIMITS, FITS & TOLERANCES

Limits, fits, and tolerances constitute fundamental principles within engineering and manufacturing. They serve as the cornerstone for guaranteeing the operational viability and interchangeability of mechanical components. These concepts outline the permissible deviation in dimensions and shapes of parts, thereby ensuring precise assembly while accommodating a specified degree of variability. By adhering conscientiously to these standards, engineers and manufacturers can strike a delicate equilibrium between stringent clearances for accuracy and precision and the requisite adaptability for streamlined production processes. The outcome is the fabrication of dependable, accurately fitting, and interchangeable components pivotal to operating the machinery and devices that shape our contemporary world.

### 4.1.1 KEY TERMINOLOGIES TO UNDERSTANDING LIMITS, FITS, AND TOLERANCE

1. Basic Size: Basic size, also known as nominal size, represents the exact theoretical size determined during the design phase. This is a nominal or target dimension of parts, serving as a reference point for manufacturing and inspection. It represents the ideal size without considering any allowances or deviations.
2. Actual Size: The actual size refers to the measured dimension of a part after manufacturing. Due to manufacturing processes and tolerances, it may vary from the basic size.
3. Deviation: Deviation denotes the difference between the actual size of a part and its basic size. It quantifies how much the manufactured part varies from its intended dimension. There exist four distinct types of deviations.
    i. Upper Deviation: This represents the algebraic variance between the maximum diameter of the job size and its basic diameter.
    ii. Lower Deviation: Lower Deviation signifies the algebraic difference between the minimum diameter of the job size and its basic diameter.
    iii. Actual Deviation: Actual Deviation quantifies the algebraic difference between the actual size of a job and its basic size.
    iv. Fundamental Deviation: Fundamental Deviation is either the lower or upper deviation, delineated concerning the zero lines. It plays a critical role in determining the fit and tolerance parameters for the component.
4. Allowance: Allowance is the intentional dimension difference between mating parts, designed to achieve specific fits and functionalities during assembly. It ensures that

parts can fit together correctly while accommodating variations in manufacturing processes. There are two primary types of allowances:

a. Maximum Allowance: This is the difference between the upper limit of a hole size and the lower limit of a shaft size. It ensures that the largest possible shaft can fit into the smallest hole within the specified tolerances.

b. Minimum Allowance: Conversely, Minimum Allowance denotes the difference between the lower limit of a hole size and the upper limit of a shaft size. It guarantees that the smallest acceptable shaft can fit into the largest acceptable hole while maintaining the desired fit and clearance.

### 4.1.2 LIMITS

Limits refer to the permissible range of dimensions assigned to a specific component, defining the lower and upper thresholds within which the component's dimensions must fall to meet desired specifications. To illustrate this concept, let's consider a cylindrical shaft with a design specification requiring a diameter of 50 mm, with a tolerance of ±0.2 mm. Calculating the limits involves:

Lower Limit (LL): This is obtained by subtracting the tolerance from the desired dimension. In this case, LL = 50 mm—0.2 mm = 49.8 mm.

Upper Limit (UL): Determined by adding the tolerance to the desired dimension. Here, UL = 50 mm + 0.2 mm = 50.2 mm.

In summary, the limits for the shaft's diameter in this example are 49.8 mm (LL) and 50.2 mm (UL).

These limits are crucial for ensuring that the actual diameter of the sharf remains within the predefined range during manufacturing. Deviating below 49.8 mm or exceeding 50.2 mm would render the shaft out of tolerance and fail to meet specified requirements.

### 4.1.3 FITS

"Fits" refer to the relationship between two components when joined during assembly, dictating the degree of tightness or looseness and influencing the presence of clearance or interference. Engineers select fit types based on factors such as assembly function, required precision, ease of assembly, and environmental conditions.

### *Types of Fits*

Clearance Fit: The maximum dimension of the hole exceeds the minimum dimension of the shaft In a clearance fit, resulting in a gap or clearance upon assembly is illustrated in Figure 4.1.

Example: A bolt inserted into a nut demonstrates a classic clearance fit, allowing easy insertion and removal.

Interference Fit: In an interference fit, the maximum dimension of the hole is smaller than the minimum dimension of the shaft, leading to a tight connection upon assembly.

Example: Press-fitting a bearing into a housing showcases an interference fit, where force or temperature manipulation is required for assembly.

Transition Fit: Transition fits provide a balance between clearance and interference, offering slight clearance for assembly ease while providing some interference for stability.

Example: Assembling a piston into a cylinder represents a transition fit, allowing for easy assembly while ensuring proper sealing and stability.

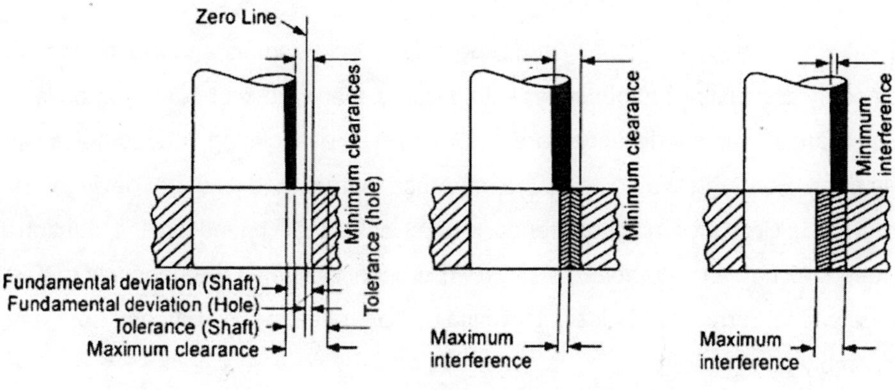


*Figure 4.1 Types of Fits*

### *Hole Basis and Shaft Basis for Fits*

1. Hole basis system: In this system, the different clearances and interferences are obtained in associating various shafts with a single hole, whose lower deviation is zero. In the hole basis system, the clearances and interferences between mating parts are determined by associating various shafts with a single hole. In this system, the hole serves as the reference feature, and its lower deviation is considered zero. The

clearance or interference is then calculated based on the relationship between the hole and the shaft. This system is advantageous when the focus is on ensuring a specific fit for a range of shafts within a single hole, providing versatility and ease of assembly.

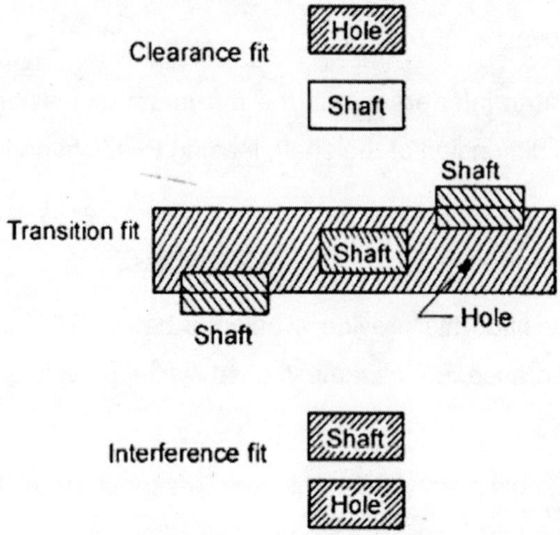


*Figure 4.2 Arrangement of tolerance zones for fittings*

2. Shaft basis system: In this system, the different clearances and interferences are obtained by associating various holes with a single shaft whose upper deviation is zero. The clearances and interferences are determined by associating various holes with a single shaft. Here, the shaft acts as the reference feature, and its upper deviation is set to zero. The clearance or interference is then calculated based on the relationship between the shaft and the hole. This system is beneficial when the priority is to ensure a specific fit for a range of holes with a single shaft, offering flexibility and consistency in assembly processes.

***Selection of Fits***

Various factors, including manufacturing processes, tooling capabilities, and functional requirements, influence the selection of fits in engineering applications. The hole basis system is frequently preferred due to practical considerations associated with hole production tools. Producing holes with odd sizes using fixed character tools is challenging, making the hole basis system more useful and widely utilized. Table 4.1

provides a comprehensive overview of commonly used types of fits, categorized based on shaft sizes and their resulting fits.

*Table 4.1 Fits and their class of shaft*

| Type of Fit | Description | Class of Shaft | Fits with Holes | Example Applications |
|---|---|---|---|---|
| Clearance Fit | Parts have a slight gap between them. | 'a to 'h' | 'A' to 'H' | - Shaft in a bearing<br>- Lid on a container |
| Interference Fit | Parts have a very tight fit. | 'j' to 'n' | 'J' to 'N' | - Press-fit pin in a hole<br>- Gear on a shaft |
| Transition Fit | Intermediate fit between clearance and interference. | 'p' onwards | 'P' onwards | - Parts requiring precise alignment but need to be disassembled for maintenance.<br>- Parts with machined locating surfaces. |

### 4.1.4 TOLERANCE

Tolerance denotes the allowable degree of variation in the dimensions of a component from its specified or nominal dimension. This critical specification ensures that even when absolute precision is lacking in the manufacturing process, the component remains functional and seamlessly integrates into the designated assembly.

Let's consider a cylindrical shaft with an intended diameter of 50 mm and a tolerance of ±0.1 mm. In this case, the nominal dimension is 50 mm, and the specified tolerance is ±0.1 mm, indicating that the actual diameter of the shaft may fluctuate within a range of 50 mm ± 0.1 mm.

Lower Limit (LL): Calculated by subtracting the tolerance from the nominal dimension, the lower limit is LL = 50 mm – 0.1 mm = 99.9 mm.

Upper Limit (UL): Conversely, the upper limit is computed by adding the tolerance to the nominal dimension. In this case, UL = 50 mm + 0.1 mm = 50.1 mm.

Therefore, for this specific example, the tolerance range for the shaft's diameter spans from 49.9 mm to 50.1 mm. Tolerance is pivotal in ensuring that the dimensions of the manufactured component reside within this predefined range. If the actual diameter of the shaft measures below 49.9 mm or exceeds 50.1 mm, it would be considered out of tolerance.

### *Types of Tolerance*

Various tolerance types are employed in engineering and manufacturing to precisely define the acceptable degree of variation in a component's dimensions. These tolerance categories offer precise insights into intended functionality and manufacturing requisites. Unilateral Tolerance specifies allowable variation solely on one side of the nominal dimension, which proves invaluable when a part's functionality relies on a specific direction of variation. Bilateral tolerance delineates allowable variation on both sides of the nominal dimension, which is applicable when no preference for variation direction exists. Limit Tolerance establishes allowable variation by specifying lower limit (LL) and upper limit (UL) values for a given dimension. It is typically employed when adherence to a prescribed range is paramount. Geometric tolerance dictates acceptable variation in geometric aspects such as form, orientation, location, and profile, commonly denoted using specific symbols to control geometric properties essential for functionality and assembly.

### *Standard Tolerances*

Standard tolerances are crucial parameters defined by the Bureau of Indian Standards (BIS) to ensure uniformity and precision in engineering and manufacturing processes. BIS outlines 18 standard grades of tolerances, each designated with specific classifications from ITO1to IT16. These designations provide engineers and manufacturers with standardized guidelines for determining acceptable levels of dimensional variation in components and products.

The classification system begins with ITOI, which represents the most precise tolerance grade, and progresses sequentially to IT16, indicating a broader tolerance range. Each designation signifies a predetermined level of permissible deviation from the nominal dimension, allowing for consistent quality control and reliable performance across diverse applications.

$$\text{Standard tolerance, } i = 0.45\, D^{1/3} + 0.001D$$

Where *i* is the standard tolerance unit in µm and D is the diameter in mm.

*Table 4.2 Standard tolerances*

| **Grade** | IT5 | IT6 | IT7 | IT8 | IT9 | IT10 | IT11 | IT12 | IT13 | IT14 | IT15 | IT16 |
|---|---|---|---|---|---|---|---|---|---|---|---|---|
| **Value** | 7i | 10i | 16i | 25i | 40i | 64i | 100i | 106i | 200i | 400i | 640i | 1000i |

*Table 4.3 Applications of Different Tolerance Grades*

| ***Tolerance Grade*** | ***Typical Application*** | ***Description*** |
|---|---|---|
| IT01 | Exceptionally Precise | Used for gauge blocks, calibration tools, and critical aerospace components requiring extremely high precision. |
| IT2 - IT3 | Very High Precision | Suitable for high-precision measuring tools, precision mechanical parts, and critical fits in aerospace and scientific instruments. |
| IT4 - IT5 | High Precision | Common for precision measurement tools, high-precision fits of small parts, and shaft and housing fits with high-tolerance roller bearings. |
| IT6 - IT7 | Precision | Often used for precision parts in machinery, gauges for checking tolerances of IT8-IT11 parts, and shaft and housing fits with medium-tolerance roller bearings. |
| IT8 - IT10 | General Engineering | Widely applied for parts requiring good interchangeability and functionality in general machinery, tools, and instruments. |
| IT11 - IT12 | Coarse Engineering | Suitable for parts in general machinery where precise fit is not critical, but functionality and interchangeability are still important. |
| IT13 - IT15 | Medium Sheet Metal Work | Common for sheet metal parts with moderate dimensional requirements, allowing for efficient production with some variation. |
| IT16 | Coarse Sheet Metal Work | Used for sheet metal parts with less stringent dimensional requirements, prioritizing formability and production speed over tight tolerances. |

## 4.2 SELECTIVE ASSEMBLY

Selective assembly refers to a strategic concept in manufacturing where subcomponents are carefully chosen and assembled to achieve a final assembly that meets the highest tolerance specifications. This approach involves meticulously selecting and matching individual parts based on their dimensional accuracy and other critical factors to ensure the overall assembly conforms precisely to the desired specifications. By employing selective assembly techniques, manufacturers can optimize the quality and performance of the final product while minimizing variations and defects. This method is particularly beneficial in industries where tight tolerances are crucial, such as aerospace, automotive, and precision engineering.

Selective assembly involves thorough inspection and testing of components to identify those with the most precise dimensions and characteristics. These selected parts are assembled, leveraging their strengths to achieve the desired accuracy and functionality in the final product. The selective assembly consists of the following process steps.

1. Measurement and Sorting: Individual parts (typically mating pairs like shafts and holes) are measured for their actual dimensions.
2. Grouping by Size: Parts are then sorted into groups based on their measured size. These groups typically correspond to specific tolerance ranges.
3. Assembly with Matched Parts: Parts from corresponding size groups are paired together during assembly. For example, a shaft from a larger size group would be assembled with a hole from a larger size group.

***Advantages***

- Improved Fit: Selective assembly reduces variability in clearance or tightness between mating components by ensuring that parts with compatible sizes are assembled. This leads to a more consistent and predictable final product.
- Reduced Scrap: Parts with slight dimensional deviations outside the intended tolerance range can still be paired with compatible counterparts. This minimizes waste and improves material utilization.
- Enhanced Performance: Tighter control over fit can improve the assembled product's performance. For example, in a bearing assembly, selective pairing can minimize friction and wear.

***Applications***

- The selective assembly is applied where the precision in fit is crucial. This includes applications like bearings, gears, and valve assemblies where tight tolerances are essential for smooth operation and long lifespan. High-volume production is desired: Selective assembly can streamline production without compromising final product quality by allowing for some variation in individual parts.

- Utilizing parts that might otherwise be scrapped due to slight dimensional deviations can be a cost-effective advantage.

***Limitations:***

1. Implementing selective assembly adds an additional sorting and pairing step to the manufacturing process, which can increase complexity and, potentially, production time.
2. Accurate measurement of individual parts is crucial for effective selective assembly, requiring additional inspection equipment and procedures.
3. Selective assembly is most beneficial for parts with well-defined tolerances and mating relationships. It may be unsuitable for simpler assemblies or components with less critical dimensional requirements.

### 4.2.1 INTERCHANGEABILITY

Traditionally, manufacturing workflows exhibited limited output. Skilled artisans were responsible for creating and fitting components, achieving the desired fit through manual adjustments. The advent of mass production, however, revolutionized contemporary manufacturing practices. Modern industrial environments witness the fabrication of parts by specialized workers across geographically dispersed facilities, followed by their subsequent assembly at separate locations. Within this decentralized framework, the dimensional consistency of mating parts becomes paramount. Each component must strictly adhere to pre-defined dimensional specifications and tolerance limits to guarantee seamless assembly during the final product integration stage. This stringent adherence is critical to accommodate the geographically dispersed nature of modern manufacturing, where parts originating from various sources must integrate flawlessly.

To facilitate smooth assembly amidst such a decentralized environment, an interchangeable system is employed. This system ensures dimensional uniformity among parts, enabling them to be swapped and integrated without requiring manual adjustments. An interchangeable system fosters a standardized approach to part creation, allowing for seamless assembly regardless of the source of individual components. Interchangeability often called the principle of dimensional standardisation, entails establishing consistent specifications for the constituent elements of components, connections, and mechanisms employed in design processes. This principle facilitates the autonomous production of these elements, allowing them to be seamlessly assembled or replaced without necessitating additional processing steps. By aligning with the technical specifications of the product, interchangeability streamlines manufacturing operations and supports rapid assembly and maintenance procedures. Consequently, adherence to interchangeability principles enhances production efficiency, promotes ease of scalability, and facilitates the integration of new technologies or design iterations within the framework of the product's requirements.

***Advantages of Interchangeability***

1. Mass production: Achieving interchangeability relies on manufacturing parts with small tolerances. Consequently, the practical application of interchangeability is paramount in mass production settings.
2. Increased productivity: In mass production, multiple workers operate various machines to manufacture similar products. As each worker consistently handles the same tasks throughout the day, the daily output rises, leading to an increased rate of production. Consequently, the company's overall productivity improves, enabling it to meet growing demand more efficiently.
3. Lower production costs: The decentralization of manufacturing allows different components to be produced in various regions based on factors such as raw material availability, skilled labor, and infrastructure. This decentralized approach significantly reduces production costs.
4. Reduced maintenance costs: The ease of replacing or repairing worn-out or defective parts contributes to a significant reduction in maintenance expenses in mass production systems.
5. Enhanced quality: By assigning workers to specialize in specific tasks, such as the production of identical components, mass production fosters skill development and expertise. This specialization results in improved quality control and consistency in the manufacturing process, ultimately leading to higher-quality products.
6. Time efficiency: The implementation of tight tolerances for manufacturing mating components ensures interchangeability, thereby streamlining the assembly process. As a result, the assembly of mating components requires minimal time, contributing to overall time efficiency in mass production operations.

## 4.3 HOLE AND SHAFT BASIS SYSTEMS

***Hole Basis Systems***

The holes and shaft basis systems are fundamental concepts in engineering design and manufacturing, particularly in fits and tolerances. These systems provide a framework for establishing the relationship between mating components, such as shafts and holes, in mechanical assemblies. In the hole basis system, the dimensions and tolerances of the hole are used as the basis for defining the fit. This means that the hole is manufactured to a specific size, and the shaft is then designed with varying sizes to fit into the hole within specified tolerance limits. The tolerance zone is centred on the nominal size of the hole, allowing for variation in the shaft size while ensuring proper assembly. This system is commonly used in applications where the size and accuracy of the hole are critical, such as bearing housings or mounting points.

The hole basis system operates by designating the hole's nominal size, with a zero lower deviation (fundamental deviation), as the basic size. Varied clearances or interferences are then achieved by adjusting the limits of the mating part, typically the shaft, to attain different classes of fit. Essentially, the hole's limits remain fixed while those of the shaft are adjusted to achieve the desired type of fit. This means that the dimensional range of the hole stays constant across different fits of the same accuracy level.

In contemporary engineering practices, the hole basis system is predominantly favoured due to its inherent advantage of the ease of adjusting shaft sizes compared to hole sizes. This preference is largely driven by the widespread use of drills, reamers, and similar tools for producing the majority of holes in engineering works. The necessity of employing a large number of tools of varying sizes to adjust hole dimensions poses a logistical challenge, making it more convenient to modify shaft sizes instead. This simplifies manufacturing processes and reduces the complexity associated with tooling requirements. However, there are situations where the shaft basis system proves to be more advantageous than the hole basis system. Notably, in the manufacturing of large-sized parts, the shaft basis system may offer benefits such as increased flexibility and efficiency in achieving desired fits.

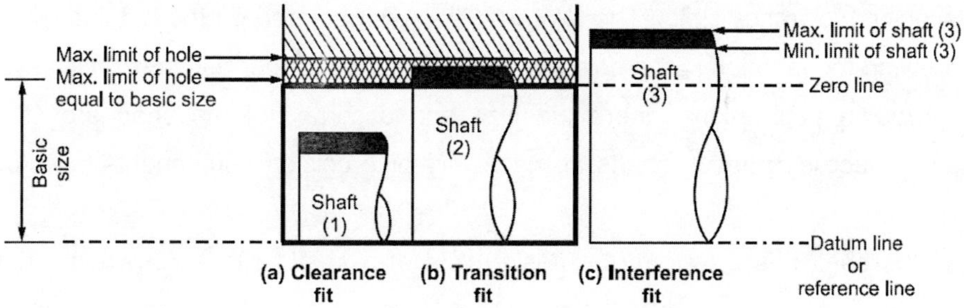


*Figure 4.3 Hole-basis system*

### *Advantages of the Hole Basis System*

1. Easy and Cost-effective Hole Fabrication: Using drills and reamers, holes can be made accurately and affordably.
2. Flexibility in Shaft Sizing: Shaft dimensions can be easily adjusted using turning and grinding techniques to suit specific fit requirements.
3. Simplified Shaft Inspection: Inspection of shafts is simplified using adjustable gauges, as external measurements are easier and quicker than internal ones.

### *Disadvantages of the Hole Basis System*

1. Limited Flexibility for Hole Sizing: Unlike the shaft basis system, where hole sizes can be adjusted to achieve desired fits, the hole basis system restricts alterations to shaft dimensions. This limitation may lead to constraints in design and assembly processes.
2. Increased Complexity in Shaft Fabrication: Modifying shaft sizes to achieve desired fits may require more intricate machining processes, potentially increasing production time and costs compared to the shaft basis system.
3. Challenges in Hole Inspection: Inspecting holes for accuracy and compliance can be more challenging in the hole basis system, as internal measurements are typically more intricate and time-consuming than external measurements. This complexity may result in slower inspection processes and potential inaccuracies.

### *Shaft Basis Systems*

Conversely, in the shaft basis system (Figure 4.4), the dimensions and tolerances of the shaft serve as the basis for defining the fit. In this system, the shaft is manufactured to a specific size, and the hole is then designed with varying sizes to accommodate the shaft within specified tolerance limits. The tolerance zone is centered on the nominal size of the shaft, allowing for variation in the hole size while ensuring proper assembly. This system is often utilized in applications where the size and accuracy of the shaft are of utmost importance, such as rotating shafts in machinery or precision components in automotive engines.

In the shaft basis system, the design size of a shaft, with a zero upper deviation (fundamental deviation), serves as the basic size. Varied clearances or interferences are then achieved by adjusting the limits of the hole to attain different types of fit. In essence, the limits of the shaft remain constant while those of the holes are varied to achieve the required fit.

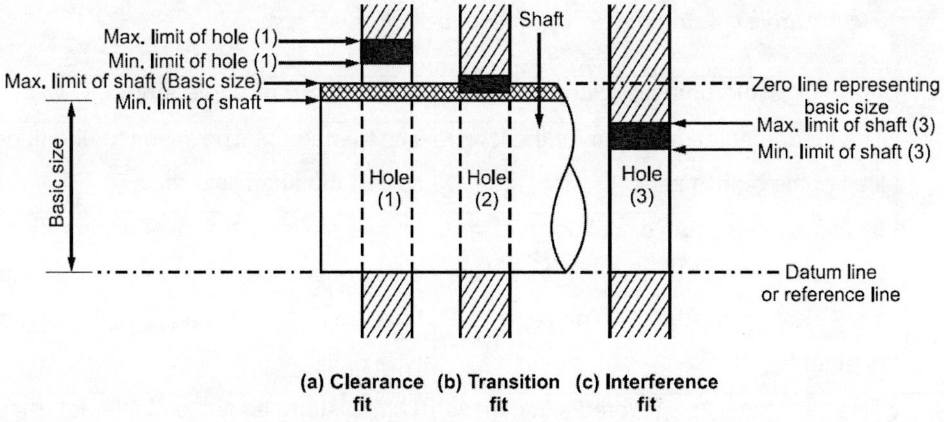


*Figure 4.4 Shaft-basis system*

### *Advantages of Shaft Basis System*

The shaft basis system is advantageous when mounting different accessories, such as pulleys, bearings, and gears, onto a single large shaft. This system allows for versatile fits to efficiently accommodate diverse components on the same shaft.

### *Disadvantages of Shaft Basis System*

1. In mass production, implementing the shaft basis system necessitates a substantial investment in tools (drills, reamers, broaches, punches, etc.) to produce holes of varying sizes. This requires significant capital expenditure and storage space, making it less favorable for mass production scenarios.
2. As the limits of holes are adjusted to achieve the desired fit, internal diameter measurements become necessary. Internal measurements are inherently challenging due to the complex construction of measuring instruments, adding complexity to the manufacturing process.
3. Internal measurements tend to be more time-consuming compared to external measurements. This can slow down production processes and affect overall efficiency.
4. The accuracy of internal measurements depends largely on the skill of the operator. Skilled labor is required to ensure precise measurements, which can increase the cost of inspection due to higher wages for skilled workers.

*Table 4.4 Comparison of hole and shaft basis systems*

| S.No | Hole basis system | Shaft basis system |
|---|---|---|
| 1 | The fundamental deviation for the lower limit of the hole is zero. | The fundamental deviation for the upper limit of the shaft is zero. |
| 2 | In this system, the dimensions of the hole are held constant while those of the shaft are adjusted to achieve the desired fit. | In this system, the dimensions of the shaft remain constant while those of the hole are adjusted to achieve the desired type of fit. |
| 3 | This system is favored in mass production due to its ease, convenience, and cost-effectiveness in producing holes of accurate size. | The system is not suitable for mass production because it is challenging and inconvenient to produce shafts of precise dimensions. |
| 4 | It is much easier to adjust the sizes of shafts according to the required fit. | It is relatively challenging to adjust the sizes of holes according to the required fit. |
| 5 | Less capital investment and smaller storage space are required to produce shafts of various sizes. | Large capital investment and extensive storage space are required for tool storage, as a significant number of tools of varying sizes are necessary to produce holes of different sizes. |
| 6 | Gauging of shafts can be readily performed using Go and No-Go adjustable gap gauges. Gauging refers to determining whether the size of a component (such as a shaft or hole) manufactured falls within specified limits or not. | As internal measurements, gauging of holes poses a challenging process. |

## 4.4 TAYLORS PRINCIPLE

William Taylor formulated a concept concerning the measurement of components to assess specific dimensions and geometric features. This concept, known as Taylor's Principle, is fundamental in the design of limit gauges.

According to Taylor's principle, "GO" and "NO GO" gauges are designed to verify maximum and minimum material conditions as follows:

**"GO" Limit:** This designation applies to "maximum material conditions," specifically the upper limit of the shaft and the lower limit of the hole.

**"NO GO" Limit:** This designation applies to "minimum material conditions," including the lower limit of the shaft and the upper limit of the hole.

*For checking holes:*

(i) "GO" Plug Gauge: Verifies the size of the minimum limit of the hole.

(ii) "NO GO" Plug Gauge: Verifies the size of the maximum limit of the hole.

*For checking shafts:*

(i) "GO" Snap or Ring Gauge: Verifies the size of the maximum limit of the shaft.

(ii) "NO GO" Snap or Ring Gauge: Verifies the size of the minimum limit of the shaft.

Taylor's principle specifies that "GO" gauges should be of full form, allowing them to simultaneously check all possible dimensions (such as roundness, taper, and location). Conversely, "NO GO" gauges should focus on checking only one dimension at a time.

The maximum material condition occurs at the upper limit of a shaft and the lower limit of a hole, while the minimum material condition occurs at the lower limit of a shaft and the upper limit of a hole. In the case of plug gauges, the "Go" side corresponds to the size of the minimum limit of the hole, ensuring full circular section and alignability. However, it cannot assess the degree of ovality. The "No Go" side verifies the upper limit of the hole and is shorter than the "Go" gauge. For slightly elliptical holes, the "No Go" gauge can be modified into a pin form to assess circularity by detecting errors at various cross-sections. In the context of snap gauges, the "Go" snap gauge aligns with the maximum limit of the shaft, while the "No Go" snap gauge corresponds to the minimum limit. Snap gauges necessitate rigidity and durability to ensure proper functionality and size maintenance. The disparity in size between the "Go" and "No Go" gauges is typically equivalent to the tolerance of the tested "hole" or "shaft."

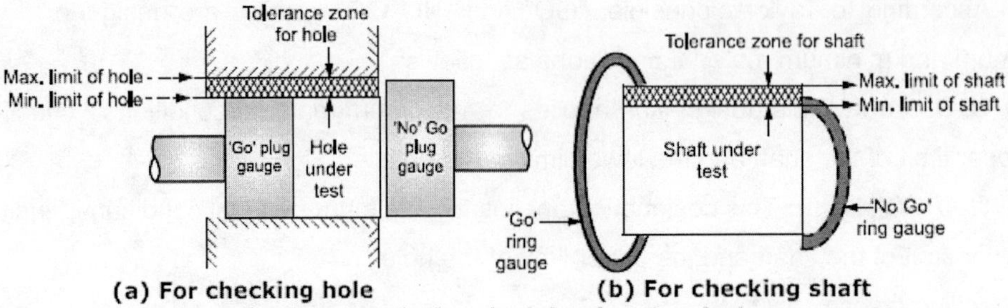


*Figure 4.5 Gauge design using Taylor's Principle for hole and shaft*

Maximum Material Condition (MMC) and Minimum Material Condition (MMC) are critical concepts in engineering design and manufacturing, especially concerning fits and tolerances. In the context of a shaft and a hole both having a specified dimension of 40 ± 0.05 mm.

Maximum Material Condition refers to the state where the shaft or hole contains the maximum material allowed within the specified tolerance. For the shaft, Maximum Material Condition occurs at the upper limit of the dimensional tolerance range, meaning the shaft would have a diameter of 40.05 mm (40 + 0.05 mm). Conversely, for the hole, the Maximum Material Condition occurs at the lower limit of the dimensional tolerance range, resulting in a diameter of 39.95 mm (40 - 0.05 mm). In Maximum Material Condition, the parts have the tightest fit possible within the specified tolerance range. The Minimum Material Condition refers to the state where the shaft or hole contains the minimum amount of material allowed within the specified tolerance. For the shaft, the Minimum Material Condition occurs at the lower limit of the dimensional tolerance range, resulting in a diameter of 39.95 mm (40 - 0.05 mm). For the hole, Minimum Material Condition occurs at the upper limit of the dimensional tolerance range, meaning the hole would have a diameter of 40.05 mm (40 + 0.05 mm). In Minimum Material Condition, the parts have the loosest fit possible within the specified tolerance range.

## 4.5 ANGULAR MEASUREMENT

Length standards like the foot and meter are human inventions, created arbitrarily. Due to challenges in replicating these standards accurately, the wavelength of light has become a reference standard for length. However, the standard for angles, derived from circles, is not man-made but inherent in nature. Whether termed as degrees or radians, angles have a direct relationship with circles, which are formed by a line revolving around one of its ends.

Whether defined as the circumference of a planet or the orbit of an electron, circles maintain a consistent relationship with their parts.

In metrology, the science of precise measurement, angular measurement plays a vital role in ensuring the accuracy of objects and their functionality. It's crucial for tasks like verifying angles of cuts, slopes, and tapers on machine parts. Metrology demands high precision, and various instruments like protractors, sine bars, and angle gauges are employed to achieve this. The selection of the appropriate tool and the most fitting unit (degrees or radians) depend on the specific requirement and the desired level of accuracy. Accurate angle measurement is crucial in various industrial settings, from workshops to tool rooms, for assessing interchangeable parts, gears, jigs, and fixtures. Measurements include taper angles of bores, gear flank angles, seating surface angles of jigs, and taper angles of jibs. Interestingly, in machine part alignment assessment, angle measurement serves to detect errors in straightness, parallelism, and flatness, often with highly sensitive instruments like autocollimators. A spectrum of angle measurement instruments exists, ranging from simple scaled devices to advanced laser interferometry-based tools. Basic types, such as vernier protractors, offer improved discrimination (least count) and are supported by mechanical mechanisms for accurate positioning and locking. Spirit levels find extensive application in mechanical and civil engineering, aiding in aligning structural elements like beams and columns. Instruments like clinometers, based on spirit level principles but with higher resolution, are popular in metrology. This chapter explores popular angle measurement devices widely utilized across industries.

### 4.5.1 INSTRUMENTS FOR ANGULAR MEASUREMENT

In metrology, a diverse array of specialized instruments serves the purpose of angular measurement, each meticulously crafted to cater to distinct measurement requirements and exacting precision standards. These instruments enable metrologists to minutely quantify angles and orientations across a broad spectrum of applications. Below are some frequently employed instruments for angular measurement:

1) **Protractors:** Renowned for their simplicity and versatility, protractors are ubiquitous tools for measuring angles in a straightforward manner. Typically comprising a semicircular or circular disc adorned with degree divisions, protractors find extensive utility in geometry, construction, and general engineering for angle assessment.
2) **Angle Gauges:** Also referred to as bevel protractors or inclinometers, angle gauges are specialized instruments tailored for the high-precision measurement of angles.

Comprising a movable arm or blade affixed to a base adorned with a calibrated scale, angle gauges are pivotal in machining, toolmaking, and metrology for verifying machine part and component angles.

3) **Sine Bars:** Sine bars emerge as precision measuring devices dedicated to facilitating accurate angular measurement and inspection endeavors. Comprising two parallel bars or cylinders mounted on a flat base, sine bars leverage trigonometric principles to achieve high-precision angle measurement by altering the relative height of one end with respect to the other.
4) **Autocollimators:** Autocollimators represent optical marvels employed for the meticulous measurement of minute angular deviations and alignments with unparalleled precision. Typically integrating a light source, collimator lens, and viewing telescope, autocollimators find widespread application in optics, astronomy, and precision engineering for alignment and calibration endeavors.
5) **Goniometers:** Goniometers represent precision instruments engineered to deliver pinpoint accuracy in angular measurement within laboratory and industrial environments. Featuring a rotating arm or platform equipped with a meticulously calibrated scale, goniometers are indispensable in fields such as optics, crystallography, and biomechanics for precise angle quantification.
6) **Theodolites:** Theodolites stand as precision optical instruments meticulously crafted for the measurement of horizontal and vertical angles in surveying and engineering applications. Consisting of a telescope mounted on a rotating platform embellished with graduated scales, theodolites are indispensable in tasks such as land surveying, construction layout, and structural alignment.
7) **Digital Angle Finders:** Rounding off the roster, digital angle finders emerge as electronic marvels harnessed for the high-accuracy measurement of angles with unparalleled ease of use. Typically featuring a digital display and integrated sensors for direct angle measurement, digital angle finders find widespread adoption in carpentry, woodworking, and metalworking for precise angle quantification in fabrication and assembly endeavors.

### 4.5.2 Universal Bevel Protractor

The universal bevel protractor is an indispensable precision instrument for acquiring accurate angle measurements across various applications. Designed with flexibility, it excels in measuring internal and external angles and surface inclinations. Central to its design is a circular base featuring a graduated scale from 0 to 360 degrees, complemented by a rotatable blade or limb adjustable to any desired angle. Coupled with a vernier scale, the blade ensures heightened measurement precision, with the protractor's dial featuring graduations in degrees, minutes, and seconds. Mounted on a movable arm, the dial can be securely locked in position for precise angle assessment, further augmented by the accuracy afforded by the vernier scale.

A hallmark feature of the universal bevel protractor is its ability to provide dual readings, facilitating measurements in both clockwise and counterclockwise directions from the zero reference point. This adaptability renders it suitable for a myriad of tasks across diverse industries. Equipped with extendable and retractable blades, the protractor accommodates measurements on various surfaces, including planar, internal, and external angles. The pivoting base enhances manoeuvrability and ease manoeuvrability of adjustment when positioning the protractor on the object under examination.

Industries reliant on precise angle measurements, such as engineering, metalworking, and woodworking, commonly employ the universal bevel protractor as a staple tool. Its utility extends to tasks like machine and tool angle adjustments and the measurement of complex shapes and surfaces.

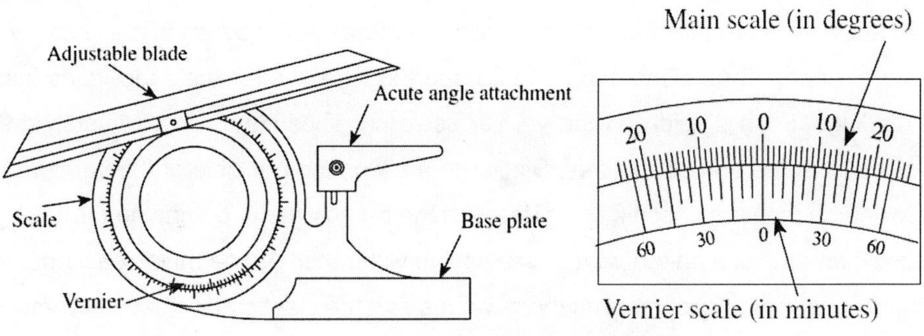


*Figure 4.6 Universal Bevel Protector*

The Universal Bevel Protractor comprises several key components:

1) **Main Body:** The central component housing the essential mechanisms and components of the protractor, providing structural support and stability.
2) **Turret:** The rotating part of the protractor that holds the scale and vernier scale.

3) **Base Plate Stock:** As the protractor's foundation, the base plate stock offers a stable platform upon which other components are mounted.
4) **Adjustable Blade:** Positioned atop the base plate stock, the adjustable blade is the primary means for measuring angles. Its flexibility and adjustability enable precise angle determination across various applications.
5) **Circular Plate with Graduated Vernier Scale Divisions:** This integral component features a circular plate adorned with graduated divisions, allowing for precise angle measurement. Including a Vernier scale enhances the instrument's accuracy, akin to the principle employed in Vernier callipers.
6) **Working Edge:** The edge of the blade from which the measurement is taken.
7) **Acute Angle Attachment:** A specialized feature designed to facilitate the measurement of acute angles, the acute angle attachment expands the protractor's versatility and utility, enabling the measurement of angles beyond 90 degrees.

***Working Principle of Universal Bevel Protractor***

The working principle of the Universal Bevel Protractor involves the interaction between its key components to enable precise angle measurement. The base plate, acting as one of the working edges, interfaces with the adjustable blade held on the circular plate. This blade, in conjunction with the circular plate, can be rotated along the main body, allowing for angular adjustments. The vernier scale, featuring 12 divisions on each side of the center zero, corresponds to 60 minutes, with each division representing 5 minutes. Aligning with the main scale, where 12 divisions equate to 23 degrees, the vernier scale facilitates accurate angle readings. Each division on the vernier scale corresponds to approximately 1.91666 degrees or 1 degree and 55 minutes. Similar to the working principle of the vernier caliper, the zero line on the vernier scale coincides with the main scale to determine the main scale reading. When divisions on the vernier scale align with those on the main scale, the vernier scale reading is noted. By combining these values with the least count of the Universal Bevel Protractor, precise angle measurements can be calculated.

In the given scenario, to determine the total reading of the Universal Bevel Protractor, we utilize the formula:

Total Reading = Main Scale Reading + (Number of divisions at which it coincides with any division on the main scale × Least count of the Vernier scale).

Given:

Main scale reading = 10°

Vernier scale reading (number of the division at which it coincides with any division on the main scale) = 3rd division

Least count of the Universal Bevel protractor = 5 minutes

Substituting the provided values into the formula:

Total Reading = 10° + (3 × 5 minutes)

Total Reading = 10° + 15 minutes

Total Reading = 10° 15'

Therefore, the total reading of the Universal Bevel Protractor in the given case is 10 degrees and 15 minutes.

***Advantages***

1. The universal bevel protractor offers precise angle measurements, crucial for accurate adjustments in various applications.
2. Capable of measuring both internal and external angles, as well as surface inclinations, it caters to a wide range of measurement needs. Its versatility makes it suitable for use in various industries and applications.
3. Its ability to provide dual readings enhances flexibility by facilitating measurements in both clockwise and counter clockwise directions.
4. Equipped with user-friendly features like extendable blades and a pivoting base, it is adaptable to different measurement scenarios.
5. Enables precise alignment of machine tools and components, enhancing operational efficiency.
6. Useful in quality control and inspection processes, ensuring products meet specifications and supports precise layout and machining tasks, aiding in accurate fabrication processes.

***Disadvantages***

1. The many number of components may pose a challenge for inexperienced users.
2. Certain models are delicate and require careful handling to avoid damage.
3. Relatively expensive compared to simpler angle measurement tools, it may be a barrier for some users.
4. Despite versatility, it may not suit high-precision applications due to its restricted measurement range.

5. Regular calibration is necessary to maintain accuracy, incurring additional time and cost for users.

***Uses of the Universal Bevel Protractor:***

1. The universal bevel protractor is instrumental in engineering and construction for accurately measuring and setting precise angles required for various tasks.
2. It aids in checking and aligning machine tool components to ensure optimal performance and accuracy in machining operations.
3. Used for creating geometric shapes with specific angles, facilitating precision in design and fabrication processes.
4. It verifies the accuracy of angles in various workpieces, ensuring they meet specified requirements and tolerances.
5. It assists in the fabrication of jigs and fixtures by providing precise angle measurements for their construction, improving workpiece stability and accuracy during machining.
6. Used in manufacturing for conducting quality control inspections to verify the accuracy of angles in machined components, ensuring compliance with standards and specifications.
7. Enables angle measurements in metalworking and woodworking projects, aiding in the fabrication of precise components and structures.
8. Supports architectural and mechanical drafting by providing accurate angle measurements for the design and layout of structures, machinery, and components.
9. Used in automotive applications to verify the alignment of vehicle components, such as wheel alignment, ensuring optimal vehicle performance and safety.
10. Facilitates angle measurements in educational settings, serving as a valuable tool for teaching geometry, trigonometry, and technical drawing concepts.

### 4.5.3 SINE BAR

A sine bar, alternatively referred to as a precision angle device, stands as a specialized tool in precision measurement within machining and metrology. It is an integral to machining and metrology, serves as a precision measuring instrument. Comprising two parallel bars featuring accurately angled surfaces, typically set at intervals of 5°, 10°, or 15°, it plays a pivotal role in the measurement of angles with utmost accuracy. Machinists rely on this tool to facilitate precise machining and inspection processes, ensuring the quality and accuracy of manufactured components. Its primary function lies in accurately measuring and setting angles with exceptional precision and accuracy. Widely utilized across machine shops, quality control laboratories, and manufacturing sectors, sine bars play a crucial role in ensuring the precise alignment and machining of workpieces at predetermined angular inclinations.

A sine bar, when paired with slip gauge blocks, emerges as a precision angular measurement tool esteemed for its accuracy in evaluating angles across machining, grinding, and inspection tasks. Renowned for its proficiency in both precise angle measurement and workpiece alignment, this instrument is crafted from high-quality, corrosion-resistant steel. Engineered with durability in mind, sine bars are designed to endure wear while retaining accuracy, rendering them indispensable for tasks demanding meticulous angle measurements and alignments.

***Construction of Sine Bar***

The construction of a sine bar involves a rigid steel gauge body featuring two equally sized rollers aligned parallel to each other along their axes. The top surface of the steel bar runs parallel to a line connecting the centers of the rollers, with the length of the sine bar precisely corresponding to the distance between these roller centers, typically set at 100 mm, 200 mm, or 300 mm. Relief holes strategically placed reduce its weight. However, a sine bar alone cannot effectively measure angles; it requires the use of slip gauges and elevation gauges.

1. **Surface Plate:** In order to ensure that the sine bar has a precise horizontal reference surface, a surface plate serves as the basis for positioning the sine bar and related parts. The sine bar's top surface must be parallel to the surface plate's horizontal planes for proper alignment, which is very important.
2. **Dial Gauge:** Dial gauges assess surface uniformity, registering zero deflections during traversal to confirm surface parallelism with its base. In the sine bar setup, dial gauges are vital for verifying the alignment of the workpiece's upper surface with surface plate or measuring the angle of the tapered sine.
3. **Block Gauges or Slip Gauges:** Block gauges, also called slip gauges, act as precise standards for height and length measurements, enhancing the accuracy of sine bar setups.
4. **Vernier Height Gauge:** Vernier height gauges determine the height of the sine bar rollers, facilitating angle measurements for larger components within the setup.

### *Working Principle*

The working principle of a sine bar is rooted in fundamental trigonometric principles. When one roller of the sine bar is positioned on a surface plate and the other roller is set at the height of the slip gauge, it establishes a triangular configuration involving the sine bar, surface plate, and slip gauge. In this triangular setup, the hypotenuse corresponds to the sine bar itself, formed by integrating vertical slip gauges with the surface plate base. If we denote the slip gauge height as H and the sine bar length as L, the sine ratio is expressed as H divided by the length of the sine bar (L). Consequently, the angle θ can be determined by calculating the inverse sine (sin^-1) of H divided by L, ensuring precise angular measurements.

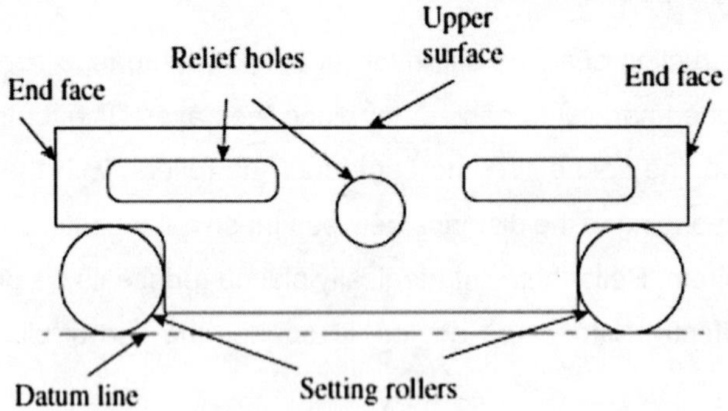


*Figure 4.7 Sine Bar*

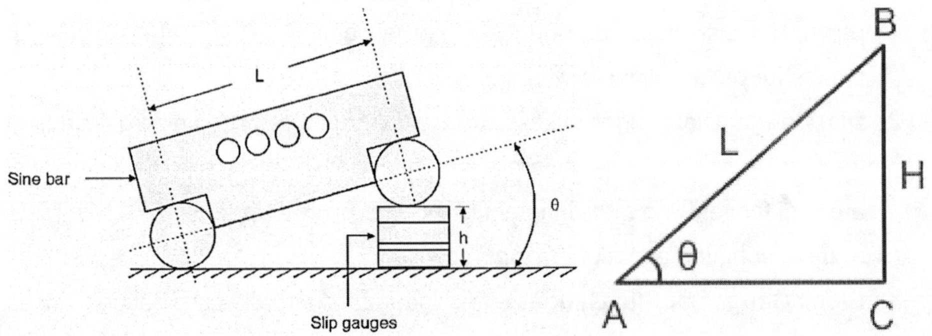


*Figure 4. 8 Working Principle of Sine Bar*

*Sine ϑ = H/L = BC/AB*

***Advantages of Sine Bar***

1. High Accuracy: Sine bars offer precise angle measurements crucial for achieving accurate machining results.
2. Repeatable: Once set, sine bars ensure consistent angle measurements and machining operations.
3. Versatility: They can measure and set various angles, making them versatile in machining tasks.
4. Simple Operation: Sine bars are relatively easy to use, requiring minimal operator skill.
5. Cost-Effective: They provide a cost-effective solution for accurate angle measurement and machining compared to more complex tools.

***Limitations of Sine Bar***

1. Limited Angle Range: Sine bars are restricted to measuring specific angles based on their length.
2. Additional Tools Required: They necessitate additional tools like slip gauges for precise measurements.
3. Angle Range Constraints: May not be suitable for measuring very small or very large angles.
4. Susceptibility to Wear: Sine bars are susceptible to wear and damage, potentially affecting accuracy over time.
5. Complex Setup: They involve a relatively complex setup compared to simple protractors.

***Uses of Sine Bar***

1. Precision Angular Measurement in Machining: Sine bars are used for precise angular measurement in machining processes.
2. Workpiece Alignment: They assist in aligning workpieces at specific angles during machining operations.
3. Surface Flatness and Parallelism Verification: Sine bars are employed to verify the flatness and parallelism of surfaces.
4. Accurate Setups in Manufacturing and Engineering: They ensure accurate setups in manufacturing and engineering applications.

5. Calibration of Other Measuring Instruments: Sine bars are also used for calibrating other measuring instruments to maintain accuracy.

### 4.5.4. SPIRIT LEVEL

A spirit level, a fundamental tool in engineering metrology, traces its origins back to practices in cold western regions. Originally filled with 'spirits of wine' to prevent freezing, these instruments earned the general term "spirit level." Functioning as an angular measuring device, the spirit level employs a bubble that consistently moves to the highest point within a glass vial. A typical spirit level comprises a base, known as the reference plane, which rests on the machine part under assessment for straightness or flatness determination. When the base is horizontal, the bubble centers on the graduated scale engraved on the glass. As the base deviates from the horizontal, the bubble shifts to the highest point of the tube. The bubble's position relative to the scale measures the machine part's angularity, with the scale calibrated to directly indicate the reading in minutes or seconds. The cross-test level, positioned at a right angle to the main bubble scale, also indicates inclination in the perpendicular plane. A screw adjustment facilitates setting the bubble to zero by referencing it with a surface plate.

The performance of a spirit level hinges on the geometric relationship between the bubble and two references: gravity acting at the center of the bubble and the scale against which the bubble position is read. Sensitivity is determined by the radius of curvature of the bubble formed against the inside surface of the glass vial and the base length of its mount. For a level with graduations at a 2 mm interval representing a tilt of 10", the angle (θ) can be calculated as $\theta_c = 10\times\pi/(180 \times 3600)$, resulting in a radius (R) of approximately 41.274 m. If the base length is 250 mm, the height (h) for a 2 mm, $\theta_c = h/250$, then the bubble movement is h=0.012mm. Sensitivity increases with a larger radius of curvature or a shorter base length, with a preferred sensitivity of 10" per division for precision measurement.

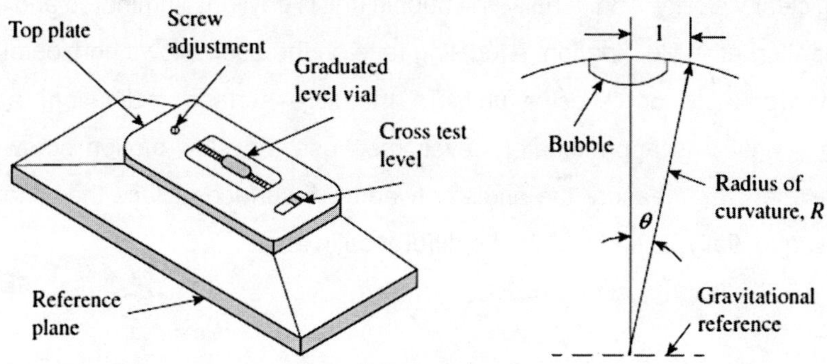


*Figure 4.9. Spirit Level*

While a spirit level is primarily used for aligning machine parts and assessing flatness and straightness rather than measuring angles, it is essential to ensure accuracy by carefully setting the vial relative to the base. To minimize error, a recommended procedure involves taking readings from both ends of the vial, reversing the base, repeating readings, averaging the four readings, and repeating the process for critical cases.

### 4.5.6 CLINOMETER

A clinometer is a specialized application of a spirit level, where the spirit level is mounted on a rotary member within a housing. One face of the housing serves as the instrument's base, while a circular scale on the housing allows for measuring the angle of inclination of the rotary member relative to its base. Clinometers are primarily used to determine the included angle between two adjacent faces of a workpiece. To achieve this, the instrument's base is placed on one face of the workpiece, and the rotary body is adjusted until a zero reading of the bubble is obtained. The angle of rotation is then noted on the circular scale against the index. A similar reading is taken on the second face of the workpiece, and the included angle between the faces is calculated as the difference between the two readings.

***Working Principle***

To determine the inclination using a clinometer (Figure 4.10), you first need to level the bubble unit, then read the scales through the reader eyepiece. The upper aperture displays two pairs of double lines and two single lines. Adjust the micrometer knob until the single line aligns precisely between the double lines, setting the micrometer scale. Then, read the main and micrometer scales, and sum their readings to obtain the desired angle. This setup cancels out any centring error of the circle. The scales are illuminated by a low-voltage lamp, ensuring clear visibility. Additionally, the bubble unit is daylight illuminated and equipped with a lamp for alternative illumination. A locating face on the back allows horizontal use with the accessory worktable or reflector unit. To measure surface inclination, adjust the clinometer's vial until it is approximately level, then use the slow-motion screw for final centering adjustment. To measure the angle between two surfaces, place the clinometer on each surface sequentially, and calculate the difference in angle.

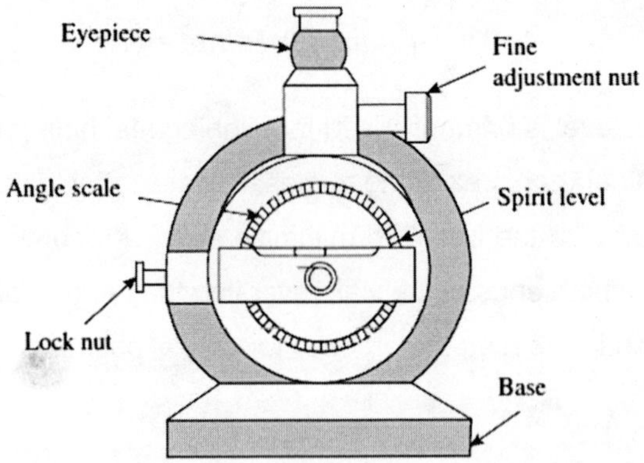


*Figure 4.10. Clinomete*

The clinometer can also be used as a precision setting tool for setting tool heads or tables at specific angles. First, set the micrometer scale, then rotate the glass scale to align the relevant graduation with the index, using the slow-motion screw for final adjustment. Tilting the work surface until the bubble is centered sets it to the specified angle relative to a level plane.

### *Applications*

Clinometers find applications in checking angular faces and relief angles on large cutting tools and milling cutter inserts. They are also used for setting inclinable tables on jig boring machines and performing angular work on grinding machines. The Hilger and Watts type of clinometer is commonly used, featuring a circular glass scale divided from 0° to 360° at 10′ intervals. A subdivision of 10′ is achievable with an optical micrometre, while a coarse scale marked every 10 degrees is provided for rough work. Some instruments include a worm and quadrant arrangement for readings up to 1′ accuracy. In certain clinometers, no bubble is present; instead, a graduated circle supported on accurate ball bearings automatically aligns with the true vertical position when released. Readings are taken against the circle with the aid of a vernier, allowing for an accuracy of up to 1 second.

### 4.5.7 ANGLE GAUGES

Dr. Tomlinson of N.P.L. developed the first combination of angle gauges. This set comprises thirteen individual gauges, combined with one square block and one parallel straight edge, enabling the setup of any angle to the nearest 3 seconds. Similar to the assembly of slip gauges to achieve linear dimensions, angle gauges can be stacked to attain a desired angle. Constructed from hardened steel and meticulously seasoned, angle gauges ensure enduring angular precision. The measuring faces undergo careful lapping and polishing to achieve high accuracy and flatness, akin to slip gauges. These gauges measure approximately 3 inches (76.2 mm) in length and 5/8 inch (15.87 mm) in width, with lapped faces accurate to within 0.0002 mm. The angle between the two ends is maintained within ± 2 seconds.

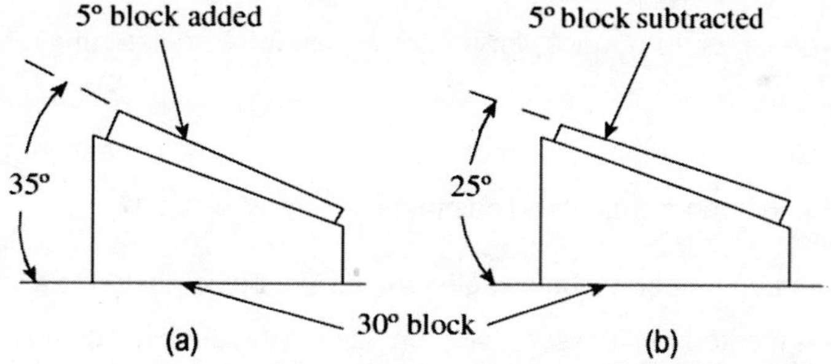


*Figure 4.11 a) Addition Angle gauge blocks b) Subtraction Angle gauge*

*Table 4.5 Angle gauge block sets*

| ***The smallest increment of the set*** | ***Number of individual blocks contained in the set*** | ***List of the blocks of the set*** |
|---|---|---|
| 1 | 6 | Six blocks of 1°, 3°, 5°, 15°, 30°, and 45° |
| 1' | 11 | Six blocks of 1°, 3°, 5°, 15°, 30°, and 45°<br>Five blocks of 1', 3', 5', 20', and 30' |
| 1" | 16 | Six blocks of 1°, 3°, 5°, 15°, 30°, and 45° |

| | | |
|---|---|---|
| | | Five blocks of 1', 3', 5', 20', and 30'<br>Five blocks of 1", 3", 5", 20", and 30" |

This diagram demonstrates how two gauge blocks can be combined to produce different angles. When a 5° angle block is paired with a 30° angle block (as shown in Fig. 5.14(a)), the resulting angle is 35°. Conversely, if the 5° angle block is reversed and combined with the 30° angle block (as illustrated in Fig. 5.14(b)), the resulting angle becomes 25°. Reversing an angle block subtracts its value from the total angle generated by the other blocks, allowing for diverse angle combinations with minimal gauges. Constructed from hardened steel, angle gauges undergo precision lapping and polishing to ensure accuracy and flatness. Typically measuring about 75 mm in length and 15 mm in width, these gauges offer surfaces accurate up to ±2". They are available in sets of 6, 11, or 16, with Table 5.2 detailing the specifications of each block in these sets. While most angles can be created in multiple ways, minimizing error is essential, especially as the number of gauges used increases. The set of 16 gauges, for instance, can form angles ranging from 0° to 99° in 1" increments, offering a total of 3,56,400 combinations. The laboratory master-grade set achieves accuracy up to one-fourth of a second, while the inspection-grade set is accurate to ½", and the tool room-grade set maintains accuracy within 1".

The diagrams illustrate how angle gauges can be combined to achieve desired angles. Each gauge is marked with the symbol '<', indicating the direction of the included angle. When adding angles, all '<' symbols should align, while for subtraction, the gauge should be flipped to align the symbol in the opposite direction.

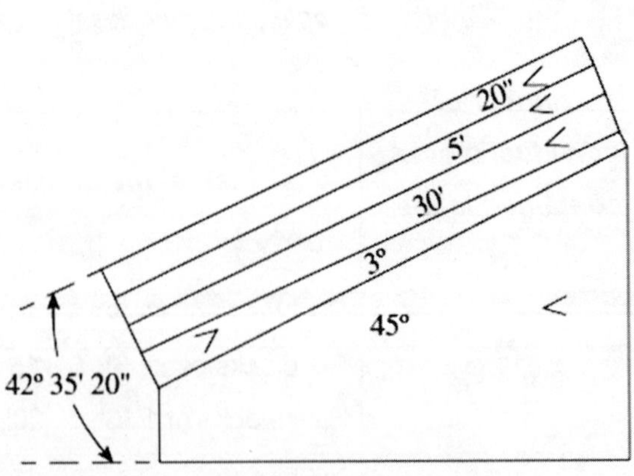


*Figure 4.12 Calibration of angle*

Let's take an example: to create an angle of 42°35′20" using a 16-gauge set, we start by subtracting a 3° block from a 45° block to get 42°. Then, combining a 30' gauge with a 5' gauge gives us 35'. Finally, we use a 20" gauge. All gauges are added except for the 3° gauge, which is reversed and wrung with the others for alignment on a surface plate. Calibrating angle gauge blocks is relatively simpler compared to slip gauges because angles are self-proving portions of a circle. For instance, three equal portions of 90° must equal 30° each. This breakdown system allows for the creation of masters of angle measurement, with each combination proven by the same method. Additionally, the accuracy of angle gauges is less sensitive to temperature changes compared to slip gauges. Therefore, a gauge block manufactured at one temperature will retain the same angle at a different temperature, provided the readings are taken after stabilization and the entire gauge is exposed to the same temperature.

Angle gauges find various uses in precision measurement and quality control processes:

- Direct Measurement of Die Insert Angles: Angle gauges are directly employed to measure the angle in a die insert. The insert is positioned against an illuminated glass surface plate or inspection light box. Using a combination of angle gauges, the built-up combination is carefully adjusted and inserted in position so that no white light can be seen between the gauge faces and die faces. The alignment is crucial, with all engraved Vs on the angle gauges in the same line for addition of angles, while those on the other side are subtracted.
- Utilization with Square Plate: Angle gauges are often paired with a square plate to enhance versatility in their application. The square plate typically guarantees 90° angles within a specific tolerance, such as 2 seconds of arc. For instances demanding exceptional accuracy, each corner of the square plate is numbered, and a test certificate accompanies the angle gauge set, detailing the measured angle of each corner. Figure 4.18 illustrates a setup to test the angle of a V-gauge with an included angle of 102°, positioned against an illuminated glass surface plate. Slip gauges may be used to facilitate the testing process.

***Advantages of Angle Gauges:***

1. Angle gauges offer precise measurement of angles, ensuring accuracy in various industrial applications.

2. They can measure a wide range of angles, making them suitable for diverse tasks such as machining, fabrication, and assembly.
3. Angle gauges are typically user-friendly, allowing operators to quickly and efficiently measure angles without extensive training.
4. Compared to more complex angle measurement tools, angle gauges are often more affordable, providing value for money.
5. Many angle gauges are compact and portable, making them convenient for on-site measurements and inspections.
6. Angle gauges can be used in conjunction with other measurement tools and equipment, enhancing their versatility and functionality.

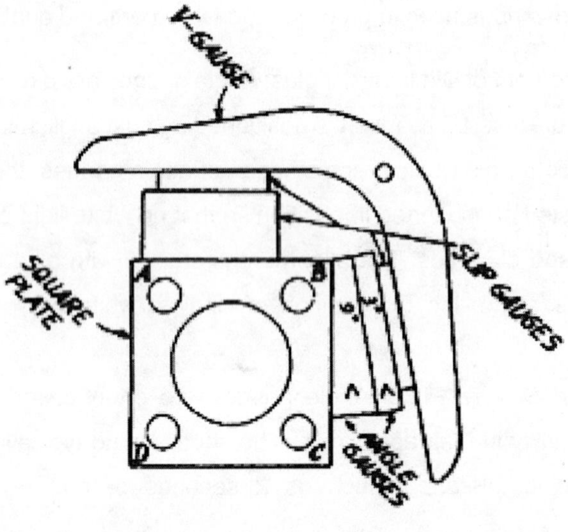


*Figure 4.13 Setup used for checking a V-gauge with an included angle of 102°*

***Disadvantages of Angle Gauges***

1. Some angle gauges may have a limited range of measurement, restricting their applicability to certain tasks.
2. Changes in temperature, humidity, or vibration can affect the accuracy of angle gauges, requiring careful calibration and handling.
3. Achieving extremely precise measurements may require complex setups or additional equipment, increasing the complexity of using angle gauges.

4. Certain types of angle gauges, especially those with delicate components or fine calibration, may be prone to damage if mishandled or subjected to rough conditions.
5. Regular calibration is necessary to maintain the accuracy of angle gauges, which can be time-consuming and may incur additional costs.

**Applications of Angle Gauges**

1. Angle gauges are essential for setting up machines, checking angles on machined components, and ensuring precise fabrication.
2. They are used in assembly operations to align parts and components at specific angles, ensuring proper fit and functionality.
3. Angle gauges play a critical role in quality control processes by verifying the accuracy of angles on manufactured parts and assemblies.
4. In welding and metalworking industries, angle gauges are used to measure and set angles for cutting, welding, and forming metal components.
5. Angle gauges are valuable tools for carpenters and woodworkers for measuring and cutting angles accurately in furniture making, cabinetry, and construction.
6. They find applications in civil engineering and construction projects for measuring angles in structural components, formwork, and concrete placements.
7. Angle gauges are utilized in automotive and aerospace industries for setting angles in vehicle components, engine parts, and aircraft structures.

## 4.6 SCREW THREAD MEASUREMENT

Screw thread gauging holds significant importance in industrial metrology, particularly due to the complexity involved compared to measurements of straightforward geometric features like length and diameter. When measuring screw threads, we must consider a range of interrelated geometric aspects such as pitch diameter, lead, helix, and flank angle, among others. These parameters collectively define the characteristics and functionality of the thread. To streamline the inspection process, it's essential to understand screw thread terminology and methods for measuring thread elements accurately. This knowledge not only ensures precision in manufacturing but also facilitates efficiency in quality control procedures. By mastering thread gauging techniques, industrial operations can maintain high standards of product integrity and performance.

Screw threads have a twofold purpose in engineering applications. Firstly, they aid in transmitting power and motion, enabling mechanisms to operate efficiently. Secondly, they play a crucial role in securely fastening two components together, often utilizing nuts, bolts, and studs to achieve this connection. The variety of screw threads is extensive, encompassing variations in form such as included angle, head angle, and helix angle, among others. This wide range of thread configurations allows engineers to choose a suitable option for specific requirements, ensuring optimal performance in various contexts.

When it comes to screw threads, they are broadly classified into two main types: external threads and internal threads. External threads are found outside a cylindrical or conical surface, while internal threads are within a hole or bore. Understanding these distinctions is fundamental in selecting the appropriate threading solution for a given application.

**Types of Screw Threads**

a) **V-screw Thread**: It is also known as V-threads, features a V-shaped profile with symmetrical flanks meeting at a 60-degree angle. They efficiently transmit power and motion while minimizing friction and providing self-locking properties. Widely used in fasteners, machinery, and precision instruments, V-threads offer reliability and ease of use across diverse applications.

b) **American National Thread:** It is also known as the Unified Thread Standard (UTS), encompasses both external (bolts and screws) and internal (nuts and tapped holes) threads. UTS is a comprehensive system encompassing both external threads, found in bolts and screws, and internal threads, utilized in nuts and tapped holes. Widely adopted in the United States and Canada for inch-based threads, UTS provides a standardized framework for thread design and interchangeability across various industries. Its versatility and widespread usage make it a cornerstone of engineering and manufacturing in North America.

c) **Metric Thread:** Metric threads form the backbone of thread standards worldwide, rooted in the International System of Units (SI). Embraced by nations adhering to the metric system, these threads offer a seamless and universal approach to thread measurement and specification. Available in coarse and fine pitch variations, metric threads cater to a broad spectrum of applications, ranging from automotive and aerospace to machinery and consumer products.

d) **Square Thread:** Renowned for their efficiency in power transmission, square threads feature a square cross-section that maximizes contact area and minimizes frictional losses. Ideal for applications where axial movement of heavy loads is paramount, square threads deliver exceptional strength and durability. Their precise geometry and high mechanical efficiency make them indispensable in machinery requiring smooth and reliable operation, from lifting systems to precision instruments.

e) **Acme Thread:** Acme threads boast a distinctive trapezoidal profile, engineered to excel in applications demanding robustness and precision. Widely employed in power screws and machinery requiring efficient load transmission and high accuracy, Acme threads ensure reliable performance under heavy loads and harsh operating conditions. Their rugged design and superior mechanical properties make them indispensable in diverse industrial settings.

f) **Whitworth Thread:** In the 19th century, Whitworth threads represented a foundational thread standard that played a pivotal role in industrialization and standardization. Although less prevalent in modern applications, Whitworth threads continue to endure in legacy equipment and historical contexts, particularly in the United Kingdom and its former colonies. Their enduring legacy is a testament to their contribution to the evolution of thread engineering and manufacturing practices.

g) **Knuckle Thread:** It feature a rounded profile, designed for smooth operation and resistance to damage. They are used in applications where durability and ease of use are essential, such as in electrical fittings. Knuckle threads provide a secure fastening while minimizing the risk of thread damage or stripping. Their rounded shape also promotes smoother engagement and disengagement, making them ideal for frequent assembly and disassembly tasks.

h) **Buttress Thread:** Characterized by one flank perpendicular to the thread axis and the other flank angled, buttress threads excel in applications requiring unidirectional load support and resistance to axial forces. Commonly found in mechanisms such as jackscrews and vices, buttress threads ensure stable and secure performance under extreme loading conditions. Their unique design provides enhanced strength and rigidity, making them ideal for applications where safety and reliability are paramount.

**Terminologies of Screw Thread**

1) ***External Thread:*** An external thread is the screw thread formed on the outer surface of a workpiece, commonly seen in bolts and studs. Conversely, an internal thread is created within the inner surface of a workpiece, as seen in the thread of a nut.

2) ***Axial Thread:*** The pitch line, or axis of a thread, is an imaginary line that passes through the screw's center longitudinally. The thread flanks are extended until they

meet, making an apex or vertex, creating the fundamental triangle (an imaginary shape).

3) ***Angle of Thread:*** The angle of a thread, also known as the included angle, is the angle between the flanks of a thread measured in the axial plane. The flank angle is the angle formed between a flank of the thread and a line perpendicular to the thread axis passing through the vertex of the fundamental triangle

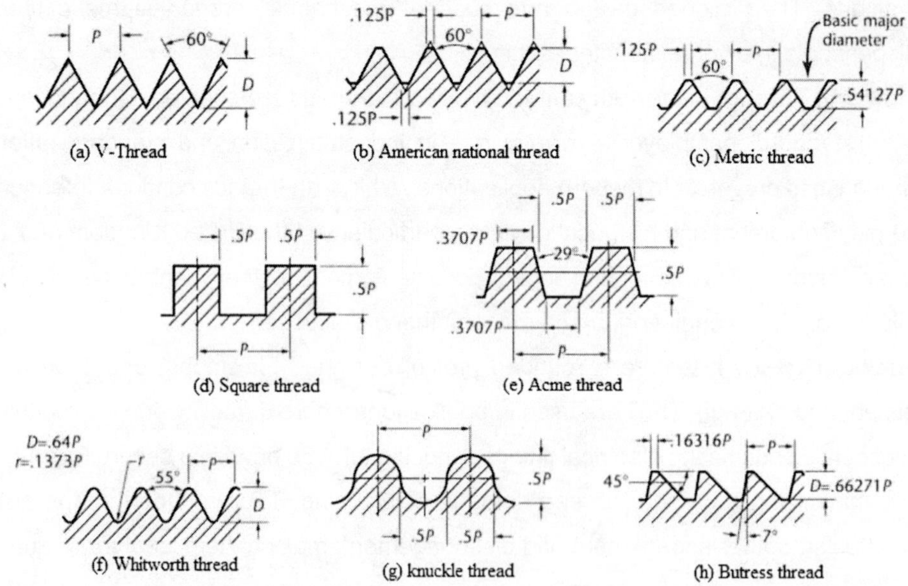


*Figure 4.14 Types of screw threads*

4) ***Pitch Line:*** The axis of a thread, also known as the pitch line, is an imaginary line that runs longitudinally through the center of the screw.
5) ***Fundamental triangle:*** The fundamental triangle is an imaginary shape formed when the thread flanks are extended until they meet, resulting in an apex or vertex.
6) ***Angle of Thread:*** The angle of a thread, also referred to as the included angle, is the angle measured between the thread flanks in the axial plane.
7) ***Flank Angle:*** The flank angle is the angle formed between a flank of the thread and a line perpendicular to the thread axis passing through the vertex of the fundamental triangle.
8) ***Pitch:*** The pitch refers to the distance between two corresponding points on adjacent threads, measured along the axis of the thread.

9) ***Lead:*** Lead indicates the axial distance covered by the screw during one complete revolution around its axis.
10) ***Lead angle:*** The lead angle represents the angle formed by the helix of the thread at the pitch line with the plane perpendicular to the axis.
11) ***Helix angle:*** The helix angle is the angle formed by the helix of the thread at the pitch line with the axis. This angle is measured in an axial plane.
12) ***Major diameter:*** In external threads, the major diameter is the diameter of the major cylinder that touches the crests of the thread. For internal threads, it's the diameter of the cylinder touching the root of the threads.
13) ***Minor diameter:*** For external threads, the minor diameter is the diameter of the minor cylinder that touches the roots of the thread. For internal threads, it's the diameter of the cylinder touching the crests of the threads, also known as the root diameter.
14) ***Addendum:*** Addendum is the radial distance between the major diameter and the pitch line for external threads. For internal threads, it's the radial distance between the minor diameter and the pitch line.
15) ***Dedendum:*** Dedendum is the radial distance between the minor diameter and the pitch line for external threads. For internal threads, it's the radial distance between the major diameter and the pitch line.
16) ***Effective diameter or pitch diameter:*** The effective diameter, or pitch diameter, is the diameter of the pitch cylinder intersecting the thread flanks to ensure equal widths of threads and spaces between them, determining the fit quality between screw and nut.
17) ***Single-start thread:*** In a single-start thread, the lead equals the pitch, meaning the screw moves an axial distance equal to the pitch during one complete revolution.
18) ***Multiple-start thread:*** The lead is a multiple of the pitch in a multiple-start thread. For example, a double-start thread moves twice the pitch distance for one complete revolution.

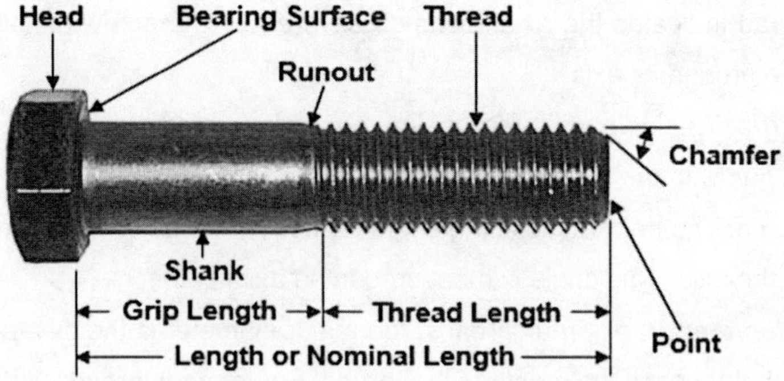


*Figure 4.15 Nomenclature of Screw Thread*

1: Angular pitch
2: Pitch
3: Major diameter
4: Pitch diameter
5: Minor diameter
6: Pitch line
7: Apex
8: Root
9: Crest
10: Addendum
11: Dedendum
12: Depth of thread

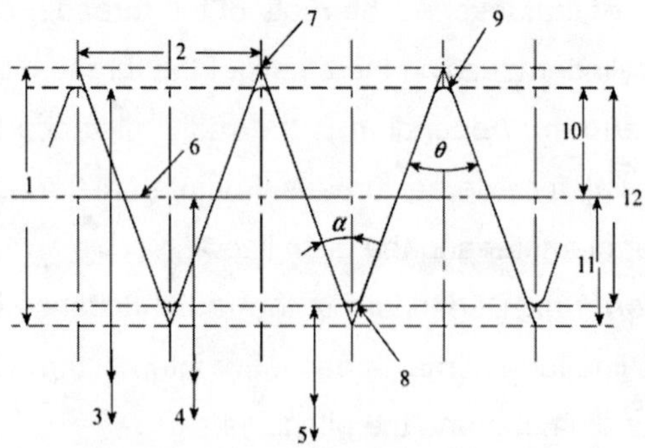

*Figure 4.16 Screw Thread Terminologies*

### 4.6.1 ISO GRADE- SCREW THREAD

The International Organization for Standardization (ISO) provides a comprehensive framework of standards governing general-purpose metric screw threads, known as the "M" series threads, with their design principles meticulously outlined in ISO 68-1. These standards are integral to ensuring uniformity and compatibility across various industries and applications. Two fundamental parameters are central to the identification and classification of ISO metric threads: the major diameter (D) and the pitch (P). These specifications are pivotal in determining thread fit, engagement, and functionality. The ISO Metric Screw Thread system is widely adopted due to its simplicity and versatility, facilitating seamless integration across diverse manufacturing processes. For instance, designations such as M6x1 signify a major diameter of 6 mm and a pitch of 1 mm. This standardized nomenclature streamlines communication and ensures precision in thread selection and application.

ISO standards play a pivotal role in ensuring the reliability and uniformity of screw threads across various industries. Here are some key ISO standards related to metric screw threads:

1. **ISO 68-1:** This standard outlines the basic profile for ISO general-purpose metric screw threads, providing fundamental design principles for thread geometry and dimensions.
2. **ISO 261:** It offers a general plan for ISO general-purpose metric screw threads, laying out the essential parameters and specifications for thread designation and classification.
3. **ISO 262:** This standard specifies selected sizes for screws, bolts, and nuts for ISO general-purpose metric screw threads, facilitating standardized sizing and interchangeability.
4. **ISO 724:** It defines basic dimensions for ISO general-purpose metric screw threads, establishing the foundational measurements essential for thread manufacturing and application.
5. **ISO 956-3**: This standard focuses on tolerances for ISO general-purpose metric screw threads, particularly deviations for constructional screw threads, ensuring consistency and quality in thread production.
6. **ISO 1502:** This standard addresses gauges and gauging for ISO general-purpose metric screw threads, providing definitions and symbols essential for accurate measurement and inspection.

***Fits of threads***

ISO threads adhere to a tolerance grade system, essential for specifying permissible variations in thread dimensions. This system determines the fit between male (external) and female (internal) threads, influencing the ease of assembly and disassembly, as well as the load-bearing capacity of the connection. The tolerance grade consists of a two-part code: a capital letter representing the external thread (e.g., E or G) and a lowercase letter indicating the internal thread (e.g., e, f, g, or h), followed by a number denoting the tolerance class. Lower numbers signify tighter tolerances, meaning smaller allowable variations in dimensions, while higher numbers represent looser tolerances, allowing for larger variations. These tolerance grades, in combination with the specified tolerance class, determine the type of fit between threads. There are three main types:

1. ***Clearance Fit:*** Characterized by a loose fit, enabling easy assembly and disassembly. Commonly employed in applications where threads do not bear significant loads, such as cover screws or access panels.
2. ***Interference Fit:*** Exhibiting a tight fit, resulting in a strong connection between threads. Ideal for applications requiring high load transmission, such as in engines or gearboxes.
3. ***Medium Fit:*** Falling between clearance and interference fits, this type is versatile and widely used across various applications where a balance between ease of assembly and load-bearing capacity is desired.

*Table 4.6. Different fit and tolerance grade of screw threads*

| Tolerance Grade | Fit | Application |
|---|---|---|
| 6g/6H | Medium | General purpose applications |
| 6g/5H | Medium-close | Applications requiring some preload |
| 6H/4g | Close | Applications requiring accurate positioning |
| 2H/2g | Very close | High-precision applications |

### 4.6.2 ERRORS IN THREADS

Errors in threads can stem from various sources, spanning initial manufacturing inconsistencies to operational wear and tear. A comprehensive understanding of these errors is imperative for upholding the integrity and functionality of threaded connections. Below is a detailed breakdown of common thread errors:

1. ***Pitch Error:*** This error arises from deviations in the distance between adjacent threads from the ideal pitch. Such deviations can lead to improper engagement between mating threads, significantly impacting the fit and functionality of the connection, potentially compromising its integrity.
2. ***Lead Error:*** Lead errors manifest as inconsistencies in the axial advancement of the thread per revolution. These variations result in uneven movement of mating components, predisposing to potential misalignment issues. Consequently, the reliability and efficiency of the threaded connection may be compromised.
3. ***Form Error:*** Form errors present as irregularities in the contour or shape of the thread profile. Whether due to excessive or insufficient material in specific areas, these

irregularities impede proper mating between threads and escalate stress concentrations. Rectifying form errors is pivotal to preserving the structural integrity of the threaded connection.

4. ***Thread Angle Error:*** Variations in the angle of the thread profile from the specified standard contribute to thread angle errors. Such deviations can lead to misalignment during assembly or operation, potentially causing binding or stripping of threads. Ensuring adherence to specified thread angles is critical to avert these detrimental effects.
5. ***Thread Depth Error:*** Thread depth errors denote differences in the depth of the thread profile from the intended specification. These discrepancies directly impact the strength and load-bearing capacity of the threaded connection. Achieving uniform thread depth is imperative to ensure the structural integrity and reliability of the connection.
6. ***Thread Runout:*** Thread runout refers to the eccentricity or wobbling of the thread axis relative to the intended axis. This phenomenon results in uneven distribution of loads and heightened wear on mating components. Minimizing thread runout is indispensable to sustain the longevity and efficiency of the threaded connection.
7. **Thread Misalignment:** Thread misalignment occurs when an offset or angular deviation occurs between mating threads. Mitigating thread misalignment is crucial to ensuring the smooth assembly and operation of threaded components.

### 4.6.3 PITCH ERRORS

Pitch errors in threads arise when the distance between adjacent threads deviates from the intended pitch. Such variations can greatly affect the interaction between mating threads, potentially resulting in an inadequate fit and compromised connection functionality. Rectifying pitch errors is essential to maintain the integrity and operational efficiency of threaded components. The pitch errors are classified into

1. Progressive Error
2. Periodic Error
3. Drunken Error
4. Irregular Error

**Progressive Error:** This type of error induces a gradual increase or decrease in the spacing between threads along the length of the thread. Typically attributed to wear on the cutting tool or machine alignment issues during manufacturing, it can adversely affect the precision and consistency of threaded components.

**Periodic Error:** Characterized by a repetitive pattern of variations in thread spacing, this error can be attributed to factors such as machine tool vibrations or inconsistencies in material properties. The periodic nature of this error necessitates careful monitoring and adjustment to ensure uniformity in threaded connections.

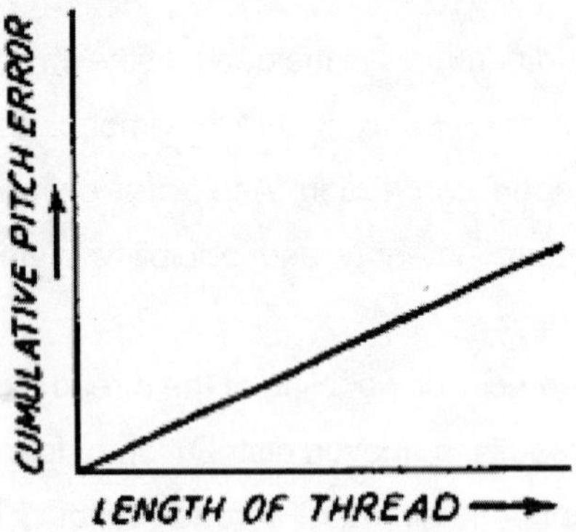


Figure 4.17

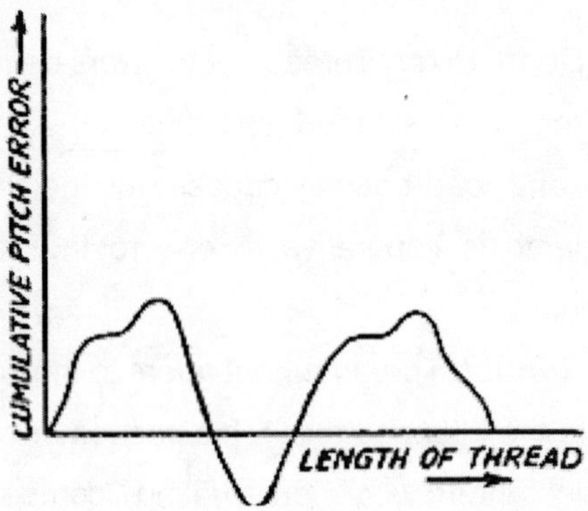


Figure 4.18

**Drunken Error:** Drunken error manifests as a significant and irregular deviation in pitch at a specific location along the thread, resembling a localized "bump" or "dip" in the thread pattern. This anomaly often results from sudden machine malfunctions or interruptions during the machining process, highlighting the importance of maintaining operational stability and consistency.

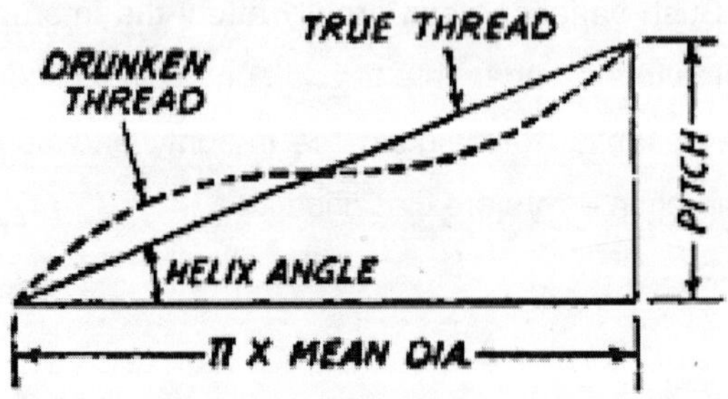


*Figure 4.19*

**Irregular Error:** This category encompasses random or unpredictable variations in pitch that do not fit into the aforementioned classifications. Such errors may stem from a combination of factors or unknown causes, underscoring the complexity of mitigating and addressing irregularities in threaded components. Vigilance and thorough analysis are essential in managing irregular errors to uphold the quality and reliability of threaded connections.

### 4.6.4 MEASUREMENT OF MAJOR DIAMETER

The major diameter of a thread refers to the diameter of the hypothetical coaxial cylinder that touches the crest of an external thread or the root of an internal thread. Conversely, the minor diameter is the diameter of an imaginary cylinder that touches the roots of an external thread or the crests of an internal thread. These diameters play a fundamental role in defining the size and geometry of threaded components, influencing their fit, function, and compatibility with mating parts. Instruments utilized for determining the major diameter include:

1. Ordinary Micrometre
2. Bench Micrometre

**Ordinary Micrometre**

A micrometre is a precision instrument utilized for measuring the exact dimensions of solid objects, including length, diameter, and thickness. It operates by employing a calibrated screw mechanism, ensuring accurate and reliable measurements. Commonly employed in mechanical engineering, machining, and various mechanical trades, micrometres are indispensable tools for ensuring precise manufacturing processes. Typically resembling callipers in structure, micrometres feature a spindle and anvil between which the object to be measured is placed. The spindle is adjusted by turning a thimble or ratchet knob until it lightly touches the object along with the anvil. This enables the user to ascertain the precise dimensions of the object with high accuracy, making micrometres indispensable tools in industries where precision is paramount.

The micrometre relies on a screw with a very fine and constant thread pitch, typically around 0.5 millimetres (mm) per revolution. This screw is connected to a thimble, a finely graduated rotating sleeve. The thimble's circumference is divided into 50 equal parts. Each division on the thimble represents a movement of the screw by 0.5 mm / 50 = 0.01 mm.

The anvil and spindle are the two key components for measurement. The screw thread is placed between the anvil and the spindle tip. By rotating the thimble, the screw drives the spindle forward until it gently contacts the screw thread. A ratchet mechanism ensures consistent pressure during contact.

Reading the measurement involves two scales:

- Sleeve Scale: This fixed scale etched on the body of the micrometre displays whole millimetres.
- Thimble Scale: As mentioned earlier, this rotating sleeve has 50 divisions, each representing 0.01 mm.

For example, if the sleeve scale aligns with the "5" mm mark and you count 23 divisions on the thimble scale, the measured diameter is 5 mm + (23 x 0.01 mm) = 5.23 mm.

**Bench Micrometre**

The bench micrometre is a specialized instrument utilized for highly accurate measurements of various dimensions, including the outer diameter of screw threads. Unlike handheld micrometres, the bench micrometre is securely mounted on a stable workbench or table, providing a rigid and vibration-free platform for precise measurements. In measuring the outer diameter of a screw thread, the screw thread sample is carefully positioned between the spindle and anvil of the bench micrometre. The spindle, controlled by a calibrated screw mechanism, is gradually adjusted until it lightly contacts the crest of the screw thread. This adjustment is typically facilitated by a precision micrometre head, allowing for extremely fine adjustments to ensure accurate measurement.

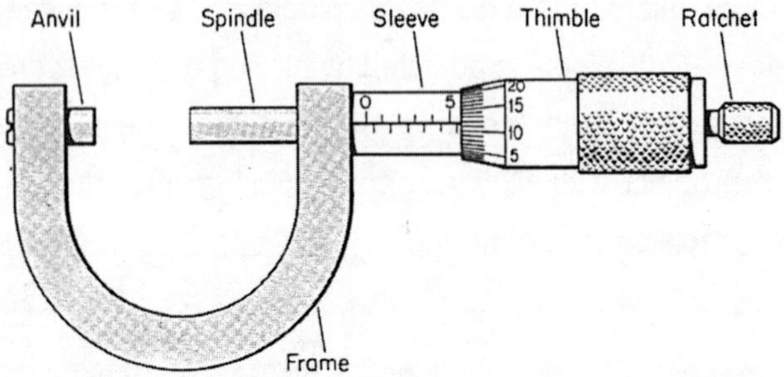


*Figure 4.20 Ordinary Micrometre*

The measurement is then read directly from the micrometre scale, which may be graduated in increments as small as 0.001 millimetres (mm) or 0.0001 inches (in), depending on the level of precision required. For example, if the micrometre scale reads 5.250 mm, it indicates that the outer diameter of the screw thread measures precisely 5.250 mm.

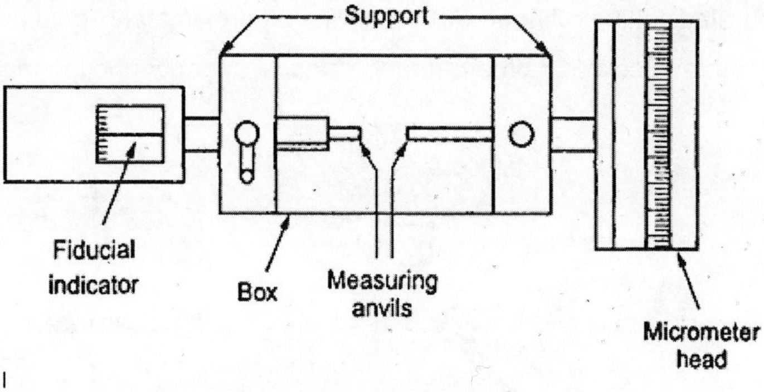


*Figure 4.21 Bench Micrometre*

Unlike the ordinary micrometre, the bench micrometre is fixed to a stable workbench or table, ensuring precise measurements with minimal vibration. Its specialized design allows for higher precision, particularly for small dimensions or tight tolerances. While both micrometres cover a wide range of measurements, the bench micrometre is preferred for larger and more complex components. It's commonly utilized in specialized manufacturing and quality control settings, whereas the handheld micrometre offers versatility for various applications, including fieldwork and general workshop tasks.

The major diameter of screw thread = $S\pm (D_2\text{-}D_1)$

The setting cylinder is a reference cylinder with a precisely known diameter (S). It's used to calibrate the micrometre before measuring the screw thread.

**Micrometre Readings:**

$R_1$: This is the micrometre reading when the two jaws of the micrometre are closed over the setting cylinder.

$R_2$: This is the micrometre reading when the two jaws of the micrometre are closed over the screw thread.

**Measurement of the Major Diameter of Internal threads**

The thread comparator utilizes a ball-ended stylus with a radius smaller than the root radius of the thread being measured. In this setup, a stylus is affixed to a floating head. This floating head maintains constant contact with the plunger of a dial indicator, thanks to the pressure exerted by a spring confined within the floating gauge. A wide range of styli are available to accommodate various thread forms and dimensions, ensuring versatility in measurement capabilities.

A calibrated setting cylinder with a diameter approximately equal to the major diameter of the internal thread serves as the reference standard for conducting measurements.

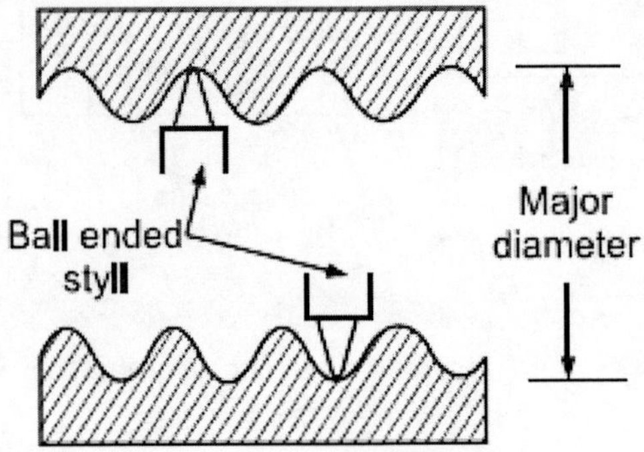


*Figure 4.22 Measurement of Major Diameter of Internal Thread*

Initially, the instrument is set on this setting cylinder, and the corresponding reading of the dial indicator is recorded. Subsequently, the floating head gauge mounted in the comparator is retracted to bring the tips of the stylus into contact with the root of the screw thread under the pressure of the spring. The reading of the dial indicator in this configuration is noted.

D represents the diameter of the cylindrical reference standard or calibrated setting cylinder, $R_1$ denotes the reading of the dial indicator on the setting cylinder, and $R_2$ signifies the reading of the dial indicator on the screw thread,

Then, the major diameter of the internal thread can be determined as follows:

**Major diameter of internal thread=$D+(R_2-R_1)$**

### 4.6.5 MEASUREMENT OF MINOR DIAMETER

The preferred method for measuring the minor diameter involves utilizing a floating carriage micrometre. This specialized equipment consists of a carriage equipped with a micrometre featuring a fixed spindle on one side and a movable spindle with its own micrometre on the opposite side. The carriage is designed to move smoothly along a finely ground 'V' guideway or an anti-friction guideway, facilitating movement parallel to the axis of the plug gauge mounted between centres.

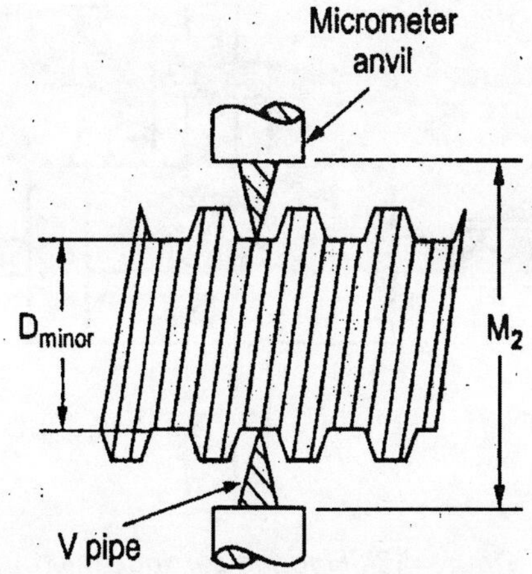


*Figure 4.23 Measurement of Minor Diameter*

The micrometre is equipped with a non-rotary spindle, offering a least count of either 0.001 or 0.002 millimetres. This level of precision makes the instrument highly beneficial for manufacturers of thread plug gauges, as well as for gauge calibration laboratories accredited under NABL and standard rooms conducting in-house gauge calibration activities.

Measurement of the minor diameter is conducted through a comparative process employing small V-pieces that make contact with the root of the threads. These V-pieces are carefully selected to ensure that their included angle is smaller than the angle of the thread. Positioned on either side of the screw, with their bases against the micrometre faces, the V-pieces facilitate accurate measurement. Initially, a reading is taken using a setting cylinder corresponding to the dimension being measured. Subsequently, the threaded workpiece is mounted between the centres, and a second reading is obtained. The difference between these two readings directly indicates the error in the minor diameter.

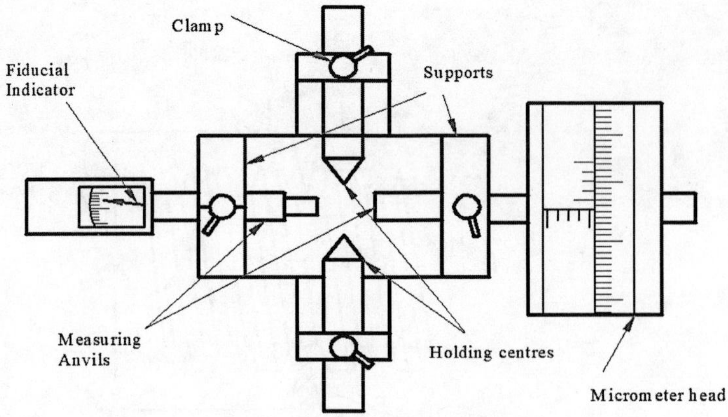


*Figure 4.24 Floating carriage micrometre*

The micrometre operates by converting rotary motion into precise linear displacement through the use of a finely threaded screw with a constant pitch. Its key components include:

- Screw: A finely threaded screw rotated by the thimble.
- Thimble: A rotatable sleeve with a finely etched scale, facilitating movement of the screw and attached spindle.
- Spindle: The movable plunger that makes contact with the object being measured.
- Anvil: The fixed jaw opposite the spindle, between which the object being measured is placed.
- Sleeve Scale: A fixed scale etched on the micrometre's body displaying whole millimetres.
- Thimble Scale: A rotating sleeve with a scale typically divided into 50 equal parts, each division representing a movement of the screw by the screw pitch (often 0.01 mm).

During the measurement procedure, the object is carefully positioned between the anvil and the spindle tip of the micrometre. Subsequently, the thimble is rotated to drive the spindle forward until it lightly contacts the object, ensuring consistent pressure throughout the measurement process. The measurement is then determined by reading two scales: the sleeve scale and the thimble scale. Firstly, the graduation line on the sleeve scale is noted, aligned with the edge of the thimble, providing the whole millimetre value. Secondly, the number of divisions on the thimble scale past the reference point on the micrometre body is counted, representing hundredths of a millimetre. Finally, the final measured diameter is obtained by summing the readings from the sleeve scale and the value from the thimble scale. This comprehensive approach ensures accurate and precise measurements of the object's diameter using the micrometre.

**Measurement of the Minor Diameter of Internal threads**

To measure the minor diameter of a thread, two commonly employed methods are:

(i) Taper Parallels: This method involves using taper parallels, which are precision machined blocks with gradually increasing thickness. By inserting the taper parallels between the thread flanks and measuring the gap, the minor diameter can be determined.

(ii) Rollers and Slip Gauges: In this method, rollers are placed between the thread flanks, and slip gauges (precision ground blocks) are used to measure the distance between the rollers. This distance corresponds to the minor diameter of the thread.

**Taper Parallels**

When the diameter of the screw is less than 200 mm, taper parallels are commonly utilized in combination with a micrometre for measuring the minor diameter of the thread. Taper parallels consist of pairs of wedges with parallel outer edges. These wedges can be adjusted to alter the diameter across their outer edges by sliding them over each other, as illustrated in Fig 4.25. provide a reference to the figure if available]. This adjustment capability allows for precise fitting between the thread flanks, facilitating accurate measurement of the minor diameter when used in conjunction with a micrometre.

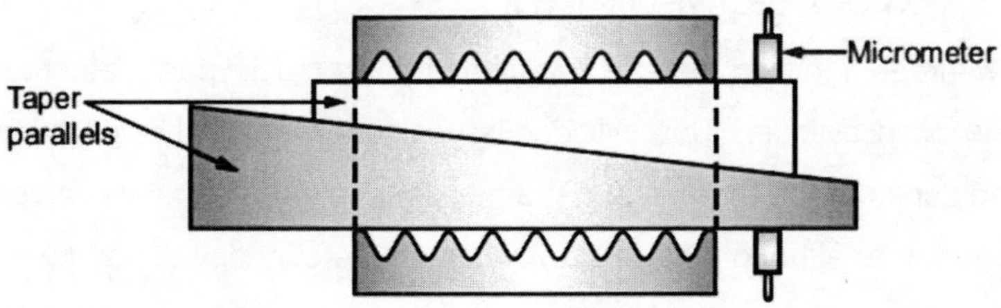


*Figure 4.25 Measurement of the Minor Diameter of Internal threads using Taper Parallels*

Taper parallels are inserted inside the thread and adjusted until they are perfectly aligned with each other to measure the minor diameter of a thread. This adjustment ensures a firm contact is established with the minor diameter of the thread. Once the taper parallels are correctly positioned, the diameter over their outer edges is measured using a micrometre. This measured diameter corresponds to the minor diameter of the thread.

When dealing with large mirror diameters of internal threads, a combination of two rollers with known diameters and a set of slip gauges is employed to measure the minor diameter. The process involves spanning the inner diameter using the rollers and slip gauges. The minor diameter is calculated using the formula:

$$\text{Minor diameter} = d1 + d2 + l$$

Where, d1 and d2 represent the diameters of the rollers,

$l$ denotes the length of the slip gauge set.

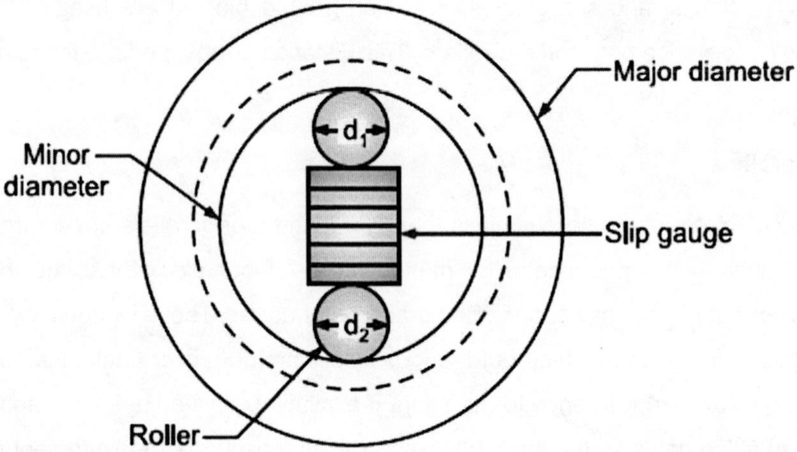


*Figure 4.26 Internal diameter Measurement of screw thread with slip gauges and rollers*

### 4.6.6 MEASUREMENT OF EFFECTIVE DIAMETER

In screw thread analysis, the effective diameter is a crucial parameter representing the diameter of the pitch cylinder. This cylinder is positioned coaxially with the screw's axis, intersecting the flanks of the threads in a manner that ensures equal widths of threads and spaces between them. Although the effective diameter is conceptual and cannot be directly measured, various indirect methods are employed to ascertain its value. Among these methods, the thread measurement by wire technique stands out as a simple and widely utilized approach.

The wire method involves the use of small, hardened steel wires, commonly referred to as best-size wires. These wires are carefully placed within the thread groove, and measurements are taken over them to determine the effective diameter. The technique offers versatility and accuracy, making it a preferred choice in thread measurement applications.

There are three primary variations of the wire method:

1. One-Wire Method: In this approach, a single wire is placed within the thread groove, and measurements are taken over it to calculate the effective diameter.
2. Two-Wire Method: Utilizing two wires placed on opposite sides of the thread groove, this method offers improved accuracy by accounting for potential thread angle variations.
3. Three-Wire Method: Considered the most accurate among the wire methods, the three-wire method involves placing three wires at specific locations within the thread groove. By taking measurements over these wires and applying a mathematical formula, the effective diameter can be precisely determined.

**Two-Wire Method**

In this method, two steel wires with the same diameter are positioned on opposite sides of a screw, as illustrated in Fig 4.27. The distance between the wires (M) is measured using a micrometre. Then, the effective diameter is calculated using the formula De = T + P, where T is the dimension beneath the wires and P is the correction factor.

$T = M - 2d$

where $d$ is the diameter of the best-size wire.

To establish the relationships between two wires of equal size and a screw thread, refer to the figure. The wires must be chosen in such a way that they touch the screw thread on the pitch line. It is important to note that the equations mentioned earlier hold true only if this prerequisite is fulfilled.

Accordingly, from triangle OFD, OF $= \frac{d}{2}$ cosec (x/2)

FA $= \frac{d}{2}$ cosec (x/2) $- \frac{d}{2} = \frac{d}{2}$ [cosec(x/2) − 1

FG = GC cot (x/2) $= \frac{p}{2}$ cot (x/2) (because BC = pitch/2 and

GC = pitch/4)

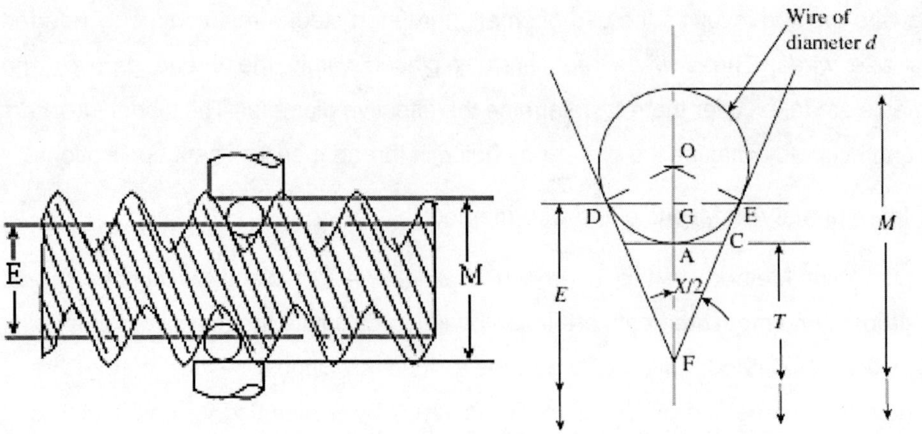


*Figure 4.27 Measurement in Two-Wire Method*

Therefore, AG = FG − FA = $\frac{p}{2}$ cot (x/2) – $\frac{d[\text{cosec}(x/2) - 1}{2}$

As AG accounts for the correction factor on only one side of the screw, we need to multiply it by 2 on the opposite flank to get the total correction factor.

P = 2 AG = $\frac{p}{2}$ cot (x/2) − d[cosec(x/2) − 1]

Although M, the distance over the wires, can be measured using an ordinary micrometre, this method is prone to errors.

Using the best size wire for measuring the effective diameter ensures accuracy by minimizing errors caused by variations in thread form or angle. The best size wire is one that touches the thread flank at the mean diameter line within ±1/5 of the flank length. This choice ensures that the wire accurately represents the true diameter of the thread, providing reliable measurements. If a wire of any diameter is used that touches the true flank of the thread, the obtained values may differ from those obtained with the best size wire, especially if there are errors in the thread angle or form.

In triangle OAB, sin (AOB) = AB/OB

that is, sin (90 − *x*/2) = AB/OB

or, OB = $\frac{AB}{\sin(90 - x/2)} = \frac{AB}{\cos(x/2)}$ = AB sec (*x*/2)

Diameter of the best-size wire (d) = 2(OB) = 2(AB) sec (*x*/2)= (*p*/2) sec (*x*/2).

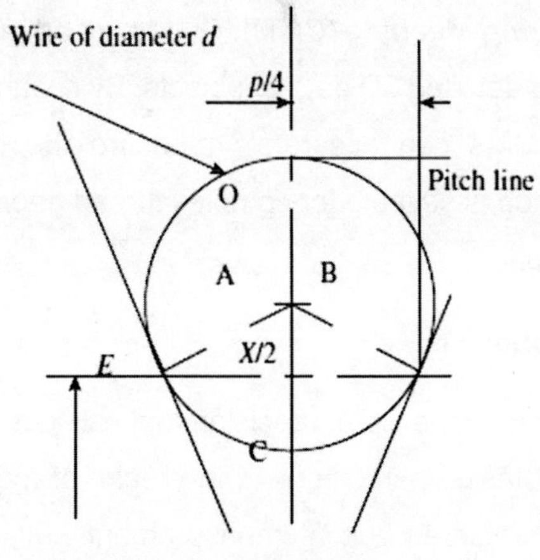


*Figure 4.28 Best wire size*

### 4.6.7 PITCH MEASUREMENT

The measurement of pitch in threads refers to determining the distance between adjacent threads along the axial direction. Pitch can be measured using various methods, depending on the type of thread and the equipment available.

1. ***Pitch Gauge:*** A pitch gauge typically consists of a set of blades or pins, each marked with a specific thread pitch. Users select the blade or pin that matches the thread they want to measure. The pitch can be read directly from the gauge by aligning the gauge with the threads and finding the best fit.
2. ***Thread Micrometre:*** This specialized tool is designed to measure the pitch diameter of threads. It features anvils or contact points that are precisely shaped to fit into the thread grooves. The pitch diameter can be determined by measuring the distance between these contact points. Thread micrometres are suitable for both internal and external threads.
3. ***Thread Wires***: Thread wires are thin, precision wires used in conjunction with a micrometre or caliper to measure the pitch diameter of threads. The wires are wrapped around the thread, and the distance between their contact points is measured using the measuring instrument. This method is highly accurate and commonly used in manufacturing settings.
4. ***Optical Comparator:*** An optical comparator is a device that projects a magnified image of the thread profile onto a screen. The pitch can be determined visually by comparing the thread profile against a calibrated scale. Some optical comparators come equipped with specialized features for measuring thread pitch accurately.

5. ***Coordinate Measuring Machine (CMM):*** CMMs are advanced metrology instruments capable of capturing detailed 3D data of objects. By scanning the thread profile with a probing system, CMMs can accurately measure the pitch of threads with high precision. This method is suitable for complex thread geometries and stringent quality control requirements.

### Tool Makers Microscope

A Tool Maker's Microscope is a precision optical instrument designed for highly accurate measurement tasks, particularly in the realm of metrology and manufacturing. Specifically tailored for screw pitch measurement, this microscope incorporates specialized features and capabilities to ensure precise analysis and assessment of screw threads.The optical head, comprising the lens system responsible for image magnification, is securely affixed to the supporting column via a clamping screw, ensuring structural integrity during operation. The supporting column serves as the vertical axis, providing stability and support for both the optical head and the stage. Facilitating lateral movement of the stage, the micrometre screw enables precise scanning of the specimen across the field of view. Complementarily, the micrometre screw for longitudinal movement grants control over the vertical positioning of the stage, facilitating accurate focusing on the specimen. The stage, acting as a flat platform, serves as the surface upon which the specimen is positioned for examination. Finally, the base, situated at the bottom of the microscope, plays a crucial role in providing overall stability to the instrument.

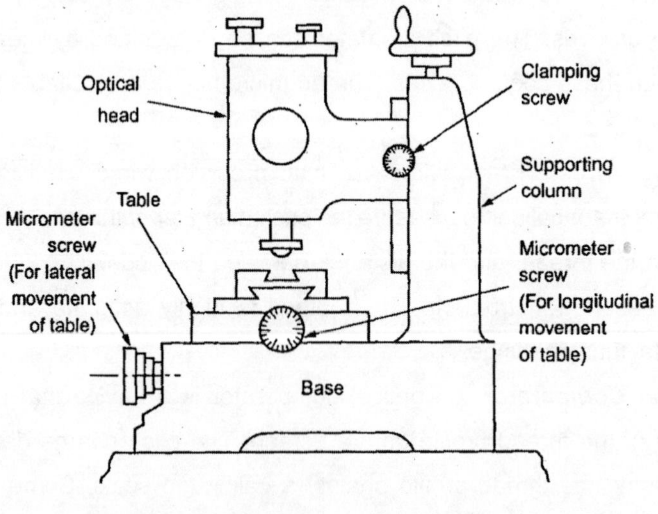


*Figure 4.29 Tool Maker's Microscope*

To utilize a tool maker's microscope effectively, follow a systematic approach. Firstly, place the threaded workpiece onto the microscope stage, ensuring it is securely positioned. Then, align specific points on the thread with the crosshairs of the microscope. Utilize the precision micrometres integrated into the stages to make precise adjustments as needed for measurement. Once aligned, read the measurements displayed on the microscope's micrometres and protractor. These readings provide valuable data regarding lateral and longitudinal movements, as well as angular measurements if necessary. Finally, calculate the differences between parameters such as diameter, pitch, or thread angle to determine the characteristics of the workpiece accurately. Tool maker's microscopes are invaluable tools for inspecting the dimensions and tolerances of precision-engineered components such as machine parts, gears, and electronic circuits, ensuring high standards of quality and accuracy in manufacturing processes.

**Pitch measuring machine**

A Screw Pitch Measuring Machine is a sophisticated instrument used in manufacturing and quality control processes to accurately measure the pitch of threaded components such as screws, bolts, nuts, and gears. Thread pitch, defined as the distance between adjacent threads, is a critical parameter that directly influences the performance and functionality of threaded assemblies. The Screw Pitch Measuring Machine employs advanced measurement techniques and precise instrumentation to ensure reliable and precise determination of thread pitch, contributing to the overall quality and integrity of threaded components in various industries.

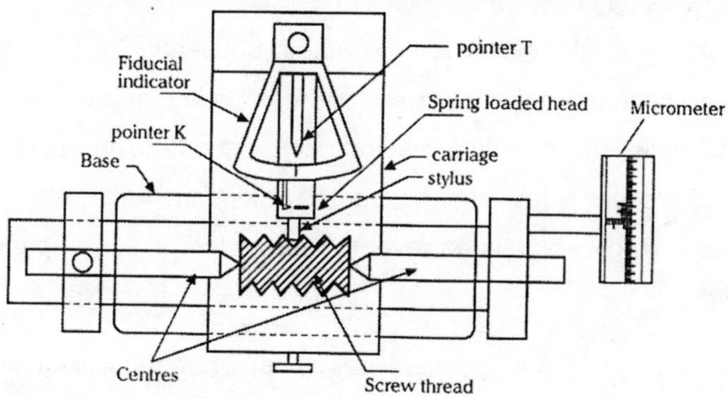


*Figure 4.30 Pitch measuring machine-2D view*

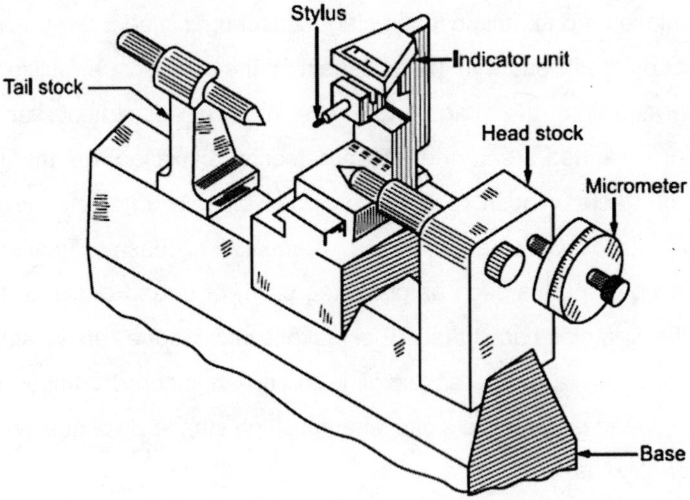


*Figure 4.31 Pitch measuring machine*

*Figure 4.31 Pitch measuring machine*

The working principle of a Screw Pitch Measuring Machine revolves around the precise detection and measurement of thread features to determine the pitch accurately. The operation of the Screw Pitch Measuring Machine is facilitated by its spring-loaded head, which enables the stylus to traverse up the flank of the thread and down into the subsequent space as it moves along the thread. Accurate positioning of the stylus between the two flanks is ensured by maintaining alignment between the pointer T and its index mark when readings are recorded. This alignment guarantees precision in measurement. Upon achieving the correct position, the micrometre reading is noted. Subsequently, the stylus is advanced into the next thread space by rotating the micrometre, allowing for a second reading to be taken. The difference between these two readings corresponds to the pitch of the thread being measured. This process is repeated sequentially along the entire length of the screw thread until comprehensive coverage is achieved, ensuring thorough and precise measurement of the thread pitch.

Screw pitch measuring machines offer numerous advantages in precision measurement processes. Their foremost benefit lies in their ability to provide highly accurate measurements of thread pitch, ensuring the quality and integrity of threaded components in manufacturing and quality control settings. Additionally, these machines enhance operational efficiency by facilitating rapid and systematic measurement procedures, thereby optimizing productivity and reducing inspection time. Many modern screw pitch measuring machines feature automation capabilities, minimizing the potential for human error and streamlining the measurement process. Moreover, their versatility enables them to measure a wide range of threaded components, from screws and bolts to nuts and gears, making them invaluable tools across various industries. Furthermore, these machines often come equipped with software for generating comprehensive reports, enabling efficient documentation and traceability of measurement data for quality control purposes. However, despite their numerous advantages, screw pitch measuring machines may present challenges such as high initial costs, complex operating procedures requiring specialized training, susceptibility to damage, limited applicability to certain thread types or components, and the necessity for regular calibration and maintenance to ensure accuracy and reliability.

### 4.6.8 THREAD GAUGE MICROMETRE

A thread gauge micrometre, also known as a screw thread micrometre, is a sophisticated measuring instrument employed in industries where precise thread measurements are essential, such as manufacturing, engineering, and quality control. This specialized micrometre is designed to accurately measure various parameters of threaded components, including the pitch of the thread, its average diameter, and the core diameter of

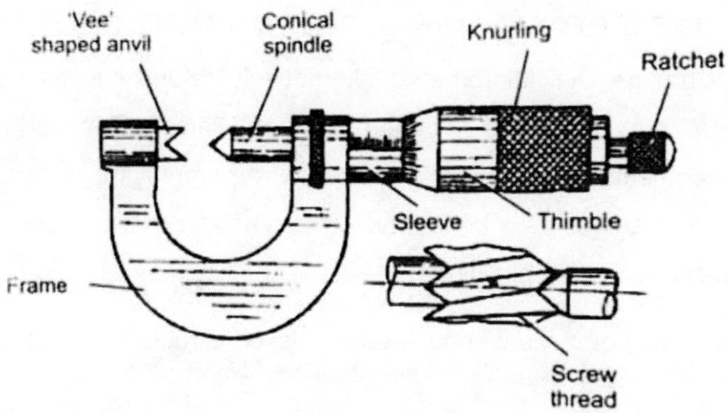


*Figure 4.32 Thread gauge micrometre*

the screw.

The construction of a thread gauge micrometre is meticulously engineered for high precision and reliability. It typically consists of a 60-degree pointed spindle and a double V-shaped swiveling anvil. The spindle and anvil are precisely machined to ensure smooth movement and accurate alignment during measurements. Additionally, the micrometre may feature a finely calibrated thimble and barrel mechanism for precise adjustment and measurement reading. One of the key features of a thread gauge micrometre is its ability to zero effectively. When the micrometre is zeroed, the pitch line of the spindle and the anvil coincide, ensuring that measurements are taken from a consistent reference point. This zeroing capability is crucial for achieving accurate and repeatable measurements across different threaded components.

In practical use, the thread gauge micrometre is applied by placing the threaded component between the spindle and the anvil. The micrometre is then gently closed until the thread comes into contact with both the spindle and the anvil. By rotating the thimble or barrel, the user can precisely measure the pitch diameter, major diameter, and minor diameter of the thread. The data obtained from a thread gauge micrometre is vital for ensuring the quality and compatibility of threaded components in various applications. For example, in manufacturing processes, accurate thread measurements are essential for verifying the conformity of machined parts and ensuring proper assembly of mechanical systems. Similarly, in quality control procedures, thread gauge micrometres play a critical role in inspecting and validating the dimensions and tolerances of threaded components to meet industry standards and specifications.

### 4.6.9 WORKING PRINCIPLE OF FLOATING CARRIAGE DIAL MICROMETRE

The Floating Carriage Dial Micrometre, alternatively referred to as the "Effective Diameter Measuring Micrometre" or the "Floating Carriage Diameter Measuring Machine," operates on the fundamental principle of a micrometre, employing a screw and nut mechanism. Essentially, it serves as a bench micrometre affixed to a carriage machine for precision diameter measurement applications.

The Floating Carriage Diameter Measuring Machine is constructed with several notable features:

Robust Cast Iron Base: Ensures stability and durability for reliable performance.

Dimensional Stability: Designed to maintain precise measurements over time.

Precision Ground Internal Ways: Achieved through meticulous grinding to ensure utmost accuracy.

Micrometre Least Count: Typically set at 0.002 mm with a non-rotary spindle for fine measurement resolution.

The machine comprises three primary units:

1. Base Casting: Houses a pair of meticulously aligned centers where the threaded workpiece is securely mounted, constituting the first carriage.
2. Lower Carriage: Positioned atop the first carriage at a precise 90-degree angle, capable of parallel movement along the thread axis.
3. Upper Carriage: Mounted on the lower carriage, this unit features V-ball slides enabling movement perpendicular to the thread axis.

The upper carriage is equipped with a micrometre thimble featuring a graduated cylindrical scale, enabling measurements with a resolution of up to 0.002 mm. Additionally, a fiducial indicator replaces the fixed anvil on one end, facilitating consistent measurements under uniform pressure. Both the micrometre thimble and fiducial indicator are outfitted with specialized exchangeable anvils tailored to accommodate various thread forms.

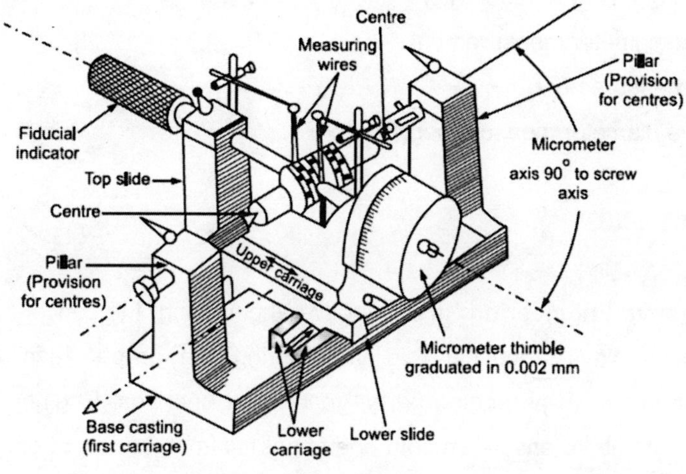


*Figure 4.33 Setup of Floating Carriage Dial Micrometre*

The Floating Carriage Diameter Measuring Machine operates on the following principles:

- Setup: The workpiece with threads to be inspected is securely placed between two centers, supported by pillars on the machine's base.
- Adaptability: The distance between the centers can be adjusted to accommodate different lengths of the threaded workpiece.

- Alignment: After inserting the workpiece, the lower carriage is adjusted to ensure proper alignment and positioning.
- Calibration: The anvils of both the micrometre and the fiducial indicator are finely adjusted to make precise contact with the threaded screw, while the fiducial indicator is set to zero.
- Orientation: With the fiducial indicator and micrometre spindle aligned perpendicular to the line between the centers, measurements are taken from the cylindrical scale on the micrometre thimble.
- Consistency: The fiducial indicator, equipped with a single index line, is designed to maintain a consistent measuring pressure for accurate and repeatable readings.
- Additional Support: For measuring effective diameter, supplementary supports are provided above the micrometre carriage to accommodate wires, V-pieces, etc.

Applications of the Floating Carriage Diameter Measuring Machine include:

(i) Pitch measurement.
(ii) External diameter measurement.
(iii) Internal diameter measurement.
(iv) Angle measurement.
(v) Effective diameter measurement.

## 4.7 APPLICATIONS

- **Automotive Engineering:** In automotive engineering, the concept of limits, fits, and tolerances plays a critical role in ensuring the proper functioning of various components such as engine parts, gears, and bearings. Engineers need to select appropriate fits to ensure smooth operation, minimal wear, and optimal performance of the vehicle.
- **Manufacturing Industry:** In the manufacturing industry, selective assembly techniques are used to achieve interchangeability of parts. By understanding the principles of limits, fits, and tolerances, manufacturers can produce components with precise dimensions, facilitating assembly processes and minimizing production costs.
- **Machinery Design and Construction:** The hole and shaft basis system is widely employed in machinery design and construction to establish standardized fits between

mating parts. Engineers utilize Taylor's Principle to design plug and ring gauges, ensuring the quality and accuracy of manufactured components as per standards such as IS 919-1993 and IS 3477-1973.

- **Quality Control and Inspection:** Multi-gauging and inspection techniques are essential in quality control processes to verify the dimensional accuracy and interchangeability of manufactured parts. By employing advanced measurement tools and gauges, manufacturers can detect deviations from specified tolerances and ensure compliance with design requirements.
- **Precision Instrumentation:** Angular measurement plays a crucial role in precision instrumentation and alignment tasks. Instruments such as universal bevel protractors, sine bars, spirit levels, and angle gauges are utilized to measure and set precise angles, ensuring the alignment and accuracy of mechanical systems and instruments.
- **Screw Thread Manufacturing:** Screw thread measurements are vital in industries such as aerospace, automotive, and machinery manufacturing. Engineers need to adhere to ISO grade and fits standards to produce threads with specified tolerances and ensure compatibility between mating parts. Measurement techniques such as the two-wire method and thread gauge micrometers are employed to accurately measure thread dimensions and detect errors such as pitch errors.
- **Quality Assurance in Aerospace:** In the aerospace industry, where precision is paramount, the application of limits, fits, and tolerances is crucial in ensuring the reliability and safety of aircraft components. Stringent quality assurance measures, including precise screw thread measurements and angular alignments, are employed to meet stringent regulatory requirements and ensure the integrity of aerospace systems.
- **Medical Device Manufacturing:** In the manufacturing of medical devices and equipment, adherence to strict tolerances is essential to ensure the functionality and safety of the products. Limits, fits, and tolerances are carefully considered in the design and production of components such as implants, surgical instruments, and diagnostic equipment to meet regulatory standards and quality requirements.
- **Consumer Electronics:** In the consumer electronics industry, where miniaturization and precision are key, the application of limits, fits, and tolerances is critical in the design and manufacturing of electronic components and assemblies. Precise fits and

tolerances are necessary to ensure the proper functioning and reliability of electronic devices such as smartphones, laptops, and tablets.

- **Energy Sector:** In the energy sector, particularly in the production and maintenance of power generation equipment such as turbines and generators, limits, fits, and tolerances are vital for ensuring efficiency, reliability, and safety. Proper fits and tolerances are maintained during manufacturing and assembly processes to minimize friction, wear, and the risk of failure, thereby optimizing energy production and reducing downtime.

These applications demonstrate the diverse range of industries and sectors where the concepts of limits, fits, and tolerances are applied to ensure quality, precision, and reliability in engineering design, manufacturing, and maintenance processes.

## 4.8 UNIT SUMMARY

This unit covers essential concepts in precision engineering:

- Understanding the significance of limits, fits, and tolerances.
- Selective assembly techniques and interchangeability principles.
- Introduction to hole and shaft basis systems for fit determination.
- Taylor's principle and design considerations for plug and ring gauges.
- Multi-gauging and inspection techniques for quality control.
- Angular measurement instruments and their application.
- ISO grade, thread fits, and measurement methods for screw threads.

## 4.9 EXERCISES

### Multiple Choice Questions

1. What is the purpose of selective assembly in metrology?

   A) To ensure uniformity in manufacturing processes

   B) To achieve specific functional requirements

   C) To minimize production costs

   D) To simplify inspection procedures

2. Which system is commonly used to specify the relationship between holes and shafts in engineering designs?

A) Geometric dimensioning and tolerancing (GD&T)

B) Hole and shaft basis system

C) Threaded fastener system

D) Linear dimensioning system

3. Taylor's Principle in metrology is primarily concerned with:

A) Ensuring precise measurement accuracy

B) Optimizing manufacturing processes

C) Selecting appropriate measuring instruments

D) Maximizing production efficiency

4. What is the purpose of plug and ring gauges in metrology?

A) To measure the dimensions of cylindrical objects

B) To check the roundness of holes and shafts

C) To verify the accuracy of internal and external threads

D) To calibrate angular measurement instruments

5. Which standard provides guidelines for limits, fits, and tolerances in engineering designs?

A) IS 919-1993

B) IS 3477-1973

C) ISO 9001:2015

D) ASTM International

6. Which instrument is commonly used for precise angular measurements in metrology?

A) Vernier caliper

B) Micrometer screw gauge

C) Universal bevel protractor

D) Depth gauge

7. What is the principle behind the operation of a sine bar in metrology?

A) Interference of light waves

B) Magnetic induction

C) Trigonometric relationships

D) Electrostatic attraction

8. Which method is commonly used for measuring pitch errors in screw threads?

A) Two-wire method

B) Direct visual inspection

C) Surface profilometry

D) Ultrasonic testing

9. What is the purpose of a floating carriage dial micrometer in screw thread measurements?

A) To measure the effective diameter of threads

B) To calibrate thread pitch gauges

C) To detect pitch errors

D) To ensure parallelism of thread surfaces

10. Multi gauging and inspection in metrology involve:

A) Using multiple gauges simultaneously for increased accuracy

B) Inspecting multiple dimensions of a part in a single operation

C) Employing multiple inspectors for redundancy

D) Performing gauge R&R studies for process validation

**Answers**

**1. B, 2. B, 3. B, 4. C, 5. A, 6. C, 7. C, 8. A, 9. A, 10. B.**

**Subjective Type Questions**

1) Define the concept of limits, fits, and tolerances in metrology. How are these concepts crucial in ensuring the proper functioning of mechanical assemblies?
2) Discuss the significance of selective assembly and interchangeability in
3) manufacturing processes. How do they contribute to efficient production and product quality?
4) Explain the hole and shaft basis system in metrology. How does it facilitate the design and production of mechanical components with precise fits?
5) Elaborate on Taylor's Principle in metrology. How is it applied in the design and usage of plug and ring gauges according to IS 919-1993 standards?
6) Describe the concept of multi-gauging and inspection in metrology. How does it enhance the accuracy and reliability of measurement processes in manufacturing?
7) Discuss the concept of angular measurement in metrology. Explain the working principles and applications of universal bevel protractor, sine bar, and spirit level.

8) Explain the principle of working of clinometers in angular measurement. How are angle gauges utilized, and provide numerical examples illustrating the setting of angle gauges?

9) Define the ISO grade and fits of thread in screw thread measurements. Discuss the common errors encountered in threads and methods for their measurement and correction.

10) Describe the measurement techniques for different elements of screw threads such as major diameter, minor diameter, and effective diameter. Explain the two-wire method and the working principle of a thread gauge micrometre.

11) Explain the working principle of a floating carriage dial micrometre in screw thread measurements. How does it overcome the limitations of traditional micrometres in measuring thread pitch and diameter accurately?

## 4.10 PRACTICAL

**Problem Statement**

**PS1.** Measurement of Hole and Shaft Dimensions Using Plug and Ring Gauges

**PS2. Selective Assembly and Interchangeability Testing**

## 4.11 KNOW MORE

In addition to the comprehensive coverage provided in Unit 4 of the book on Limits, Fits, and Tolerances, there are several advanced topics and practical considerations worth exploring further.

1. **Statistical Process Control (SPC):** Understanding SPC techniques can significantly enhance the quality control process in manufacturing. It involves the use of statistical methods to monitor and control a process to ensure it operates efficiently, producing high-quality output. Topics within SPC may include control charts, process capability analysis, and the concept of variation.

2. **Geometric Dimensioning and Tolerancing (GD&T):** While Unit 4 introduces the basic principles of tolerancing, delving deeper into GD&T can provide a more detailed and standardized way of specifying and controlling the geometry of parts. GD&T utilizes symbols, tolerances, and datum references to define the permissible variations in form, size, orientation, and location of features on a part.

3. **Metrology in Advanced Manufacturing:** With the advent of advanced manufacturing technologies such as additive manufacturing (3D printing), precision machining, and automated inspection systems, it's crucial to explore how metrology practices adapt to these advancements. This could include discussions on non-contact measurement methods like laser scanning, computer-aided inspection, and the integration of metrology with digital manufacturing systems.

4. **Tolerance Analysis and Stack-Up Analysis:** Tolerance stack-up analysis is essential for predicting the cumulative variation of dimensions and clearances in an assembly due to the accumulation of part tolerances. Learning about techniques for conducting tolerance analysis, such as worst-case analysis and statistical tolerance analysis, can aid in designing assemblies that meet performance requirements while considering manufacturing variability.

5. **International Standards and Regulations:** Familiarizing oneself with relevant international standards and industry regulations pertaining to tolerancing, metrology, and quality management systems is crucial for ensuring compliance and interoperability in global markets. Standards organizations like ISO (International Organization for Standardization) and ASME (American Society of Mechanical Engineers) publish standards that govern tolerancing practices and metrology procedures.

6. **Emerging Trends in Metrology:** Stay updated on the latest trends and advancements in metrology technology and methodologies. This could include developments in measurement techniques such as optical metrology, 3D scanning, nanometrology, and the application of artificial intelligence and machine learning for data analysis and process optimization.

## 4.12 REFERENCE AND SUGGESTED READINGS

**Books**

1. "Engineering Metrology" by R.K. Jain

   - A comprehensive guide covering all aspects of metrology including limits, fits, and tolerances, with detailed explanations and practical examples.

2. "Dimensional Metrology" by Roger P. Harbison and Richard E. Kibbe

- Provides a thorough understanding of measurement principles, including selective assembly, interchangeability, and the hole and shaft basis system.

3. "Mechanical Measurements" by Thomas G. Beckwith, Roy D. Marangoni, and John H. Lienhard V

- Offers insights into Taylor's principle and the design of plug and ring gauges, along with guidelines from standards like IS 919-1993 and IS 3477-1973.

4. "Precision Measurement and Calibration" by Frank J. Spitzer

- Focuses on the concept of multi-gauging and inspection techniques, providing practical strategies for ensuring precision in manufacturing processes.

**Standards**

1. IS 919-1993: Limits, Fits & Tolerances, Gauges

- A key standard providing guidelines for establishing limits, fits, and tolerances in engineering design and manufacturing.

2. IS 3477-1973: Indian Standard for Interchangeable Tapers

- Defines standards for interchangeable tapers, essential for ensuring compatibility and interchangeability of components.

Additional Resources:

1. "Geometric Dimensioning and Tolerancing" by Gene R. Cogorno

- Explores advanced concepts in tolerancing, providing insights into geometric dimensioning practices for complex engineering designs.

2. "Handbook of Dimensional Measurement" by Mark A. Curtis and Francis T. Farago

- A comprehensive reference covering various measurement techniques, instruments, and standards, including angular measurement and screw thread measurements.

3. "Introduction to Engineering Metrology" by R. K. Jain

- A foundational text offering a broad overview of metrology principles, ideal for beginners and professionals seeking to enhance their understanding of measurement science.

### Online Resources

1. National Institute of Standards and Technology (NIST) - Metrology Handbook
    - A valuable online resource providing in-depth information on measurement techniques, standards, and best practices in metrology.
2. ISO Standards Catalogue - Thread Standards
    - Access the latest ISO standards related to screw threads, including grade and fit specifications, pitch measurement methods, and thread gauge calibration procedures.

### Dynamic QR Code for Further Reading

Angular Measurements

Limits, Fits and Tolerances

# 5 Gear Measurement and Testing

**UNIT SPECIFICS**

*This unit presents information related to the following topics:*

- *Analytical and functional inspection; Rolling test*
- *Measurement of tooth thickness (constant chord method); Gear tooth vernier*
- *Errors in gears such as backlash, runout, composite errors*
- *Machine tool testing: Parallelism, Straightness, Squareness, Coaxiality, Roundness, Runout, Alignment testing of machine tools as per IS standard procedure*

***Applications***

*This unit is designed to provide an in-depth understanding of gear measurement and testing, crucial for ensuring the accuracy and functionality of gear mechanisms in mechanical systems. It begins with the principles of analytical and functional inspection methods, including the rolling test, which is used to evaluate the overall performance and quality of gears.*

*The unit then covers specific techniques for measuring tooth thickness using the constant chord method and the use of gear tooth verniers, which are essential for maintaining the precise dimensions required for proper gear function. Various types of gear errors, such as backlash, runout, and composite errors, are also discussed, along with their impact on gear performance and how they can be measured and minimized.*

*Additionally, the unit includes comprehensive coverage of machine tool testing procedures. It explains how to test for parallelism, straightness, squareness, coaxiality, roundness, and runout, as well as the alignment of machine tools according to IS standard procedures. This knowledge is vital for ensuring that machine tools are operating correctly and producing parts within the desired tolerances.*

*Apart from this, at the end of the unit, the overall broad concepts are provided as a unit summary. Besides, a large number of multiple-choice questions as well as descriptive-type questions with Bloom's taxonomy action verbs are included. A list of references and suggested readings is given in the unit so that one can go through them for practice. It is important to note that for getting more information on various topics of interest, some QR codes have been provided in different sections which can be scanned for relevant supportive knowledge. Video resources along with QR codes are mentioned for getting more information on various topics of interest which can be surfed or scanned through mobile phones for viewing.*

**RATIONALE**

*Accurate gear measurement and testing are essential for the reliability and efficiency of mechanical systems. Gears must be manufactured to precise specifications to ensure proper fit and function, and any errors in gear production can lead to significant performance issues. Understanding the principles and techniques of gear measurement and machine tool testing enables engineers to produce high-quality gears and maintain the precision of manufacturing equipment. This unit provides the necessary knowledge and skills to achieve these goals, preparing students and professionals to excel in fields that require meticulous gear inspection and testing.*

**PRE-REQUISITES**

*Before reading this unit, the students are advised to revisit the following:*

- *Basic Mathematics: Concepts of measurement and geometry*
- *Basic Engineering Mechanics: Understanding of mechanical systems and gear functions*
- *Introduction to Manufacturing Processes*

**UNIT OUTCOMES**

*After studying this unit, students will be able to:*

- *U5-O1: Understand the principles and methods of gear inspection and testing.*
- *U5-O2: Measure tooth thickness using the constant chord method and gear tooth verniers.*
- *U5-O3: Identify and evaluate common gear errors such as backlash, runout, and composite errors.*

- *U5-O4: Perform machine tool testing for parallelism, straightness, squareness, coaxiality, roundness, and runout.*
- *U5-O5: Apply IS standard procedures for the alignment testing of machine tools.*

***EXPECTED MAPPING WITH COURSE OUTCOMES***

*(1- Weak Correlation; 2- Medium correlation; 3- Strong Correlation)*

| Unit Outcomes (U5) | CO-1 | CO-2 | CO-3 | CO-4 | CO-5 |
|---|---|---|---|---|---|
| **U5-O1** | 3 | 2 | 3 | 2 | 1 |
| **U5-O2** | 3 | 3 | 2 | 2 | 1 |
| **U5-O3** | 2 | 2 | 3 | 1 | 1 |
| **U5-O4** | 3 | 3 | 2 | 3 | 1 |
| **U5-O5** | 2 | 3 | 3 | 2 | 1 |

## 5.1 GEAR MEASUREMENT

A gear is a mechanical device that transfers power using a toothed wheel. In this gear drive, the driving and driven wheels are in direct contact with each other. Precision is the most critical aspect of gear manufacturing, as gears achieve about 99 percent transmission efficiency. Therefore, accurate testing and measurement of gears are essential. To thoroughly inspect a gear, it is important to focus on the raw materials used in production, as well as the machining, heat treatment, and tooth finishing of the blanks. Additionally, gear blanks must be evaluated for tooth thickness and dimensional accuracy across various gear forms.

### 5.1.1 GEAR TERMINOLOGIES

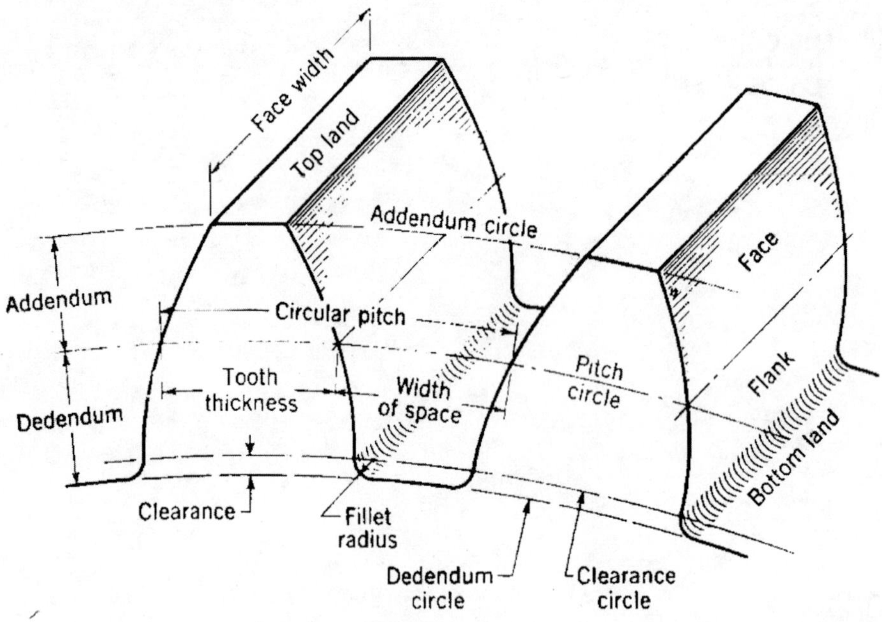


*Figure 5.1 Gear Tooth*

1) **Pitch Surface:** The surface of a theoretical rolling cylinder (or cone, etc.) that represents the toothed gear being replaced.

2) **Pitch Circle:** A cross-section of the pitch surface taken perpendicular to its axis.

3) **Addendum Circle:** The circle defining the outermost points of the gear teeth in the right section.

4) **Root (or Dedendum) Circle:** The circle defining the base of the spaces between the gear teeth in a right section.

5) **Addendum:** The radial distance between the pitch circle and the addendum circle.

6) **Dedendum:** The radial distance between the pitch circle and the root circle.

7) **Clearance:** The difference between the dedendum of one gear and the addendum of its mating gear.

8) **Face of a Tooth:** The portion of the tooth surface extending outward from the pitch surface.

9) **Flank of a Tooth:** The portion of the tooth surface extending inward from the pitch surface.

10) **Circular Thickness (or Tooth Thickness):** The thickness of the tooth measured along the pitch circle, represented as an arc length.

11) **Tooth Space:** The distance between adjacent teeth measured along the pitch circle.

12) Backlash: The difference between the circular thickness of one gear and the tooth space of its mating gear.

13) **Circular Pitch (p):** The combined width of a tooth and a space measured along the pitch circle, defined mathematically as ($p = \pi D / N$), where D is the pitch diameter and N is the number of teeth.

14) **Diametral Pitch (P):** The number of teeth per unit of pitch diameter, calculated as ($P = N / D$).

**15) Module (m):** The ratio of the pitch diameter to the number of teeth, with the pitch diameter typically given in inches or millimeters. In the case of inches, the module is the inverse of the diametral pitch.

**16) Fillet:** The small radius connecting the tooth profile to the root circle.

**17) Pinion:** The smaller gear in any pair of mating gears, with the larger gear simply referred to as the gear.

**18) Velocity Ratio:** The ratio of the rotational speed of the driving gear to that of the driven gear.

**19) Pitch Point:** The tangency point of the pitch circles in a pair of mating gears.

**20) Common Tangent:** The line tangent to the pitch circles at the pitch point.

**21) Line of Action:** The line perpendicular to the mating tooth profiles at their contact point.

**22) Path of Contact:** The trajectory traced by the contact point of a pair of tooth profiles.

**23) Pressure Angle:** The angle between the common normal at the point of tooth contact and the common tangent to the pitch circles; it is also the angle between the line of action and the common tangent.

**24) Base Circle:** An imaginary circle in involute gearing used to generate the involute curves forming the tooth profiles.

#### 5.1.1.1 Forms of Gear Teeth

The two most commonly used forms of gear teeth are:

1. Involute
2. Cycloidal

Involute gears, also known as straight tooth or spur gears, are characterized by their straight teeth, which are found on involute racks. These gears are widely used due to their efficient and reliable performance. The pressure angle for involute gears is typically either 20° or 14.5°.

On the other hand, cycloidal gears are designed to handle heavy and impact loads, making them ideal for demanding applications. Their unique tooth profile helps distribute the load more evenly, reducing stress and wear.

### 5.1.2. ANALYTICAL AND FUNCTIONAL INSPECTION

Measuring gears involves two key techniques: analytical and functional inspection, each serving a distinct purpose in ensuring performance and quality.

Analytical Inspection: This method focuses on evaluating the geometric features and dimensional accuracy of gears through precise measurements using specialized tools and equipment.

Functional Inspection: Unlike analytical inspection, functional inspection assesses how gears perform under real operating conditions. While analytical inspection emphasizes geometric conformity and dimensional accuracy, functional inspection looks at actual performance.

Gear inspection serves several purposes:

- Ensuring the necessary accuracy and quality standards.

- Reducing manufacturing costs by managing rejects and scrap.
- Regulating machines and machining techniques to sustain accuracy despite wear.
- Identifying and correcting heat treatment distortions as needed.

### 5.1.3. ROLLING TEST

- A rolling test is an essential technique in gear measuring that's used to assess the tooth contact pattern and meshing properties of gears in real-world operations.
- In this test, two mating gears engage dynamically while rotating, allowing the assessment of essential parameters like tooth contact pattern, contact ratio, pressure angle and tooth profile, backlash, noise, and vibration.
- A highly effective and convenient method for measuring gear thickness involves using two or three different-sized rollers. This approach checks for vibrations at multiple points on the gear teeth, providing accurate measurements and identifying potential issues.
- By conducting rolling tests as part of gear inspection procedures, manufacturers can ensure that their gears meet design specifications and deliver reliable operation in various applications.
- This test is done using a Parkinson Gear Tester. This test brings out any errors in tooth profile, pitch, concentricity and pitch line.
- As the gears mesh and rotate together, any deviations in the tooth profile, pitch, or concentricity of the test gear cause fluctuations in the center distance.
- These variations are detected by a dial indicator or an electronic sensor attached to the apparatus, which records the changes.
- The outcome of the rolling test is a precise measurement of the gear's manufacturing quality, highlighting any discrepancies that may affect its performance.

### 5.1.4. MEASUREMENT OF TOOTH THICKNESS

The difference between the actual and theoretical values of tooth thickness is known as the allowable error or tolerance. Since tooth thickness is often measured at the pitch circle, it is also referred to as the pitch line thickness of the tooth.

**Definition and Measurement of Tooth Thickness:**

Tooth thickness is defined as the length of an arc along the pitch circle, which presents a challenge for precise measurement. This arc length is essential for ensuring proper gear meshing and performance. Given the difficulty in measuring the exact arc length, an alternative approach is often employed: measuring the chordal thickness.

**Chordal Thickness:**

Chordal thickness is the straight-line distance (chord) between two points on the gear tooth, extending from the pitch circle across the tooth profile. This method simplifies the measurement process while providing sufficiently accurate results for most applications. Chordal thickness can be measured using calipers or specialized gear-measuring instruments, making it a practical solution for many gear inspection processes.

**Pitch Circle and Tooth Profile:**

The pitch circle is a crucial reference in gear design and inspection, as it represents the imaginary circle on which the gears theoretically mesh without slipping. Measuring tooth thickness at the pitch circle ensures consistency in gear operation. For gears with a fine pitch, the difference between the chordal thickness and the actual arc length becomes negligible, allowing for even more straightforward and effective measurement.

**Importance of Accurate Measurement:**

Accurate measurement of gear tooth thickness is critical for ensuring the proper functioning of gear systems. Incorrect thickness can lead to issues such as improper meshing, increased wear, noise, and vibration, ultimately affecting the gear's performance and lifespan. Manufacturers can maintain high-quality standards and optimize gear performance by using precise measurement techniques and understanding the difference between chordal and arc measurements.

### 5.1.4.1. Constant Chord Method

A constant chord is defined as the chord that joins the points on opposing faces of a gear tooth, where these points contact the mating teeth when the tooth's center line is aligned with the line of the gear centers.

- Constant Chord Measurement: The constant chord of a gear is measured at the points where the tooth flanks touch the flanks of the basic rack. In this context, the basic rack has straight teeth that are inclined to their center lines at the pressure angle, as illustrated in figure 5.2.

- Tooth Thickness and Depth Variation: The thickness of the tooth (w) and the depth (d) can vary depending on the number of teeth when using the gear tooth vernier calliper method. Despite these variations, for a given tooth size, contact with the rack consistently occurs at points A and B whenever the gear rotates.

$Consider\ \Delta DAE\ with\ angle\ \angle ADE\ =\ \phi.$

$$\cos\phi = \frac{AD}{DE}$$

$$AD = DEcos\varphi$$

$Thus,$

$$AD = \frac{1}{4}\cdot\pi\cdot m\cdot\cos\phi$$

$calculating\ the\ chord\ length\ AB:$

$From\ Fig. 5.1,$

$$l(DE) = l(DF) = ArcDG$$

$Given:$

$$1/4\ circular\ pitch\ = 1/4\cdot\pi\cdot m$$

$Consider\ \Delta DCA\ with\ angle\ \angle CAD\ =\ \phi.$

$$\cos\phi = CA/AD$$

$Thus,$

$$CA = AD\cdot\cos\varphi\ = \frac{1}{4}\cdot\pi\cdot m\cdot\cos\phi\ Sin\ \phi = cos^2\phi.\pi\cdot m/4$$

$From\ Fig. 5.1:$

$$chord\ length\ AB = 2\cdot l(CA) = 2\cdot cos^2\phi.\pi\cdot m/4$$

$The\ depth\ h\ can\ be\ calculated\ as\ follows:$

$From\ \Delta DAC,$

$$\sin\phi = CD/AD$$

*Thus,*

$$CD = AD \cdot \sin\phi = 14 \cdot \pi \cdot m \cdot \sin\phi \cdot \cos\phi$$

$$GD = GC + CD$$

$$Where, GD = addendum = module$$

GD=m

$$CD = 1/4 \cdot \pi \cdot m \cdot \sin\phi \cdot \cos \quad \phi,$$

$$GC = depth = h$$

$$m = h + \frac{1}{4} \cdot \pi \cdot m \cdot \cos\phi \cdot \sin\phi$$

$$h = m - 1/4 \cdot \pi \cdot m \cdot \cos\phi \cdot \sin\phi$$

$$\mathbf{Depth\ h = m(1 - 1/4 \cdot \pi} \cdot \cos\phi \cdot \sin\phi\,)$$

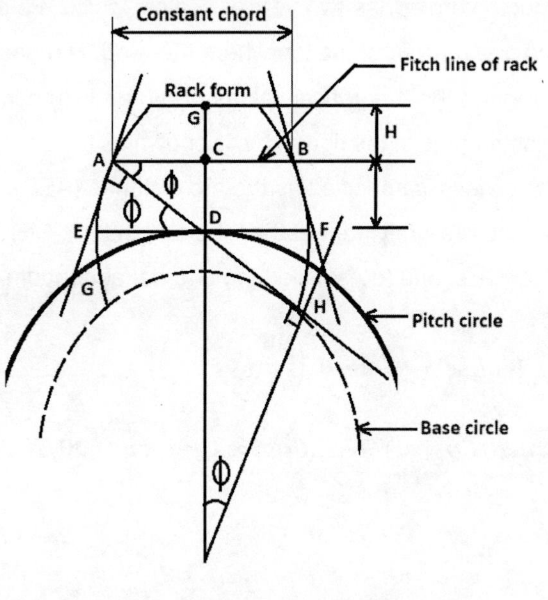


*Figure 5.2 Constant Chord Thickness Method*

The concept of a constant chord is crucial in gear measurement and ensures that the gear teeth maintain consistent contact points with the basic rack, leading to reliable and accurate gear operation.

### 5.1.4.2 Gear Tooth Vernier

The Gear Tooth Vernier method is used to measure the thickness of gear teeth at the pitch line, also known as chordal thickness, and the distance from the top of a tooth to this chord.

- The measurement process involves an adjustable tongue, with each part being independently adjusted using screws on graduated bars. It's important to account for zero errors to ensure accuracy.
- This method is simple and cost-effective but requires different settings for different numbers of teeth for a given pitch. The accuracy is limited by the least count of instruments, and wear on the calliper jaws needs regular calibration to maintain measurement precision.
- A gear tooth vernier is particularly convenient for measuring tooth thickness. Given that the thickness varies from the tip to the base circle of the tooth, the instrument must measure at a specific position, typically at the pitch circle, referred to as the pitch-line thickness.
- The gear tooth vernier has two vernier scales, which are adjusted for the tooth width (w) and the depth (d) from the top where the width is measured.
- For a gear tooth, the theoretical values of (w) and (d) can be calculated and verified using the instrument. In the figure, (w) is shown as the chord (ADB) in Figure 5.3, while the tooth thickness is specified as the arc distance (AEB). The depth (d), adjusted on the instrument, is slightly greater than the addendum (CE). Therefore, (w) is called the chordal thickness, and (d) is called the chordal addendum.

$$w = (Nm_n / Cos^3 \propto) [sin \left(\frac{90}{N} Cos^3 \propto\right)]$$

$$d = (Nm_n / Cos^3 \propto) [l + 2Cos^3 \propto / N - cos (90/N \, Cos^3 \propto)]$$

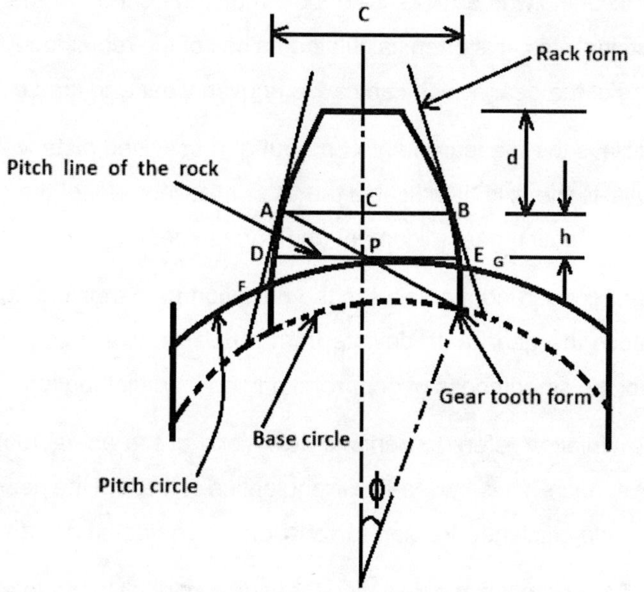


*Figure 5.3 Gear Tooth Vernier Method*

### 5.1.4 ERRORS IN GEARS

1. Profile Error: The profile error is defined as the maximum distance between any point on the actual tooth profile and the design profile. This error indicates how much the actual gear tooth shape deviates from the intended design, affecting the smoothness and efficiency of gear meshing.

2. Pitch Error: Pitch error refers to the difference between the actual pitch (the distance between corresponding points on adjacent teeth) and the design pitch. Accurate pitch is crucial for ensuring proper gear engagement and minimizing noise and vibration during operation.

3. Cyclical Error: Cyclical error is a recurring deviation that occurs with each complete revolution of the gear. This type of error can lead to periodic variations in gear performance, potentially causing torque and speed transmission fluctuations.

4. Runout: Runout is the total variation in measurement observed on a fixed indicator as the contact points are rotated around a fixed axis without any axial movement. It represents the total deviation of the gear surface from a true circular path, impacting gear accuracy and performance.

5. Eccentricity: Eccentricity is a measure of how much the center of the gear deviates from its intended rotational axis. It is often calculated as half of the radial runout, indicating the off-center positioning of the gear, which can cause uneven wear and load distribution.

6. Wobble: Wobble is the measurement of runout at a specified distance from the rotational axis, taken parallel to the axis. It indicates the tilt or misalignment of the gear face relative to its axis of rotation, affecting gear alignment and engagement.

7. Radial Runout: Radial runout measures the deviation perpendicular to the rotational axis. It shows how much the gear teeth deviate from a true circular path in the radial direction, which can impact the smoothness of gear rotation and load distribution.

8. Undulation: Undulation refers to periodic deviations of the actual tooth surface from the intended design surface. These wave-like irregularities can affect the gear's ability to transmit motion smoothly and efficiently, leading to variations in contact stress and wear.

9. Axial Runout: Axial runout is the deviation measured parallel to the rotational axis while the gear is rotating. It indicates the axial displacement of the gear teeth, affecting the alignment and engagement with mating gears and potentially leading to increased wear and noise.

By understanding and controlling these various types of errors, it is possible to ensure higher precision, better performance, and longer life for gear systems.

The inspection of gears involves identifying potential manufacturing errors in the following elements:

i. Runout
   - Pitch-circle eccentricity refers to the deviation of the gear's pitch circle from its true center, causing the gear to vibrate periodically with each rotation. This vibration can lead to premature gear tooth failure. To measure runout, eccentricity testers are used.
   - The testing process involves mounting the gear on a mandrel. The tester's dial indicator is equipped with a specially designed tip that matches the gear's module. This tip is placed between the gear's tooth spaces. As the gear is rotated tooth by tooth, the dial indicator measures any deviations, revealing variations in the gear's pitch circle. This method ensures accurate detection of eccentricity, allowing for corrective measures to be taken to prevent gear failure.

ii. Backlash

- Backlash refers to the amount of rotation a gear can have before its nonworking flank comes into contact with the teeth of its mating gear. It is measured numerically at the point of the pitch circle where the gears mesh the tightest.
- There are two categories of backlash:

  1. Circumferential Backlash
  2. Normal Backlash

  To calculate backlash, the following steps are performed:

  1) Lock one of the two mating gears in place.
  2) Rotate the other gear forward and backward.
  3) Use a comparator to measure the maximum displacement during this rotation.

- Circumferential backlash is the measure of this displacement, taken as a tangent to the comparator stylus's locking location relative to the reference cylinder. This method ensures an accurate measurement of the rotational play between the gear teeth, helping to identify and correct excessive backlash that can lead to gear noise, wear, and decreased accuracy.

iii. Composite

- Composite testing of gears involves evaluating the variation in center distance as a gear meshes tightly with a master gear. This testing method helps identify errors in gear manufacturing by measuring how gears interact under operating conditions. In composite gear checking, two main types of variations are assessed: tooth-to-tooth composite variation and total composite variation.
- Composite testing provides a comprehensive gear quality assessment by highlighting localized and overall manufacturing errors. By measuring tooth-to-tooth and total composite variations, manufacturers can identify and rectify issues that impact gear performance, ensuring higher precision, reliability, and longevity in gear applications.

## 5.2. MACHINE TOOL TESTING

The accuracy of machine tools determines the accuracy of components that are created. The rigidity and stiffness of the machine tool and its parts determine the quality of the workpiece. Alignment of various components with respect to one another, as well as the precision and quality of the control and driving mechanisms. The inherent quality and accuracy of the machine tools determine the accuracy of the components that are being manufactured in that machine.

It can be classified into

i) Static tests
ii) Dynamic tests

Machine tool accuracy can be assessed through two primary types of evaluations: static evaluations and dynamic evaluations.

1) Static tests

Static evaluations refer to tests conducted to examine the alignment of a machine tool's components in a stationary environment. These tests do not involve any dynamic loading conditions and focus solely on the precision of the machine parts when at rest. Static evaluations are essential for ensuring the foundational accuracy and alignment of the machine tool components before they are subjected to operational stresses.

2) Dynamic tests

Dynamic evaluations involve tests conducted under dynamic loading conditions, where the alignment and performance of the machine tool are examined while it is in operation. These tests are crucial for understanding how the machine tool behaves under actual working conditions, including the effects of cutting forces and vibrations. Dynamic evaluations provide a comprehensive assessment of the machine's operational accuracy and stability.

Dynamic tests are classified further into two types

i. Geometrical Tests:

Geometrical tests involve checking machine tool components' dimensions, positions, and relative displacements. These tests ensure that each part of the machine is correctly aligned and positioned according to design specifications, which is crucial for maintaining overall accuracy and precision during operation.

ii. Practical Tests:

Practical tests involve machining test pieces using the machine tool. These test pieces are specifically chosen to reflect the fundamental purpose for which the machine has been designed. By machining these test pieces, practical tests evaluate the machine's ability to produce parts that meet the required quality and precision standards under real-world operating conditions.

### 5.2.1 PURPOSE OF MACHINE TOOL TESTING

- The measurements, geometry, and surface finishes of any workpiece are determined by the precision of the machine tool used in its production.
- High accuracy is essential for the numerous components produced in mass manufacturing to ensure seamless assembly without introducing errors.
- The increasing demand for precisely machined components has driven significant improvements in the geometric precision of machine tools.
- To achieve and maintain this level of precision, comprehensive inspections of the machine tool's various components are conducted regularly.
- These inspections ensure that every aspect of the machine tool, from its alignment and rigidity to the accuracy of its control and driving mechanisms, meets the stringent requirements necessary for producing high-quality, error-free components.

### 5.2.2. TYPE OF GEOMETRICAL CHECKS ON MACHINE TOOLS

Different types of geometrical tests conducted on machine tools include the following:

1. Straightness:

    - This test evaluates whether the machine tool's movement or surface follows a straight line. Any deviation from a true straight path can affect the precision of the machined components. Straightness tests ensure that linear guides and machine movements are accurate and free from significant deviations.

2. Flatness:

- Flatness testing determines whether a surface lies in a single plane. This is crucial for surfaces that require uniform contact with other components or workpieces. Flatness errors can lead to inaccuracies in machining operations and poor surface finishes. This test ensures that the machine's worktables, bases, and other flat surfaces are correctly aligned.

3. Parallelism, Equi-distance, and Coincidence:

- Parallelism checks if two lines or surfaces run parallel to each other, ensuring that parts and tools move in unison without angular deviation.
- Equi-distance involves verifying that two points maintain a consistent distance from each other throughout their entire range of motion.
- Coincidence ensures that different axes or points align perfectly when they are supposed to intersect or coincide. These tests are crucial for multi-axis machines where precise relative positioning is necessary.

4. Rectilinear Movements or Squareness of Straight Line and Plane:

- This test examines the accuracy of linear movements and the squareness between different axes and planes. Ensuring that movements along one axis are perpendicular to those along another is essential for maintaining geometric integrity in machined parts. It checks for any angular deviation that could lead to errors in part dimensions and shapes.

5. Rotations:

- Rotational tests assess the accuracy of rotating components, such as spindles and rotary tables. These tests measure the concentricity, runout, and angular positioning accuracy. Accurate rotational movements are vital for operations like drilling, milling, and turning, where the precise circular motion is required.

6. Coaxiaility

- Coaxiality tests determine whether multiple components share a common axis. This is critical for operations involving rotating parts, such as spindles and chucks, where misalignment can cause vibrations, uneven wear, and inaccuracies in the machined product. Coaxiality ensures that all relevant components align perfectly along the same axis, maintaining the integrity of the rotational movements and the overall machining process.

### 5.2.3. ALIGNMENT TESTING OF MACHINE TOOLS

Alignment testing using laser equipment enhances accuracy and can cover greater distances compared to traditional methods. This method is recognized for its precision and efficiency in various industrial applications, including aircraft production and shipbuilding. The following outlines the alignment testing procedure using laser equipment according to IS standards:

1) Preparation
   - Ensure the machine tool and environment are clean and free from obstructions.
   - Verify that the machine is properly leveled and stabilized.
   - Calibrate the laser equipment according to the manufacturer's instructions.
2) Straightness Tests
   - Laser Setup: Position the laser emitter to establish a straight reference line. The laser produces a real straight line, which is superior to the imaginary line provided by traditional alignment telescopes.
   - Measurement: Use a laser receiver or detector to measure deviations along the machine's bed ways or movement paths. Record the deviations as the laser detects any misalignment over long distances.
3) Flatness Tests
   - Surface Check: Place the laser emitter perpendicular to the surface to be tested. Direct displacement measurements are taken using the laser receiver.
   - Recording Deviations: Move the laser receiver across the surface and record any deviations from flatness. The data can be used to create a detailed map of the surface profile.

4) Parallelism Tests
    - Baseline Setup: Establish a laser baseline parallel to the reference surface or component.
    - Measurement: Using the laser receiver, measure the distance from the laser line to the component at various points to ensure parallelism. Adjust the components as necessary to achieve the required parallelism.
5) Squareness Tests
    - Optical Square: Use an optical square in conjunction with the laser equipment to establish a square reference relative to the laser baseline.
    - Measurement: Position the laser receiver at various points to measure the squareness of components relative to the established laser line. Adjust as necessary to correct any deviations.
6) Coaxiality Tests
    - Alignment Setup: Align the laser emitter with the rotational axis of the machine tool.
    - Measurement: Use the laser receiver to measure the coaxiality of rotating components, such as spindles and tailstocks. Ensure that all components share a common axis and adjust if necessary.
7) Operational Verification
    - Component Alignment: Check the alignment of multiple components to a predetermined straight line established by the laser. This is particularly important for components spaced at long distances.
    - Machined Surface Check: After adjustments, perform a test run to verify the accuracy of the machining process.
8) Documentation:
    - Record all measurements and deviations observed during the testing process.
    - Compare the results with the permissible limits specified in the IS standards.
9) Calibration and Adjustment:
    - If any deviations are found, calibrate and adjust the machine components accordingly.
    - Re-test the machine tool to ensure compliance with the standards.

The Indian Standards (IS) for alignment tests on machine tools are specific to different types of machines and their components. Here are some key IS standards that outline the procedures and requirements for alignment tests:

1) IS 2063:1988 - "Test Charts for Lathes"
   - This standard specifies the test procedures for general-purpose lathes, covering geometric and practical tests.
2) IS 2200:1988 - "Test Charts for Milling Machines"
   - This standard provides the test procedures for milling machines, including tests for geometric accuracy.
3) IS 12449:1988 - "Test Charts for Vertical Turning and Boring Machines"
   - This standard outlines the alignment tests for vertical turning and boring machines.
4) IS 13022:1991 - "Test Charts for Radial Drilling Machines"
   - This standard covers the alignment tests for radial drilling machines.
5) IS 12181 (Parts 1 to 4):1992 - "Acceptance Conditions for Vertical Turning and Boring Lathes"
   - These standards specify the acceptance conditions, including alignment tests for vertical turning and boring lathes.
6) IS 13275:1992 - "Test Charts for Horizontal Boring and Milling Machines"
   - This standard outlines the tests for checking the accuracy of horizontal boring and milling machines.
7) IS 13936 (Parts 1 to 5):1994 - "Acceptance Conditions for Machining Centres"
   - These standards include tests for the accuracy and alignment of machining centers.
8) IS 13550:1992 - "Acceptance Conditions for General-Purpose Horizontal Spindle and Vertical Spindle Milling Machines"
   - This standard specifies the alignment and accuracy tests for general-purpose milling machines.

These IS standards provide detailed procedures and acceptable tolerances for conducting alignment tests on various types of machine tools, ensuring they meet the necessary precision and operational requirements.

## 5.3 APPLICATIONS

***Gear Measurement***

**Quality Control in Manufacturing**

- Ensures gears meet design specifications and tolerances, crucial for the reliable performance of mechanical systems in various industries.
- Prevents defects and reduces waste in production, leading to cost savings and improved efficiency.

**Automotive Industry**

- Essential for the production of transmission systems, differentials, and other critical components.
- Helps in maintaining smooth and efficient power transfer, reducing noise and vibration in vehicles.

**Aerospace Industry**

- Critical for the manufacturing of precision gears used in aircraft engines, landing gear, and control systems.
- Ensures safety and reliability by adhering to stringent quality standards.

**Industrial Machinery**

- Applied in the production and maintenance of gears for heavy machinery, conveyors, and robotic systems.
- Enhances the durability and performance of industrial equipment.

**Consumer Electronics**

- Used in the manufacturing of gears for household appliances, power tools, and electronic devices.
- Ensures smooth operation and longevity of consumer products.

**Medical Devices**

- Critical for producing high-precision gears used in medical equipment such as MRI machines, surgical robots, and diagnostic devices.
- Ensures accurate and reliable performance in healthcare applications.

***Machine Tool Testing***

**CNC Machining**

- Ensures the accuracy and reliability of CNC machines, which are widely used in manufacturing complex and high-precision parts.

- Critical for industries such as aerospace, automotive, and electronics.

**Metalworking and Fabrication**

- Maintains the precision of machine tools used in cutting, shaping, and forming metal components.
- Ensures high-quality finishes and dimensional accuracy in fabricated products.

**Woodworking**

- Ensures the proper functioning and alignment of woodworking machinery, leading to precise cuts and improved product quality.
- Reduces material waste and increases efficiency in furniture and cabinetry production.

**Tool and Die Making**

- Critical for producing molds, dies, and other tools used in manufacturing processes.
- Ensures the dimensional accuracy and longevity of these tools, which are essential for mass production.

**Heavy Equipment Manufacturing**

- Ensures the proper alignment and functioning of machine tools used in producing parts for construction, mining, and agricultural machinery.
- Enhances the performance and reliability of heavy equipment.

**Quality Assurance and Maintenance**

- Regular testing and calibration of machine tools ensure they remain within specified tolerances.
- Prevents machine downtime and reduces maintenance costs by identifying and correcting issues early.

### *Standards Compliance*

**Adherence to International Standards**

- Ensures that manufacturing processes and products meet global quality standards.
- Facilitates international trade by ensuring compatibility and reliability of components and machinery.

**Certification and Auditing**

- Supports the certification processes for various industries, ensuring that products and processes comply with regulatory requirements.
- Enhances customer confidence and marketability of products.

By integrating these gear measurement and machine tool testing techniques into their processes, industries can achieve higher precision, reliability, and efficiency, which are essential for maintaining competitiveness and meeting the ever-increasing demands for quality and performance.

## 5.4 UNIT SUMMARY

This unit focuses on the critical aspects of gear measurement and the testing of machine tools, ensuring high precision and reliability in mechanical systems.

Gear Measurement involves both analytical and functional inspections. Analytical inspection uses precise instruments and mathematical methods to evaluate gear parameters theoretically, while functional inspection assesses gear performance under actual operating conditions. An essential practical evaluation in gear measurement is the rolling test, which checks the smoothness and accuracy of gear operation by observing its interaction with a master gear or gear rolling tester.

One of the precise methods for measuring gear teeth is the constant chord method, which measures tooth thickness at a specific point to ensure proper meshing and load distribution. Additionally, the gear tooth vernier is a **specialized** tool that provides quick and accurate measurement of tooth thickness at the pitch circle diameter, crucial for maintaining quality control.

Understanding and identifying errors in gears is vital for their proper function. Backlash, the clearance between mating gear teeth, must be controlled to avoid binding and ensure smooth operation. Runout, the deviation from the ideal circular path, can cause vibration and noise, while composite errors, the combined effects of various individual gear errors, can significantly impact overall gear performance and reliability.

Machine Tool Testing includes evaluating several key parameters to ensure the precision and alignment of machine tools. Parallelism ensures that surfaces or axes are parallel, which is crucial for accurate machining. Straightness verifies that components like guideways and spindles maintain a straight line, essential for precision work. Squareness checks the perpendicularity of surfaces and axes, guaranteeing that machined parts meet design specifications.

Coaxiality measures the alignment of multiple axes or cylindrical features to a common centerline, important for the proper functioning of rotating parts. Roundness assesses the circularity of cylindrical parts to ensure uniform diameter and surface finish. Run-out evaluates the deviation of a rotating part from its intended axis of rotation, affecting balance and functionality.

Finally, alignment testing of machine tools as per Indian Standard (IS) procedures ensures that all components are correctly aligned to meet standardized performance and precision criteria. This comprehensive approach to gear measurement and machine tool testing is essential for maintaining the quality, efficiency, and reliability of mechanical systems.

## 5.5 EXERCISES

### Multiple Choice Questions

1. What is the primary purpose of analytical inspection in gear measurement?

   A) To test gear performance under operational conditions

   B) To analyze detailed gear geometry and tolerances

   C) To clean the gears before assembly

   D) To test the gear's resistance to corrosion

2. Functional inspection of gears typically includes which of the following tests?

   A) Noise testing

   B) Chemical composition testing

   C) Gear material hardness testing

   D) Temperature resistance testing

3. The rolling test for gears is primarily used to:

   A) Measure the chemical properties of the gear material

   B) Check the smoothness and accuracy of gear meshing

   C) Determine the gear's resistance to thermal expansion

   D) Assess the electrical conductivity of the gear

4. In the constant chord method, tooth thickness is measured:

A) At the pitch circle diameter

B) At the root of the gear tooth

C) At a fixed distance from the base circle

D) At the tip of the gear tooth

5. The constant chord method is particularly useful in:

A) Low-precision gear manufacturing

B) High-precision applications like watchmaking

C) Testing gear lubricants

D) Verifying gear hardness

6. Gear tooth verniers are primarily used for:

A) Measuring gear hardness

B) Quick and onsite inspection of gear teeth

C) Cleaning gears before inspection

D) Applying lubricants to gears

7. Which gear error is defined as the clearance between mating gear teeth?

A) Runout

B) Backlash

C) Pitch error

D) Tooth thickness error

8. Minimizing runout in gears is crucial for:

A) Low-speed applications

B) Highspeed applications like turbine engines

C) Static applications

D) Applications requiring high thermal resistance

9. Composite errors in gears are evaluated to:

A) Determine the gear's electrical properties

B) Ensure overall gear performance

C) Measure the gear's thermal expansion

D) Test the gear's resistance to corrosion

10. Parallelism testing in machine tools ensures:

A) The gears are lubricated correctly

B) Machine parts move along parallel paths

C) Electrical circuits are functioning properly

D) Thermal expansion is minimized

11. Straightness testing is essential for:

A) Ensuring parallelism in machine tools

B) Checking the straight travel paths of machine components

C) Testing the chemical composition of machine parts

D) Verifying electrical connectivity

12. Squareness testing is important in machines where:

A) Accurate 3D movements are required

B) Only 2D movements are performed

C) High thermal resistance is needed

D) Chemical properties need to be tested

13. Coaxiality testing ensures:

A) Machine components are square

B) Spindle alignment in rotating machines

C) Parallel movement of machine parts

D) Proper chemical composition of machine tools

14. Roundness testing is particularly crucial in:

A) Static machinery

B) Bearing manufacturing and highspeed rotating equipment

C) Low-speed applications

D) Testing electrical properties

15. Runout testing in high-precision machining helps to:

A) Ensure the machine's chemical resistance

B) Achieve high-quality surface finishes and maintain tool life

C) Test the machine's thermal expansion

D) Verify the machine's electrical connectivity

Answers: 1B, 2A, 3B, 4C, 5B, 6B, 7B, 8B, 9B, 10B, 11B, 12A, 13B, 14B, 15B

**Subjective Type Questions**

1. Explain the differences between analytical and functional inspection in gear measurement. Why are both methods essential for ensuring gear quality?
2. Describe the rolling test procedure for gears. What key parameters are assessed during this test, and why are they important for gear performance?
3. Discuss the concept of tooth thickness in gears. How is tooth thickness measured using the chordal thickness method, and what are its advantages?
4. Define the constant chord method for measuring gear tooth thickness. Please explain how the constant chord remains consistent and its significance in gear measurement.
5. What is a gear tooth vernier, and how is it used to measure the chordal thickness and chordal addendum of gear teeth? What are the potential sources of error in this measurement method?
6. Identify and explain the various types of errors in gears, such as profile error, pitch error, cyclical error, runout, eccentricity, wobble, radial runout, undulation, and axial runout. How do these errors impact gear performance?
7. Describe the process of measuring runout in gears. Why is controlling runout important for gear operation, and what tools are typically used for this measurement?
8. Explain the significance of measuring backlash in gears. How is circumferential backlash calculated, and what are the implications of excessive backlash on gear performance?

9. What is composite testing in gear measurement? Describe the difference between tooth-to-tooth composite variation and total composite variation, and discuss how these tests help in assessing gear quality.

10. Discuss the importance of machine tool testing in ensuring the accuracy of manufactured components. Explain the differences between static and dynamic evaluations, and why both are necessary for a comprehensive assessment of machine tool performance.

## 5.6 PRACTICAL

### Problem Statements

**PS1.** To measure the tooth thickness of a gear using the constant chord method and understand the significance of accurate gear measurement.

**PS2.** To perform a rolling test on a pair of gears to assess the tooth contact pattern and identify any errors or irregularities in gear meshing.

## 5.7 KNOW MORE

1. **Analytical Inspection Techniques:** Explore how advanced mathematical models and high-precision instruments are used to evaluate the theoretical accuracy of gear parameters.

2. **Functional Inspection Methods:** Learn about real-world testing conditions that assess the operational performance of gears, ensuring they meet practical application standards.

3. **Rolling Test Procedures:** Understand the detailed process of conducting rolling tests, which evaluate the smoothness and precision of gear engagement.

4. **Constant Chord Method:** Delve into the specifics of measuring tooth thickness using the constant chord method, including step-by-step guidelines and tools required.

5. **Gear Tooth Vernier Applications:** Discover how the gear tooth vernier is used for quick and accurate measurement of gear teeth, and its role in quality control processes.

6. **Common Gear Errors:** Gain insights into the types of errors that can occur in gears, such as backlash, runout, and composite errors, and learn methods to detect and mitigate these issues.

7. **Machine Tool Testing Standards:** Familiarize yourself with the IS standard procedures for testing machine tools, ensuring alignment, precision, and reliability in machining operations.
8. **Advanced Testing Techniques:** Investigate advanced techniques and instruments used to test parallelism, straightness, squareness, coaxiality, roundness, and run out in machine tools.

This unit provides a thorough understanding of both gear measurement and machine tool testing, equipping you with the knowledge and skills needed to ensure high standards of mechanical precision and performance.

## 5.8 SUGGESTED READINGS

### References

1. Gear Design and Application" by David W. Dudley
   - ❖ This comprehensive guide covers gear design principles, measurement techniques, and error analysis, providing a solid foundation for understanding gear mechanics and quality control.
2. Fundamentals of Gear Manufacturing" by Stephen P. Radzevich
   - ❖ This book offers detailed insights into gear production processes, including analytical and functional inspection methods, rolling tests, and measurement techniques.
3. Handbook of Gear Design" by G.M. Maitha
   - ❖ An essential resource for understanding various gear measurement methods, including the constant chord method and the use of gear tooth verniers, along with common gear errors.
4. Indian Standard IS 2063: Gear Tooth Vernier Calliper Specifications
   - ❖ This standard provides detailed specifications for the gear tooth vernier calliper, including usage guidelines and accuracy requirements.
5. Indian Standard IS 11731: Machine Tool Alignment Testing
   - ❖ This standard outlines the procedures for alignment testing of machine tools, ensuring compliance with IS standards for parallelism, straightness, squareness, and other critical parameters.

## Suggested Readings

1. Gear Metrology" by J. Derek Smith
   - This book delves into the metrology of gears, covering various measurement techniques, tools, and error analysis in detail.
2. Precision Gear Metrology: Gear Measurement and Inspection" by J.W. Dudley
   - Focuses on precision measurement techniques for gears, including analytical and functional inspection methods, rolling tests, and error identification.
3. Principles of Machine Tool Design" by N.K. Mehta
   - Covers the principles and practices of machine tool design, including alignment testing and the evaluation of key parameters such as parallelism, straightness, and squareness.
4. Advanced Metrology" by P. Hockel
   - Explores advanced metrology techniques for machine tools and gears, including roundness, coaxiality, and runout measurement.
5. Machine Tool Practices" by Richard R. Kibbe
   - Provides a practical approach to machine tool testing, with detailed explanations of testing procedures for alignment, parallelism, and other critical factors.
6. Metrology and Measurement" by Anand K. Bewoor and Vinay A. Kulkarni
   - A comprehensive textbook covering various aspects of metrology, including gear measurement and machine tool testing techniques.

**Dynamic QR Code for Further Reading**

How to Select Gears

Machine Tool Standards

# Measurements and Metrology Lab

## MEPC 210 Measurements & Metrology Lab

| Sl. No | LIST OF EXPERIMENTS |
|---|---|
| 1 | Measure the diameter of a wire using micrometer and compare the result with a digital micrometer |
| 2 | Measure the angle of the machined surface using a sine bar with slip gauges. |
| 3 | Measure the angle of a V-block / Taper Shank of Drill / Dovetail using a universal bevel protractor. |
| 4 | Measure the dimensions of ground MS flat/cylindrical bush using Vernier Caliper compared with Digital/Dial Vernier Caliper. |
| 5 | Measure the geometrical dimensions of V-Thread using a thread Vernier gauge. |
| 6 | Measure the thickness of ground MS plates using slip gauges |

| EX. NO.:1 | MEASUREMENT OF WIRE DIAMETER USING MICROMETER AND DIGITAL MICROMETER | DATE: |
|---|---|---|

**OBJECTIVE:**

The objective of this experiment is to measure the diameter of a wire using a micrometer and a digital micrometre and to compare the results obtained from both instruments.

**MATERIALS REQUIRED:**

1. Wire sample
2. Micrometer
3. Digital micrometer
4. Vernier caliper (for reference)

**DESCRIPTION:**

The micrometer is a precise linear measuring instrument. It consists of an accurate screw with 10 to 20 threads per centimeter that rotates inside a fixed nut. One end of the screw acts as a measuring tip, while the fixed anvil acts as the other tip. The screw has threads cut for a certain length, leaving the remaining portion called the sleeve. The spindle moves towards or away from the fixed anvil by rotating the thimble. The spindle is placed inside the barrel to slide freely over it, which is firmly fixed with the frame. The barrel has 20 divisions per centimeter, constituting one complete revolution. However, the thimble has 25 divisions around its circumference, meaning each revolution is divided into 25 divisions. As a result, each division equals 0.02mm, making the least count of the micrometer 0.02mm.

A digital micrometer is a precision measuring tool used for accurately determining the dimensions of small objects with high precision. Unlike traditional micrometers, which rely on manual reading of scales, digital micrometers feature an electronic display that shows measurements directly. This electronic display makes reading measurements easier and less prone to human error. Digital micrometers often have additional features such as data output capabilities for recording measurements digitally, making them suitable for integration into automated measurement systems. They are widely used in industries like manufacturing, engineering, and research where precise measurements are crucial.

**PROCEDURE:**

In preparation for the experiment, ensure that both the micrometer and digital micrometer are calibrated and operational, and select a suitable wire sample for measurement. Create a clean and organized workspace to facilitate accurate measurements. Begin by using the micrometer: open it, clean its measuring faces, place the wire sample between the anvil and spindle, gradually tighten the spindle to secure the wire, and record the measurement displayed on the micrometer barrel. Then, proceed to the digital micrometer: turn it on, position the wire sample between its anvil and spindle, gently close it until firm contact is made with the wire, and record the measurement shown on the digital screen. Next, compare the measurements obtained from both instruments and calculate any differences. Record observations and analysis accordingly. Optionally, verify the wire diameter using a vernier caliper and note any disparities or consistencies with the micrometer and digital micrometer measurements. Finally, clean both instruments after use to maintain their functionality.

**OBSERVATION:**

**Specimen's Name** : ______________________________

**Specification** : ______________________________

| Sl. No. | Main Scale Reading (M.S.R) (mm) | Vernier Scale Division (V.S.D) (Div) | Correct Reading CR=MSR+(VSD×LC) (mm) | Average Reading (mm) | Reading from Digital Micrometer | Error |
|---|---|---|---|---|---|---|
| 1 | | | | | | |
| 2 | | | | | | |
| 3 | | | | | | |
| 4 | | | | | | |
| 5 | | | | | | |

**DIAGRAM:**

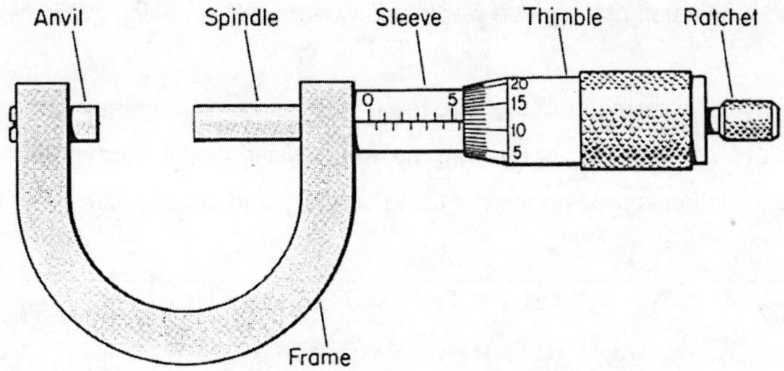


*Ordinary Micrometer*

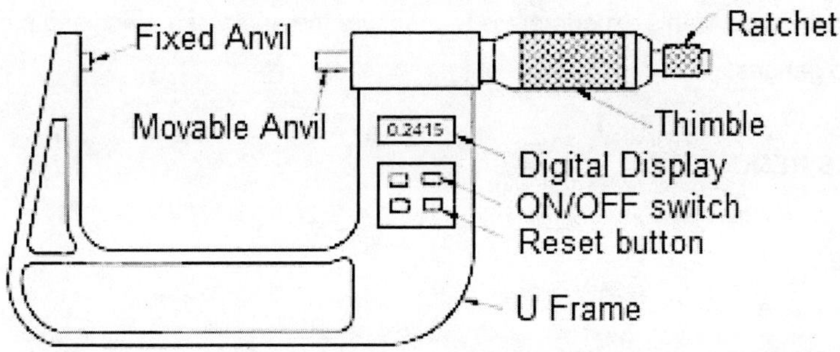


*Digital Micrometer*

**MODEL CALCULATION:**

**RESULT:**

Thus the dimension of the given workpiece was measured using micrometer and digital micrometer.

1. The average diameter of the wire measured using micrometer = ________ mm
2. The average diameter of the wire measured using digital micrometer = _______mm
3. The deviation in measurements using ordinary and digital micrometer = _______mm

| EX. NO.:2 | MEASURE THE ANGLE OF THE MACHINED SURFACE USING SINE BAR WITH SLIP GAUGES | DATE: |
|---|---|---|

**OBJECTIVE:**

The objective of this experiment is to measure the angle of a machined surface using a sine bar with slip gauges.

**MATERIALS REQUIRED:**

1. Sine bar
2. Slip gauges
3. Surface plate or flat surface
4. Dial indicator (optional)
5. Vernier protractor (optional)
6. Height gauge (optional)

**DESCRIPTION:**

Sine bars are indispensable tools in metrology, often paired with slip gauges for precise angle measurements. Crafted from high-quality materials like high carbon, high chromium steel, they undergo meticulous hardening, grinding, and calibration processes to ensure accuracy and durability. These bars typically feature two parallel cylinders, with standardized distances between them, commonly 100mm, 200mm, or 300mm. To streamline handling and reduce weight without compromising structural integrity, relief holes are strategically incorporated into the design of sine bars.

**PROCEDURE:**

1. Ensure cleanliness and functionality of the sine bar, slip gauges, and other measuring instruments.
2. Place a stable platform, such as a surface plate or flat surface, for the experiment.
3. Position the sine bar on the surface plate with its precision-ground surface facing upwards.
4. Adjust the height of the sine bar as needed for stability.
5. Choose appropriate slip gauges based on the desired angle using the formula provided.
6. Elevate one end of the sine bar by placing the selected slip gauges underneath.
7. Confirm cleanliness and secure placement of slip gauges for accurate measurements.
8. Align the machined surface with the precision-ground surface of the sine bar.
9. Utilize a dial indicator, vernier protractor, or height gauge for precise alignment and contact.
10. Optionally, use a dial indicator or height gauge to measure the height difference between the machined surface ends.
11. Calculate the angle using the provided formula and compare it with the desired angle for validation.
12. Clean all equipment post-experiment and return them to designated storage areas.

**FORMULA:**

$$Sin\ \theta = \frac{h}{l}$$

Where,

$\theta$ = Angle of taper surface in degrees,

h = Height of slip gauge in mm.

l=Length between the rollers in mm

**DIAGRAM:**

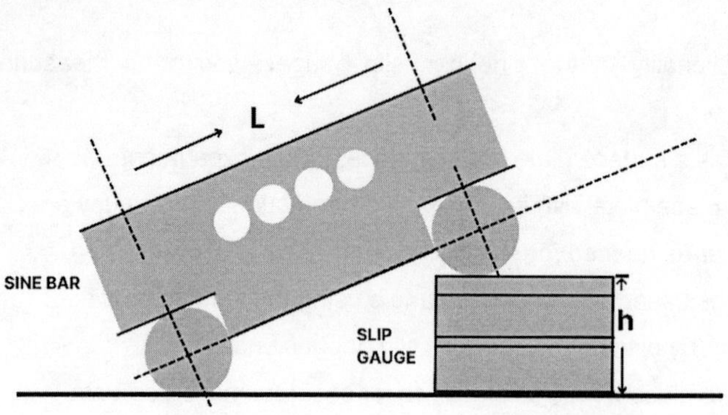


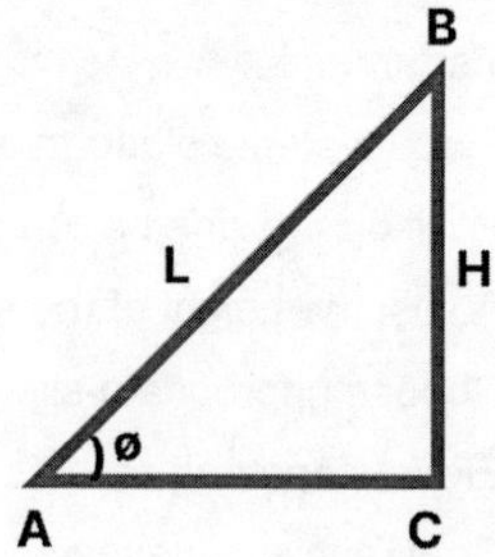


*Sine bar setup*

**OBSERVATIONS:**

| Sl. No. | Specimen's Name and Specification | Height of Slip Gauge ($h_1$) (mm) | Height of Slip Gauge on other side ($h_2$) (mm) | Angle (θ) (Deg) |
|---|---|---|---|---|
| 1 | | | | |
| 2 | | | | |
| 3 | | | | |
| 4 | | | | |
| 5 | | | | |

**MODEL CALCULATION:**

**RESULT:**

The taper angle of the given specimen is using sine bar = __________ degrees.

| EX. NO.:3 | MEASURE THE ANGLE OF A V-BLOCK / TAPER SHANK OF DRILL / DOVETAIL USING UNIVERSAL BEVEL PROTRACTOR. | DATE: |
|---|---|---|

**OBJECTIVE:**

To measure the angles of a V-block, taper shank of a drill, and a dovetail using a universal bevel protractor.

**APPARATUS:**

1. Universal bevel protractor
2. V-block
3. Taper shank drill
4. Dovetail workpiece
5. Surface plate

**DESCRIPTION**:

A universal bevel protractor is a precision instrument used to measure angles with high accuracy. It consists of a base, a protractor head, a blade, and a vernier scale for fine measurements. The tool can measure both internal and external angles, making it versatile for various mechanical tasks. An angular graduated main scale is used to note a specimen's angle accurately. The least count of the universal bevel protractor is 0.001°.

**PROCEDURE:**

**Calibration of the Protractor:**

- Ensure the universal bevel protractor is clean and free from debris.
- Place the protractor on a surface plate to check its initial zero setting.

**Measurement of the V-block Angle:**

- Place the V-block on the surface plate.
- Position the protractor blade along one side of the V-block.
- Adjust the protractor head to align with the second side of the V-block.

- Read the angle directly from the protractor scale.

**Measurement of the Taper Shank of Drill:**

- Secure the drill in a vertical position on the surface plate.
- Align the protractor blade along the taper shank.
- Rotate the protractor head until it is flush with the shank.
- Record the angle from the protractor scale.

**Measurement of the Dovetail Angle:**

- Place the dovetail workpiece on the surface plate.
- Position the protractor blade along one side of the dovetail.
- Adjust the protractor head to align with the adjacent side of the dovetail.
- Note the angle from the protractor scale.

**DIAGRAM:**

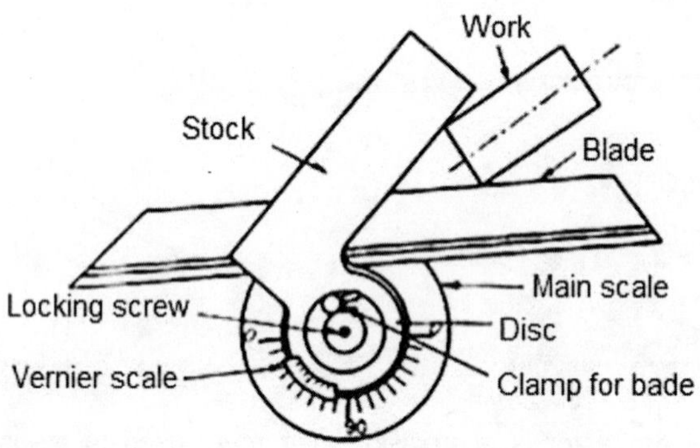


**OBSERVATION:**

| Sl. No. | MSR (Degree) | VSR (Min.) | Correct Reading |
|---|---|---|---|
| 1 | | | |
| 2 | | | |
| 3 | | | |
| 4 | | | |
| 5 | | | |

**MODEL CALCULATION:**

RESULT:

Thus, the angle of the given specimen was found by using a universal bevel protractor.

Angle of V-Block / Taper Shank Of Drill / Dovetail : ------------------ degrees.

| EX. NO.:4 | MEASURE THE DIMENSIONS OF GROUND MS FLAT/CYLINDRICAL BUSH USING VERNIER CALIPER COMPARE WITH DIGITAL/DIAL VERNIER CALIPER. | DATE: |
|---|---|---|

**OBJECTIVE:**

To measure the dimensions of a ground mild steel (MS) flat and a cylindrical bush using a vernier caliper, and to compare the measurements with those obtained using a digital/dial vernier caliper.

**APPARATUS:**

1. Vernier caliper
2. Digital/dial vernier caliper
3. Ground MS flat
4. Cylindrical bush
5. Surface plate

**DESCRIPTION:**

Vernier calipers are precise instruments used to measure internal and external dimensions, as well as depths, with high accuracy. They consist of two scales: the main scale and the Vernier scale, which moves along the main scale. The caliper is placed on the object to be measured, and the fine adjustment screw is rotated until the jaws fit tightly against the workpiece. Readings from the main scale and the Vernier scale are then taken. The main principle of the Vernier caliper is that two scales of different sizes are used to measure dimensions with high accuracy. The least count of a

Vernier caliper is 0.02mm.

A digital vernier caliper is a precision tool used to measure internal and external distances accurately. It features a digital display for easy and precise readings. With a typical range of 0 to 150 mm (6 inches) and an accuracy of ±0.02 mm, it ensures high precision. It can measure dimensions, depths, and steps. This tool is essential in engineering, manufacturing, and metalworking for exact measurements.

**PROCEDURE:**

**Calibration of calipers:**

- Ensure both the vernier caliper and digital/dial vernier caliper are clean and free from debris.
- Check the zero setting on both instruments by closing the jaws completely and verifying the zero reading.

**Measurement of ground MS flat:**

***Using vernier caliper:***

- Place the ground MS flat on a stable surface.
- Open the jaws of the vernier caliper and position them around the flat's thickness.
- Close the jaws gently to make contact with the flat and take the reading from the vernier scale.
- Repeat for length and width if needed.

***Using digital/dial vernier caliper:***

- Repeat the same steps as above using the digital/dial vernier caliper.
- Note the digital/dial reading.

**Measurement of cylindrical bush:**

***Using vernier caliper:***

- Position the cylindrical bush on a stable surface.
- Open the jaws of the vernier caliper and position them around the bush's outer diameter.
- Close the jaws gently to make contact with the bush and take the reading from the vernier scale.
- Measure the inner diameter by adjusting the small jaws inside the bush and read the measurement.
- Measure the height of the bush by positioning the depth rod at the bottom and noting the reading.

**Using digital/dial vernier caliper:**

- Repeat the same steps as above using the digital/dial vernier caliper.
- Note the digital/dial reading.

**FORMULA:**

$$\text{Least count} = \frac{main\ scale\ reading}{no.of\ vernier\ scale\ divisions} = 0.02\text{mm}$$

**DIAGRAM:**

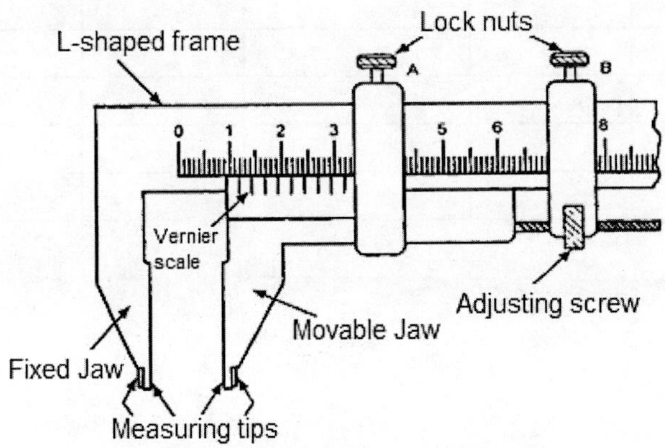


*Ordinary vernier caliper*

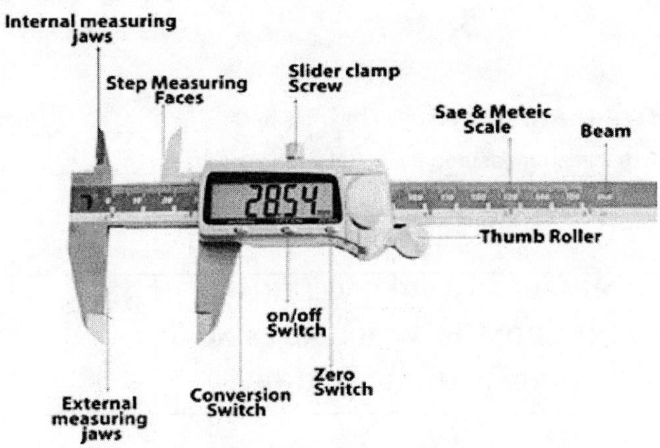


*Digital vernier caliper*

**OBSERVATIONS:**

**Specimen's Name & Specification:**______________________________

| Sl. No. | Main Scale Reading (M.S.R) (mm) | Vernier Scale Division (V.S.D) (Div) | Correct Reading CR=MSR+ (VSD×LC) (mm) | Average Reading (mm) | Digital vernier caliper reading | Deviation |
|---|---|---|---|---|---|---|
| 1 | | | | | | |
| 2 | | | | | | |
| 3 | | | | | | |
| 4 | | | | | | |
| 5 | | | | | | |

**MODEL CALCULATION:**

**RESULT:**

Thus, the dimension of the given specimen was measured by using vernier caliper and digital vernier caliber.

1. The dimension of specimen measured by vernier caliber = ______________ mm
2. The dimension of specimen measured by digital vernier caliber = ______________ mm
3. The deviation/error in measurements = _________ mm.

| EX. NO.:5 | MEASURE THE GEOMETRICAL DIMENSIONS OF V-THREAD USING THREAD VERNIER GAUGE | DATE: |
|---|---|---|

**OBJECTIVE:**

To measure the geometrical dimensions of a V-thread using a thread vernier gauge.

**APPARATUS:**

- Thread vernier gauge
- V-thread workpiece
- Surface plate (optional for stability)
- Magnifying glass (optional for better reading accuracy)

**DESCRIPTION**:

A V-thread is a type of screw thread with a triangular cross-section. It is commonly used for power transmission due to its high strength. The thread vernier gauge is a measuring instrument specifically designed for measuring thread dimensions. It has two scales: a main scale and a vernier scale. The main scale provides coarse readings, while the vernier scale allows for precise readings by taking advantage of the slight difference in size between the main scale divisions and the vernier scale divisions.

**PROCEDURE:**

***Calibration of the Thread Vernier Gauge:***

- Ensure the thread vernier gauge is clean and free from debris.
- Close the gauge completely and check the zero setting to ensure accuracy.

**Measurement of V-Thread Dimensions:**

***Major Diameter:***

- Open the thread vernier gauge and place the jaws over the external crests of the V-thread.
- Close the jaws gently until they make contact with the crests.
- Read the measurement from the main scale and the vernier scale for precise reading.

***Minor Diameter:***

- Insert the internal jaws of the gauge into the thread roots.
- Open the jaws until they make contact with the roots.
- Read the measurement from the main scale and the vernier scale.

***Pitch Diameter:***

- Use the appropriate thread inserts provided with the thread vernier gauge for measuring the pitch diameter.
- Place the inserts into the gauge, ensuring they match the thread profile.
- Position the gauge over the thread, making sure the inserts fit into the thread flanks.
- Close the gauge until it makes contact with the thread flanks.
- Read the pitch diameter from the gauge.

***Repeat Measurements:***

- Repeat each measurement (major diameter, minor diameter, and pitch diameter) multiple times to ensure accuracy and consistency.
- Record all readings carefully.

**DIAGRAM:**

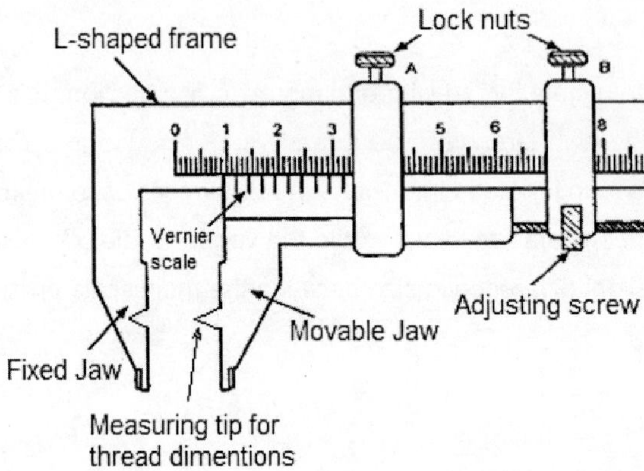


*Thread vernier gauge*

**OBSERVATIONS:**

| Sl. No. | Main Scale Reading (M.S.R) (mm) | Vernier Scale Division (V.S.D) (Div) | Correct Reading CR=MSR+ (VSD×LC) (mm) | Average Reading (mm) |
|---|---|---|---|---|
| Major diameter of the thread | | | | |
| 1 | | | | |
| 2 | | | | |
| 3 | | | | |
| Minor diameter of the thread | | | | |
| 1 | | | | |
| 2 | | | | |
| 3 | | | | |
| Pitch diameter of the thread | | | | |
| 1 | | | | |
| 2 | | | | |

| 3 | | | | |
|---|---|---|---|---|

**MODEL CALCULATION:**

**RESULT:**

Thus, the dimension of the given specimen was measured by using thread vernier caliper.

1. The major diameter of the given thread = ____________ mm
2. The minor diameter of the given thread = ____________ mm
3. The pitch diameter of the given thread = ____________ mm.

| EX. NO.:6 | MEASURE THE THICKNESS OF GROUND MS PLATES USING SLIP GAUGES | DATE: |
|---|---|---|

**OBJECTIVE:**

To determine the thickness of a ground mild steel (MS) plate using a set of slip gauges.

**APPARATUS:**

- Set of slip gauges
- Micrometer (optional, for verification)
- Surface plate (flat, smooth reference surface)
- Cleaning cloth

**DESCRIPTION:**

Slip gauges, also known as gauge blocks, are precision-made rectangular blocks with very accurate dimensions. They come in a variety of thicknesses and are used individually or in combination to achieve a desired gauge length for various measuring tasks. By building a stack of slip gauges with their thicknesses known, we can indirectly measure the thickness of the object placed between the stack and a flat reference surface.

**PROCEDURE:**

***Preparation:***

- Clean the surface plate and the plate whose thickness needs to be measured with a cleaning cloth to remove any dirt or oil that might affect the measurements.
- Arrange the slip gauges on the surface plate for easy selection.

***Building the Stack:***

- Estimate the thickness of the plate based on visual inspection or any provided information.
- Select slip gauges from the set with thicknesses that will add up to a value slightly greater than the estimated thickness.
- Carefully place the selected slip gauges on the surface plate, building the stack next to the plate.

**Adjustment**:

- Gently place the plate on top of the slip gauge stack. There should be a slight gap between the bottom of the plate and the surface plate.
- Systematically remove or replace individual slip gauges from the stack until the gap becomes minimal and offers slight resistance when a thin sheet (like cigarette paper) is inserted between them.

**Taking Measurements:**

- Note the thickness values of each slip gauge used in the final stack.
- Add the individual thicknesses of all the slip gauges in the stack. This sum represents the measured thickness of the plate.

***Data Recording:***

- Record the individual thicknesses of each slip gauge used in the final stack.
- Calculate and record the total thickness of the slip gauge stack (measured thickness of the plate).

**OBSERVATIONS:**

| Sl. No. | Types of Slip gauges used | Total no of slip gauges | Total Thickness of slip gauge (Gap between two parallel MS flat plates) |
|---|---|---|---|

| | | | |
|---|---|---|---|
| 1 | | | |
| 2 | | | |
| 3 | | | |
| 4 | | | |
| 5 | | | |

**RESULT:**

Thus, the gap between two parallel MS flat plates was measured by using slip gauges. The thickness of the gap = ______________ mm.

# SUGGESTED READINGS AND REFERENCES


## Books

1. R.K. Jain, Engineering Metrology, Khanna Publishers, 2007.
2. I.C. Gupta, Engineering Metrology, Dhanpat Rai Publications, 2008.
3. Terry L.M. Bartel, Measurement and Instrumentation: Theory and Application, CRC Press, 2014.
4. E.O. Doebelin, Measurement Systems: Application and Design, McGraw-Hill, 2004.
5. Thomas G. Beckwith, Roy D. Marangoni, John H. Lienhard V, Mechanical Measurements, Pearson, 2010.
6. S.P. Venkateshan, Mechanical Measurements, Ane Books, 2015.
7. A.K. Sawhney, A Course in Electrical and Electronic Measurements and Instrumentation, Dhanpat Rai & Co., 2012.

## Standards

1. ISO 9001:2015 - Quality management systems – Requirements.
2. ISO 10012:2003 - Measurement management systems – Requirements for measurement processes and measuring equipment.
3. ISO 17025:2017 - General requirements for the competence of testing and calibration laboratories.
4. IS 919-1993 - Limits, Fits and Tolerances.
5. IS 3477-1973 - Specifications for measuring instruments.

## Online Resources

1. National Institute of Standards and Technology (NIST)

   [www.nist.gov](https://www.nist.gov)

2. International Organization for Standardization (ISO)

   [www.iso.org](https://www.iso.org)

3. American Society for Quality (ASQ)

   [www.asq.org](https://www.asq.org)

4. IEEE Xplore Digital Library

   [ieeexplore.ieee.org](https://ieeexplore.ieee.org)

## CO - PO ATTAINMENT TABLE

Attainment of Programme Outcomes (1- Weak; 2- Medium; 3- Strong)

| Programme Outcome (PO) | CO-1 | CO-2 | CO-3 | CO-4 | CO-5 | CO-6 | Average Attainment |
|---|---|---|---|---|---|---|---|
| PO-1 | | | | | | | |
| PO-2 | | | | | | | |
| PO-3 | | | | | | | |
| PO-4 | | | | | | | |
| PO-5 | | | | | | | |
| PO-6 | | | | | | | |
| PO-7 | | | | | | | |
| PO-8 | | | | | | | |
| PO-9 | | | | | | | |
| PO-10 | | | | | | | |
| PO-11 | | | | | | | |
| PO - 12 | | | | | | | |

**Action Steps Based on Gap Analysis**

1. Identify Weak Areas:
    - Highlight POs with low average attainment scores (e.g., scores of 1 or 2).
2. Determine Causes:
    - Review course content, teaching methods, and assessment techniques to identify why certain POs are not being strongly attained.
3. Plan Improvements:
    - Course Deliver: Modify the course lesson plan to better address weak POs.
    - Teaching Methods: Incorporate new teaching strategies or tools that may improve understanding and performance related to the weak POs.
4. Implement Changes:
    - Update the course syllabus, teaching plan, and assessments based on the planned improvements.
5. Monitor and Review:
    - After implementing changes, continue to monitor the attainment of POs in subsequent course offerings and make further adjustments as necessary.

By filling out this table and performing a thorough analysis, teachers can ensure continuous improvement in course design and delivery, leading to better attainment of program outcomes.

# INDEX